# HISTORY OF CLASSICAL SCHOLARSHIP

U. von Wilamowitz-Moellendorff

# HISTORY OF CLASSICAL SCHOLARSHIP

*Translated from the German by Alan Harris*

*Edited with Introduction and Notes by*
Hugh Lloyd-Jones
*Regius Professor of Greek
in the University of Oxford*

The Johns Hopkins University Press
Baltimore, Maryland

First published in German in 1921 as
*Geschichte der Philologie*
by B. G. Teubner Verlag

First published in English in 1982 by
Gerald Duckworth & Co. Ltd
The Old Piano Factory
43 Gloucester Crescent, London NW1
and
The Johns Hopkins University Press
Baltimore, Maryland 21218

Library of Congress Catalog Card Number 81–48182
ISBN 0–8018–2801–5

Photoset by
Specialised Offset Services Limited, Liverpool
and printed in Great Britain by
Redwood Burn Limited, Trowbridge, Wiltshire

# Contents

63,948

# Introduction
# by Hugh Lloyd-Jones

There is no adequate short account of the history of classical scholarship written in the English language. The history in three volumes published in 1908 by Sir John Sandys[1] is still a very useful book; but it is long, and it is useful as a store of factual information, not as a critical study of the subject. We are fortunate to possess a history of classical scholarship written in English by Rudolf Pfeiffer, whose first volume goes from the beginnings to the end of the Hellenistic age and whose second covers the period between 1300 and 1850.[2] This is a work of high quality; but it too is long, and the treatment of the subject from the middle of the seventeenth century is by no means equal to the earlier part of the work. In particular, the nineteenth century is inadequately handled; and that period is particularly important for the modern reader.

Almost any competent person would agree that the best short history of the subject is the *Geschichte der Philologie*[3]

---

[1] See Bibliography.

[2] See Bibliography. The Italian translation of vol. i, *Storia della filologia classica*, tr. Marcello Gigante and Salvatore Cerasuolo, 1973, has an excellent introduction by Gigante; see also his article 'Dal Wilamowitz al Pfeiffer: Storici della Filologia Classica' in *PP* 156, 1974, 3f., and the discussion by L.E. Rossi in *RIFC* 104, 1976, 98f. See also the reviews of vol. i by A.Momigliano, *RSI* 80, 1968, 377f. = *QC* 893f. and N.G. Wilson, *Cl.Rev.* 19, 1969, 366f., and my obituary notice of Pfeiffer in *BG* ch. 22. On vol. ii, see G. Chiarini, *ANSP*, 1977, 1629.

[3] It first appeared in the second (1921) edition of *Einleitung in die Altertumswissenschaft*, ed. A. Gercke and E. Norden, 3rd edn., 1927, but is now available separately. There are other short histories in German by W. Kroll, *Geschichte der klassischen Philologie*, 1908, A. Gudeman, *Grundriss der Geschichte der klassischen Philologie*, 1909, and E. Drerup, *Der Humanismus*, 1934; in Italian by C. Giarratano, in *Indroduzione alla filologia classica*, 1951, A. Bernardini and G. Righi, *Il concetto di filologia e di cultura classica nel pensiero moderno*, 1947, and G. Righi, *Breve storia della filologia classica*, 1962.

written by the great Hellenist Ulrich von Wilamowitz-Moellendorff (1848-1931), which first appeared in 1921 and was reissued in 1927. It may seem surprising that a book first published sixty years ago should still be the best of its kind. But the author's astounding energy enabled him to keep in touch with almost every branch of the subject; he could speak of scholars and their achievements with unique familiarity and with unique authority; and he wrote with great clarity and with great liveliness.[4]

Of course, Wilamowitz, like all human beings, had his failings. First, he often trusted his wonderful memory too far and made trivial mistakes in detail; that need not worry us, and I have done my best to correct such errors in the notes, using such material as others have provided. Next, his judgments are sometimes arbitrary, as is inevitable in what Pfeiffer calls 'an individual and quite brilliant survey'.[5] 'It is a very subjective review of classical scholars,' Pfeiffer writes, 'made by a great master who calls up the dead heroes of the past from the other world and praises or blames them.' Pfeiffer himself has protested against some of Wilamowitz's judgments; where that is so, I have signified as much.

In the brief notes appended to the text I have tried first of all to supply the reader with the facts that will help him follow the argument. To supply a chronological framework, I have given in most cases the dates of birth and death of the persons mentioned; and I have referred to the chief treatments of them in Sandys, in Pfeiffer, in the valuable *Scribes and Scholars* of my Oxford colleagues, L.B. Reynolds and N.G. Wilson,[6] and in other works. Wilamowitz's way of writing is allusive, and some of his allusions may puzzle even a well-informed reader;

---

[4] Fausto Codino in the introduction to his admirable Italian version of this book (*Storia della filologia classica*, no. 91 in the series Piccola Biblioteca Einaudi, 1967, p.1) applied to it the words used of E. Zeller's history of Greek philosophy by Wilamowitz himself: 'Works of such high quality ought to be left as the author wrote them. We want to know what he said, even in the places where he would speak differently if he were alive today.' Codino's translation drew interesting comments from B. Hemmerdinger, 'Supplément à la "Geschichte der Philologie" de Wilamowitz', Belfagor 27, 1972, 653f.

[5] *HSC* i, ix.

[6] See Bibliography.

not all are equally important, but any may provoke curiosity, and this I have done my best to satisfy. Where I have detected factual errors I have corrected them; and where a judgment seems to me specially controversial I have said so. In many places I have mentioned modern works that may give a notion of the recent development of research into the topic mentioned in the text. Sometimes the works I mention are surveys intended for the general reader; but I have not hesitated to quote specialist publications, including some in foreign languages. I hope that the general reader will not be alarmed by the latter nor the advanced reader by the former type of reference; to anyone who complains that I am inconsistent I reply that my aim is to be useful. The works which I have made most use of will be found listed in the bibliography on p.179, together with the abbreviations by which I have denoted them.

But one aspect of Wilamowitz's book must receive attention here. The standpoint from which he wrote is not that of a man of our own time; and the difference needs explanation and discussion.

The translation is called, 'History of Classical Scholarship'; but the original is called 'Geschichte der Philologie'. The translation could not be called 'History of Philology', because for most English people 'philology' has come to mean 'comparative philology', and 'comparative philology' means 'comparative study of language'. Yet if one uses terms exactly, linguistics is only one section of philology, a word which came into use in Alexandria as early as the third century before Christ and which properly denotes the love of literature, of thought, of all that is expressed in words. This is the meaning of the word in the titles of the Philological Societies which flourish in Oxford and Cambridge, and this is its meaning on the Continent; it is deplorable that we in England have ceased to use this valuable term correctly. Strictly speaking 'philology' should not include the study of monuments, though it should include that of history and of philosophy. But Wilamowitz' account of it includes archaeology and art history, because for him philology was not separable from these disciplines. For Wilamowitz a student of philology must be a student of *Altertumswissenschaft*, 'the science of antiquity', a term invented by German scholars of the nineteenth century to describe the study, conceived as a unity, of everything connected with the ancient world. That concept had taken many centuries to come into being, as Wilamowitz' history shows. The humanists of fourteenth-century Italy were passionately eager to rediscover ancient literature, art, science and medicine, because they wanted to improve their own; their aims were not theoretical, but strictly practical. Likewise they thought that a knowledge of the early Church could benefit their Christianity; the scholarly interests of the greatest figure of the late Renaissance, Erasmus, centred upon the Bible and the Christian Fathers.

We come closer to a scientific concept of philology when we arrive at the great French scholars of the second half of the sixteenth century, Scaliger and Casaubon. Scaliger's massive researches, resting on a learning by no means confined to Greek and Latin, laid the whole foundation of our knowledge of the chronology of the ancient world; Casaubon with vast erudition described all kinds of facts and objects connected with antiquity. Yet even now philology as a separate discipline did not exist; men studied the classics in the interests of divinity, law, medicine or science, not for the sake of classical learning in itself.

With the coming of the wars of religion, the spring almost ran dry. The study of ancient authors issued in heavy variorum editions, repeating the learning of past scholars, or in huge volumes of 'antiquities', deadly to the reader. The precious information which the ancients had had to give had now been yielded up and absorbed into the bloodstream of the modern world; science and medicine could now do without the ancient authors. The Battle of the Books – *La Querelle* – marked the moment at which modern Europe consciously threw off the leading-strings of ancient Europe. France had taken the lead in civilised progress from the start of the sixteenth century, and during that century made an immense contribution to classical studies; and it was France that now took the lead in their abandonment.

But there was to be a second revival of interest in classical antiquity. Before the seventeenth century was over, its beginnings might have been discerned. In Holland and in

England critical methods were developed which were to make possible an enormous increase in knowledge and in understanding of the ancients. Here Bentley was the leader in discovery. People who think of him merely as the author of ingenious emendations are quite unaware of the real nature of his importance, which was not noticed before F.A. Wolf and which is better explained by Wilamowitz in a few pages of this book (pp. 79ff.) than it has ever been by any of Bentley's countrymen.

The new methods were to be taken up and exploited on a vast scale by the scholars of nineteenth-century Germany; but this process could never have begun had it not been for a new wave of interest in antiquity that had something in common with the Italian Renaissance. Wilamowitz rightly emphasises the importance of the part played by men who are not counted among classical scholars, men like Lessing, Goethe and Herder. Till now, Europe had seen ancient civilisation for the most part through Roman spectacles; now, reacting against the now decadent baroque and against the formalism of the age of reason, these men turned to Greek art and literature for their examplars. Here Winckelmann played the decisive role; he was able to approach the Greeks directly, and inspired others to do the same.

The tremendous impact of Greek art and literature was bound in the end to penetrate even the universities and the education they provided. The Jacobites of Oxford who poured scorn on the Elector of Hanover and his countrymen would have been surprised to learn that his dominions included a university in classical learning incomparably superior to their own, that of Göttingen. After Gesner (see pp.93-4) came Heyne, and after Heyne, Wolf; and when Wolf, asked whether he wished to matriculate as a student of theology, law or medicine, insisted on being put down as a student of philology,[7] at last that subject began an independent existence in schools and universities. At the end of the century, when English universities set up examinations for their degrees, classical scholarship figures prominently in the curriculum.

[7] I know Wolf was not the first (see E.J. Kenney, *The Classical Text*, 1974, 98, i), but his action is significant.

For Goethe, and even for Wilhelm von Humboldt and those who helped him found that University of Berlin which quickly became a model for the universities of the world, the chief value of classical studies was aesthetic rather than historical. Such men did not desire knowledge for its own sake; like the humanists of the earlier renaissance, they desired it for the sake of their own work. By the middle of the nineteenth century, the movement they had initiated had taken on a very different character.

The existing tradition of textual scholarship was greatly strengthened by the new enthusiasm deriving from the literary and artistic cult of Greek antiquity. It reached a new height in the work of Gottfried Hermann (1772-1848), whose contribution to the improvement of the texts of the principal Greek poets can never be surpassed. But the new movement brought into being a new school of classical scholarship, which unlike the school of Hermann was more specifically German than European; and before long the two schools became involved in bitter controversy. The occasion of the quarrel was the publication in 1833 by Karl Otfried Müller of an edition of Aeschylus' *Eumenides* which though vulnerable to attack by so great a linguistic scholar and textual critic as Hermann had the importance of a pioneer work, embodying the notion, already propounded by Welcker, that art and archaeology should contribute to the understanding even of a work of literature. Boeckh made a large contribution to the study of the poets; but he is chiefly famous for having built up the first detailed picture of the working of government and public economy in ancient Greece, giving a quantity of detailed illustration, much of it derived from the new study of epigraphy, which no modern historian of government at that time could match. Soon after, Niebuhr with his well-reasoned criticism of Roman traditions revolutionised the approach to Roman history. Scholars like him and Boeckh belonged to the same movement as such contemporary modern historians as Ranke. Like him they were influenced in their conception of history by the Romantics; not content with a narrative of battles, kings and parliaments, they aimed to portray a whole civilisation, not omitting its social and economic aspects.

From a fusion between the school of Boeckh and the school

of Welcker and Karl Otfried Müller came the concept of *Altertumswissenschaft* which I have mentioned. Such a study had to combine several different disciplines. History must use not only historical and other written texts, but inscriptions and (when these became available in large numbers) papyri; with it must be combined literary and linguistic study. Linguistic study must be applied not only to literary texts, but to every other kind of document; the new science of comparative linguistics was to throw new light upon Greek and Latin, and even upon history. Art as well as literature was to be studied with a new degree of thoroughness; both were to be studied not only for themselves, but for their social and historical significance. Such a vast programme demanded a large measure of specialisation. Humble scholars were content to devote their whole lives, if necessary, to the completion of arduous but necessary tasks, like the decipherment of a precious but barely readable palimpsest or the editing of a necessary but barely readable author. Vast corporate projects for the systematic publication of huge corpora of inscriptions or works of art were set in motion; numerous scholars, many of them nameless, toiled like the Nibelungen under the direction of gigantic figures like Boeckh and later Mommsen.

This programme naturally led to the adoption of a sternly realistic view of ancient society. The impulse to portray the factual and material background of ancient life had come to the historians from the romantics; it was bound to issue in realism, as in the novel romantic theory had led to the realism of Balzac and finally of Zola. The view of antiquity as providing ideal standards for emulation could no longer be sustained; and as the old classicists' picture of the ancient world became remoter, the afflatus that had set in motion the whole vast development became feebler. A dry and rigid positivism crept over the work of scholars; confined each within the bounds of his narrow specialism, they became increasingly unable to see the wood of antiquity for its innumerable trees. By the sixties, when Nietzsche (1844-1900) became Professor of Philology at Basle, the engines driving on the mighty juggernaut of German *Altertumswissenschaft* seemed to be running down.

The name of Nietzsche is not to be found in Wilamowitz'

history, and it is not a name that Wilamowitz heard with pleasure. Nietzsche was educated at Schulpforta, the most famous classical school in Germany, and later at the University of Bonn; Wilamowitz, four years younger, followed him at both these institutions. At Bonn Nietzsche won the high regard of the great Plautine scholar Friedrich Ritschl, whose support enabled him to gain a full professorship at Basle at the astonishingly early age of twenty-four. Three years later he published *The Birth of Tragedy*, which the twenty-two-year-old Wilamowitz assailed in a pamphlet of extreme violence. The antipathy between the two men was to some extent a consequence of an earlier quarrel between Nietzsche's patron, Ritschl, and Wilamowitz' chief friend among the Bonn professors, Otto Jahn. Further, Wilamowitz was provoked by the numerous inaccuracies and exaggerations which the book contains and by its over-excited tone; he particularly disliked the last section of it, which deals with Wagner's music and which Nietzsche afterwards regretted having published. Wilamowitz was by reason of his character not likely to appreciate the part of the work which has permanent value, the philosophical theory of the nature of tragedy. But that was not all; the two men differed widely in their views of the character and duty of philology.

Nietzsche's opinions on this subject had already taken definite shape in the notes made for a course of lectures which he gave during the summer of 1871, a year before the publication of *The Birth of Tragedy*. He is critical of the belief, which he imputes to the classicists of the age of Goethe, that the ancient classics could furnish ideal patterns for imitation; but he is still more critical of the historicism prevalent in his own time. He attacks scholars for assuming that the ancients were in general like themselves; the most important thing for a scholar, and the hardest, he says, is to enter into the life of antiquity in imagination and to feel the difference between the ancients and ourselves. He warns against the damage done by over-specialisation, and insists that the acquisition of knowledge is a means and not an end.

Later, after the violent controversy provoked by the appearance of *The Birth of Tragedy*, Nietzsche became more bitter. In the notes for 'We Philologists', which was to have been one of the *Untimely Meditations* of which four were published between 1873 and 1876, he attacked philologists for their lack of respect for antiquity, excessive respect for them-selves, sentimentality and loose rhetoric. If they really understood the nature of antiquity, he said, they would turn from it in horror. That remark is obviously relevant to his own pioneer work in drawing attention to the importance of the irrational, the violent, the terrifying elements in ancient religion and in ancient life. His picture of antiquity differed radically from that painted by the old classicists, for whom the Greeks served as the types of rational enlightenment; but he agreed with the old classicists against the new historicists in insisting that the value of the study of antiquity must lie in what it can contribute to the modern world.[8]

Not surprisingly Nietzsche ended by taking the advice given to him by his adversary Wilamowitz and giving up his chair of philology to devote himself to his philosophic and prophetic mission. His dark prophecies of the impending collapse of German philology proved, in the event, considerably exaggerated. The amazing energy of Wilamowitz and his contemporaries, inspired by the example of the aged Mommsen, checked the incipient decline and inaugurated an age of even greater triumphs than the first half of the century had seen. After them came a brilliant generation of their pupils; and though as early as 1900 the classical gymnasium lost its dominating place in German education, the great age of German philology may be said to have lasted until the coming to power of National Socialism in 1933. But after 1914 the questions first asked by Nietzsche were asked with increasing frequency, sometimes by the philologists themselves.

Wilamowitz was a unique phenomenon, and so not typical of the rest; but his conception of philology had enormous influence, and may be considered representative of the period.[9] His conscious aim was to combine the tradition of

[8] See my article 'Nietzsche and the study of the ancient world' in *Nietzsche and the Classical Tradition*, ed. James C. O'Flaherty, Timothy F. Sellner and Robert M. Helm, University of North Carolina Studies in the Germanic Languages and Literature, 1976, 1f = *BG*, ch. 14.

[9] See A. Momigliano, 'Premesse per una discussione di Wilamowitz',

literary scholarship typified by Hermann and his eminent
pupils Ritschl and Lachmann with the literary scholarship
joined with the study of religion, art and archaeology of
Welcker and the historical scholarship joined with literary
studies of Boeckh. All these disciplines were to find their place
in a single developed concept of *Altertumswissenschaft*. Since
philology could not be truly scientific unless seen as a part of
this great whole, it was identified with the science of antiquity.

But the description of the programme means little without a
description of the man. Wilamowitz came from what might
have seemed the last social background likely to produce a
great scholar, that of the Junker aristocracy settled in West
Prussia. The name does not prove that he had Polish blood;
yet in Gilbert Murray's phrase he 'united in a strange and
impressive combination the haughty *virtus* of a Prussian noble
in the Polish marches, the warm imagination of a Slav and the
beelike industry of a German savant'.[10] He never shrank from
the most arduous labour, and spent untold time working on
inscriptions; but there was nothing pedantic about him, and
nothing that he said or wrote was dull. He brought out
important editions of classical authors, such as Theocritus,
Callimachus and Aeschylus, besides publishing many new
papyri. But he also wrote commentaries of an entirely new
kind, in which the whole vast body of knowledge of antiquity
built up by scholarship was brought to bear not merely upon
the constitution of the text, but upon the interpretation of the
author. Not that Wilamowitz ever swamped his reader with a
mass of detail; he was highly selective in his choice of material
for illustration, and became more so as he grew older. The
first and most famous of his commentaries was that on the
*Heracles* of Euripides, circulated privately in an early version as
early as 1879 but given to the world only ten years later. In
the first edition the volume that contained the text and
commentary was preceded by another that comprised an
introduction to Greek tragedy which though many of its

*RSI* 84, 1972, 746f.; to his list of accounts of Wilamowitz, add K. Reinhardt,
*Vermächtnis der Antike*, 2nd edn., 1966, 361f., and U. Hölscher, *Die Chance des
Unbehagens*, 1965, 7f.
    [10] *Cl. Rev.* 45, 1931, 161.

details have been superseded remains after eighty years
necessary reading for interested persons. Later commentaries
dealt with Euripides' *Hippolytus* and *Ion*, Aeschylus' *The
Libation Bearers*, Menander's *The Arbitration*, Aristophanes'
*Lysistrata* and Hesiod's *Works and Days*. He also wrote a series
of brilliant interpretative books, containing much detailed
scholarship but written in so clear and vigorous a style that
even an ordinary reader with no pretensions to learning may
find them compulsive reading. He wrote three books on
Homer and one each on Pindar, Aeschylus, early lyric poetry,
Greek metre and the poetry of the Hellenistic Age; and the
books which he devoted to the textual histories of Euripides
and of the lyric and bucolic poets are written with his usual
liveliness and contain much that goes far beyond the problems
of transmission. When the Aristotelian *Constitution of Athens*
was published from a newly-found papyrus, he not only edited
the text together with his friend Georg Kaibel,[11] but within a
few years produced two astonishing volumes in which he used
the new material to throw a flood of light on the whole of
Athenian history and culture. Apart from several minor
books, he wrote two volumes about Plato; and at the very end
of his career appeared two volumes about Greek religion
which are among the finest of his achievements. He produced
also a history of Greek literature, an account of state and
society in Greece and a uniquely interesting anthology of
Greek literature of all kinds with concise elementary notes. A
selection from his minor writings has been published in six
volumes; their contents alone would have established their
author as a scholar of the highest rank.

The author of this amazing quantity of learned work was
above all else a teacher and only in the second place a writer.
People who knew him have unanimously testified that he
always seemed to have time for anyone who showed the
slightest interest in the ancient world, and all speak of the
powerful impression that he made on anyone who heard him
speak. This extraordinary man's approach to scholarship had

[11] On Georg Kaibel (1850-1901) see Wilamowitz, *Erinnerungen*, 2nd edn.
1929, 240f. and K.J. Dover, in *Fifty Years (and Twelve) of Classical Scholarship*,
ed. M. Platnauer, 1962, 151, n.3.

an effect upon at any rate the more intelligent of his colleagues
and disciples. The belief that most German scholars of the
later nineteenth century were dry pedants, interested only in
textual criticism, could not be held by anyone actually
acquainted with their works.

Only a small selection of the contemporaries of Wilamowitz
and of their successors can be mentioned here. Hermann Diels
(1848-1922) did much for the study of Greek philosophy,
above all by editing the remains of the Presocratics and
assembling the remains of the doxographic tradition.[12]
Friedrich Leo (1851-1914) not only contributed greatly to the
textual and interpretative study of Plautus and of other
authors, but wrote the first volume and part of the second of a
history of Roman literature both extremely learned and highly
intelligent and readable.[13] Eduard Meyer (1855-1930)
combined vast knowledge of the languages and history of the
ancient east with equal mastery of Greek and Roman history,
being perhaps the most learned ancient historian who has ever
lived.[14] Eduard Schwartz (1858-1940) made a great
contribution not only to philology and ancient history but to
the study of the Christian Church.[15] Richard Reitzenstein
(1861-1931) was eminent not only in the study of Greek and
Roman literature and of ancient scholarship, but as a
historian of ancient religion, particularly of syncretism and
the effect of Oriental influences. Eduard Norden (1868-1941)
threw light on the whole history of the elaborate formal prose
written by the ancients, wrote the best commentary on any
part of Virgil and did important work on ancient religion.[16]
Jacob Wackernagel, of Basle, (1853-1938)[17] and Wilhelm

[12] See W. Burkert's introduction to H. Diels, *Kleine Schriften zur Geschichte der antiken Philosophie*, 1969.

[13] See E. Fraenkel's introduction to F. Leo, *Ausgewählte Kleine Schriften*, 2 vols 1960 (also *KB* ii 545f.).

[14] See V. Ehrenberg, *Aspects of the Ancient World*, 1946, 221f.

[15] See Pfeiffer in *Geist und Gestalt: Biographische Beiträge zur Geschichte der Bayerischen Akademie, vornehmlich im zweiten Jahrhundert ihres Bestehens*, 1959, 135f.

[16] See H. Haffter, *Neue Zürcher Zeitung*, no. 3897, 29 September 1963. Reitzenstein and Norden used their classical scholarship to throw new light on Judaism and Christianity.

[17] See G. Pasquali, *Pagine Stravaganti ii*, 1968, 216f.

Schulze (1863-1935)[18] used their mastery of comparative philology to illuminate the Greek and Latin literature and language. All these men worked on a gigantic scale; so did several of their successors, to some of whom I will come later (see p. xxv).

No intelligent person who knew the facts could deny the greatness of Wilamowitz, or fail to see that he never forgot that his tremendous apparatus of scholarship had value only insofar as it was relevant to real life. But it would be strange if his conception of scholarship fully satisfied a later generation; and several aspects of it have been found fault with. The various disciplines linked together by his conception of *Altertumswissenschaft* are in theory on an equal footing; but in practice the rest are held together in the firm grasp of a single branch of study, history; and to regard every facet of a culture from a historical standpoint may involve some dangers. For example, modern anthropology has accustomed us to the idea, obvious enough in itself, that cultural phenomena may on occasion be viewed with profit under a synchronic as well as under a diachronic aspect. Certain elements in religion, and even in philosophy, are best understood if we are free to approach them from a standpoint that is not fixed in time; and we can now see the harm done to the understanding of ancient literature and thought by an excessive preoccupation with development. In a sense every work of literature is a historical document; but an exclusively historical approach to it may result in the error of trying to extract from literature historical evidence that is not really there. For example, Wilamowitz assumed that Pindar uttered his own personal reflections in his poetry as a romantic poet might have done; but scholars are now beginning to regard many statements of Pindar which Wilamowitz took as personal as the expression, varied according to the context, of some of the accustomed commonplaces of encomiastic poetry.[19] A strictly historical approach to poetry and religion incurs the danger of neglecting their aesthetic aspect; and here Erwin Rohde (1845-1898)[20] was

[18] See E. Fraenkel, *Cl. Rev.* 49, 1935, 217f. = *KB* ii 579f.

[19] On Wilamowitz's attitude to Pindar, see L.E. Rossi, *ASNP*, ser.3, vol. 3, 1973, 119f. and H. Lloyd-Jones, *JHS* 93, 1973, 110-1, 115f.

[20] See O. Crusius, *Erwin Rohde; ein biographischer Versuch*, 1902.

Wilamowitz' superior. Rohde had been an early friend of
Nietzsche, and as such took part in the controversy with
Wilamowitz. Later he quarrelled with Nietzsche, but he
remained faithful to many of his attitudes, and his great book
*Psyche* pursued a line of investigation of Greek beliefs about the
soul which Nietzsche's insight had done much to make
possible.

Nietzsche described, in words that find a curious echo in
Housman's Cambridge Inaugural Lecture of 1911,[21] the
increasing mechanisation and brutalisation of German
cultural life that followed the foundation of the empire after
the defeat of France in 1871. More and more the humanities
tried to emulate the concrete successes of the natural sciences;
more and more these successes were seen as contributing to
the advancement, material as well as spiritual, of the German
nation. Idealistic philosophy led directly to the worship of the
state, and the new triumphs of historical science, like those of
natural science, seemed to contribute to the state's progress.
The new developments in ethnology and linguistics had not
only helped to make Germans race-conscious, but had
reminded them of their supposed racial connection with the
Greeks. Leopardi wrote a sonnet in mockery of J.W. Kuithan,
who after obtaining his doctorate with a work attempting to
show that Pindar's encomia were really a kind of comedy
achieved a popular success with a book in which he argued
that ancient Greeks and modern Germans were the same
people and spoke the same language.[22] This kind of nonsense
naturally cut no ice with learned men; but whoever reads the
address 'On the Splendour of the Athenian Empire' delivered
by the twenty-nine-year-old Wilamowitz on the occasion of
the Emperor's birthday in 1877 cannot fail to notice that the
German Empire also was present to the speaker's mind.[23] The
vast German effort in scholarship and science was in a sense
linked with the German drive towards domination in Europe;
and though this hardly justifies a condemnation of German
scholarship, it helps to explain a growing element of

[21] Published under the title (not given by its author) *The Confines of
Criticism*, Cambridge, 1969.

[22] See S. Timpanaro, *La Filologia di Giacomo Leopardi*, 1978², 230f.

[23] 'Von des Attischen Reiches Herrlichkeit', in *Aus Kydathen*, 1880, 1f.

coarseness and mechanicality in its productions.

The great age of German philology was bound to make some impact on the rest of Europe. The country most affected by it was Italy, whose historical situation in the nineteenth century showed such significant resemblances to that of Germany and whose scholarship developed in reaction, positive or negative, to German influences. Already in the age of Leopardi, Borghesi and Peyron[24] these had been at work, and the native tradition of local antiquarian scholarship had become affected by the new historiography. Literary studies too made progress. Domenico Comparetti (1835-1927),[25] chiefly famous for his learned study of Virgil in the middle ages, was a pioneer. Later the great palaeographer Girolamo Vitelli (1849-1935)[26] became a master of the new discipline of papyrology; he and his pupils had to defend their admiration for German scholarship against a school of nationalist conservatives. Some of these were men of taste and ability, who tried to vindicate the aesthetic element in literary scholarship against German positivism. But their provincialism went against the best interests of international scholarship; the Italians were protected by Croce's aestheticism, and also by their nature, from dryness and positivism, and badly needed the discipline which German philology could give, and neither these nationalists nor their present-day successors have achieved much that is of more than local significance. Vitelli's successor as the leader of the other school was Giorgio Pasquali (1887-1952)[27] who had been taught at Göttingen by Leo, Schwartz and Wackernagel; he did important work on Horace and on the theory of textual criticism, besides exercising great personal influence. Ancient history in Italy was stimulated by the presence in Rome of the

[24] On Leopardi and Borghesi, see below p.119 and p.156; on Amedeo Peyron (1785-1870), see Treves, *SAO*, 1963, 871f.

[25] See Treves, op.cit., 1051f.; Pasquali, op.cit. (in n.17), i 119f.; Timpanaro, *Aspetti e figure della cultura ottocentesca*, 1980, 349f.

[26] See Treves, op.cit., 1113f.; Pasquali, op.cit., i 205f.; Fraenkel, *Gnomon* 35, 1963, 822f.

[27] See Fraenkel, *KB* ii 601f.; a special number of *Atene e Roma* (fasc.6, anno 2, 1952, 201f., with memoirs by various contributors; F. Klingner, *Studien zur griechischen und römischen Literatur*, 1964, 719f.

distinguished German scholar K.J. Beloch (1854-1929),[28] a
pioneer of modern statistical methods; his chief pupil was a
great scholar of very different character, the liberal Catholic
Gaetano de Sanctis (1856-1939).[29]

The country least affected by German philology was of
course France. After the *Querelle*, the amount of attention
given by France to ancient literature had remained restricted;
and the disturbed political conditions of the turn of the
century did not improve matters. Nineteenth-century France
did distinguished work in classical archaeology, and this
tradition has continued; the excavations of Delphi and Delos,
apart from the importance of their results, have trained
generations of scholars in the understanding of archaeological
technique and of Greek art, architecture and epigraphy. The
great school of linguistics associated with the Swiss scholar
Ferdinand de Saussure (1857-1913) did valuable work on
Greek and Latin as well as upon other languages; Antoine
Meillet (1866-1936) left a succession of distinguished pupils.
But French literary scholarship has not attained the same
level; it is significant that the leading literary classical scholar
of nineteenth-century France was Henri Weil, who as
Wilamowitz points out (p.138), came from Germany. French
work in this field has often suffered from provincial
complacency;[29a] yet much of it has shown the characteristic
French clarity and sound reasoning, and has suffered
undeserved neglect from foreigners. Like England, France has
used classical scholarship for her own purposes, and the
quality of her achievement is not to be measured simply in
terms of learned production.

In England a strange break in local tradition coincided with
the beginning of the great age of German philology. The new
honours schools founded in the ancient universities gave a
prominent place to classical studies; but the use they made of
them was strictly practical. The classics might furnish schools

[28] See Momigliano, *TC* 239f.

[29] See Momigliano, *SC* 299f.

[29a] Louis Gernet (1882-1962), who did brilliant work on early law and
religion, using the new sociology and anthropology, was neglected by the
French establishment, see S.C. Humphreys, *Anthropology and the Classics*, 1978,
76f.

and universities with subject-matter which was thought morally edifying as well as intellectually stimulating; they might interest the educated reader and inspire the modern writer; but they were not thought so important that large numbers of gifted persons should devote most of their lives to an attempt to throw new light on them.

Since Bentley the tradition of textual scholarship had maintained itself; Porson, and after him his followers, did textual work of high quality, mostly on the Attic drama. But so far from stimulating this tradition, the establishment of the new honours schools practically abolished it; after 1825, the year of what Housman, echoing a phrase of Wilamowitz, called 'the successive strokes of doom which consigned Dobree and Elmsley to the grave and Blomfield to the bishopric of Chester', no successors took their places. It might have been expected that scholars would be influenced by the great movement now going on in Germany; but for a long time this did not happen, and when it did, it seldom happened in the universities. John Conington (1825-1869) did, it is true, valuable work on Aeschylus as well as on Persius and Virgil; he was inspired by Hermann rather than by the newer trend. At Cambridge the Porsonian tradition kept up a kind of life, like that of a decapitated snake; at Oxford, the curriculum gave much importance to ancient history and to ancient philosophy, yet little important work on these subjects came from there. Of course some gifted people in England realised what was going on in Germany; but they were too much occupied in teaching, like Thomas Arnold (1795-1842), or in the service of the church, like Connop Thirlwall (1797-1875), or in politics, like Sir George Cornwall Lewis (1806-1863),[30] to achieve in scholarship what men of their ability would certainly have achieved, had they been born in Germany. The most important products of English nineteenth-century classical scholarship were not scholars, but were men like Matthew Arnold (1822-1888) and Walter Pater (1839-1894). The universities at least managed to provide them and others with the classical knowledge which they needed. The best learned work often came from people unconnected with the

[30] See Momigliano, *C* 249f.

ancient universities; the banker George Grote (1794-1871),[31] the author of a history of Greece of independent outlook which had international importance, was a case in point. Apart from archaeology, where scholars like Sir Charles Newton[32] contributed to what had already become an international discipline, the first Englishman to achieve real eminence in linguistic scholarship after 1825 was H.A.J. Munro (1819-1885);[33] Conington might have done so but for religious catastrophe and early death. Later came Ingram Bywater (1840-1914)[34] and Sir Richard Jebb (1841-1905),[35] both of whom were highly esteemed by Wilamowitz. Bywater derived great profit from his acquaintance with Jacob Bernays, and edited Priscianus Lydus for a series sponsored by the Berlin Academy. Jebb showed less sympathy with German methods; yet his famous edition of Sophocles would have been impossible without close study of German scholarship, most of all the work of Hermann. Another distinguished Sophoclean scholar was Lewis Campbell (1830-1908),[36] who also did valuable work in using the study of style to determine the chronology of Plato's dialogues; another who did good work on ancient philosophy was Jebb's contemporary and successor, Henry Jackson (1839-1921).[37] In the late nineteenth century and later one can trace in English scholarship, as in that of other countries, an insular and a European element. A.E. Housman (1859-1936)[38] was perfectly familiar

[31] See Momigliano, ibid. 213f.; also M.L. Clarke, *George Grote: A Biography*, 1962; cf. p.153 below.

[32] See pp.137-8.

[33] See A.E. Housman, op.cit. (in n.21 above) 20f. and A.S.F. Gow, *A.E. Housman: A Sketch*, 1936, 4-5.

[34] See below, p.144.

[35] There is a life by Caroline Jebb, 1907; cf. Wilamowitz, *Kl.Schr.* i 461f. Wilamowitz wrote that Jebb's work as an interpreter of Sophocles would remain alive as long as people made the effort to understand the language of that difficult author. Cf. *Cl. Rev.* 19, 1969, 26-7.

[36] See *Memorials in Verse and Prose of Lewis Campbell*, 1914.

[37] There is a life by R. St J. Parry, 1926; it is no more exciting than the pious memoirs of Jebb and Campbell written by their widows.

[38] See the excellent memoir by Gow cited in n.33 above, and the brilliant appreciation by D.R. Shackleton Bailey in *The Listener*, March 26, 1959; also Kenney, *CT* 133f.

with the German scholarship relevant to his interests, but chose to continue in the Porsonian tradition of textual scholarship. In his London Introductory Lecture of 1892,[39] he justified his outlook in the name of knowledge for the sake of knowledge; later he described this production as 'rhetorical and not wholly sincere'. In his Cambridge Inaugural of 1911,[40] he criticised English scholars for imputing to the ancients their own romantic literary taste and German scholars for treating textual criticism as though it resembled the exact sciences; forty years before, Nietzsche had reproached his countrymen with both these faults. Although Housman knew that the taste of the ancients was not romantic, he was as much convinced as most of his contemporaries that romantic taste must be good and that a liking for the rhetoric, the baroque, the poetry depending on wit and polish must be bad. Thus he felt guilty at the relish for the condemned type of literature which his obvious sympathy with poets like the ones he edited – Juvenal, Ovid, Lucan and Manilius – reveals. Otherwise, instead of condemning all literary studies of the ancient poets, he might have tried to substitute for the prevailing romantic attitude towards them a kind of criticism able to take account of their poetic aims and methods. Then this great scholar's name could not have been invoked, as it too often has been, in defence of a dryness which has harmed the study of the classics; and he could less easily have been sniped at by people wishing to discredit those severe and learned studies of which they know themselves to be incapable.

The best scholars among Housman's contemporaries made better use of German work than their contemporaries had done. Wilamowitz on his famous visit to England in 1908 was much impressed by Walter Headlam (1866-1908),[41] who in his work on Aeschylus and on the newly-published poems of

[39] Reprinted in A.E. Housman, *Selected Essays*, ed. John Carter, 1961 1f.

[40] See n.21 above; cf. my unsigned review of Housman's *Collected Papers*, reprinted in the volume *TLS 12: Essays and Reviews from the Times Literary Supplement*, 1974, 137 = *BG*, ch. 15.

[41] See Cecil Headlam, *Walter Headlam: his Letters and Poems with a Memoir*, 1910, a work of fraternal piety about as exciting as Parry's life of Henry Jackson.

Herodas showed not only fine literary taste but wide and comprehensive learning. Gilbert Murray (1866-1957)[42] greatly admired Wilamowitz, corresponded with him from 1894 on, and was much influenced by his work.[43] The influence was not always for good; the Ibsenian Euripides of Wilamowitz inspired the Shavian Euripides of Murray. But in textual work Wilamowitz helped to counteract the bad effects of Murray's admiration for the ingenious but disingenuous and unscholarly A.W. Verrall, whom Headlam had rightly criticised. Murray's translations of ancient drama into Swinburnian verse show him to have been guilty of the errors castigated by Housman; but this fault does not vitiate all his work. Like Wilamowitz, Murray was keenly interested in the life and literature of his own day, and though this sometimes led him into error, it gave his studies life. Unlike Wilamowitz, he was keenly interested in contemporary anthropology, and the alterations in that science since his day should not prevent him and his friends from being recognised as pioneers of a rapprochement between the disciplines that was to lead to interesting results, some of them manifest in the work of Murray's pupils. One of his associates in that approach was F.M. Cornford (1874-1943),[44] who later did important work on Plato and on presocratic philosophy and its pre-philosophical background.

In England both independent and state schools have continued, or continued till the other day, to give the solid grounding in Greek and Latin which is so effective if taken at the age when memory is at its best. Till lately, English schools taught their pupils to translate into Greek and Latin, an exercise much esteemed by Wilamowitz. Murray excelled in it, and so did J.D. Denniston (1887-1949),[45] whose book *The Greek Particles* (1933) is a powerful and sensitive instrument for

[42] See Gilbert Murray, *An Unfinished Autobiography*, 1960, and the excellent sketches of his life by M.I. Henderson in *JHS* 77, 1957, xv and in the *DNB*; also *BG*, ch. 17.

[43] See Gilbert Murray, 'Memories of Wilamowitz', in *Antike und Abendland* 4, 1954, 9f.

[44] See the memoir by W.K.C. Guthrie prefaced to Cornford's posthumous work *The Unwritten Philosophy*, 1950.

[45] See the memoir of Denniston by C.M. Bowra, *PBA* 35, 1949, 219f. (one of Bowra's best pieces of writing).

the understanding of Greek. Since Jebb's *Sophocles*, Englishmen have continued to produce good editions and commentaries. The ninth edition of Liddell and Scott's famous lexicon (1925-40) maintained its high standard; and the editing of the literary texts among the countless papyri found by Grenfell and Hunt (1899-1902) at Oxyrhynchus has been exemplary. For some of this country's contributions to archaeology and art history[46] see p.160, n.600 and p.137, n.503. Especially important is the work of Sir John Beazley (1885-1970), whose profound learning and exquisite feeling for style placed the whole study of Greek vase-painting on a new basis.

During the thirties a small band of distinguished German scholars came to England as refugees from National Socialist persecution.[47] Felix Jacoby (1876-1959)[48] continued in Oxford his colossal task of editing the fragments of the Greek historians. In teaching, Eduard Fraenkel (1888-1970)[49] had a decisive influence. A pupil of Wilamowitz, Leo and Wackernagel, he had won an early reputation with his work on Plautus, and while in England brought out a learned commentary on Aeschylus' *Agamemnon* and a sympathetic study of Horace. But for his English pupils his introduction of the German seminar and his manner of conducting it were even more important; and with other exiles he did much to bring English scholars into close relations with their colleagues on the Continent.

Wilamowitz rightly points out that in its latest phase classical learning has become increasingly international. He alludes to the early work of the Russian Michael Rostovtzev (1870-1952), and to the important work done in Scandinavia by Latinists like Einar Löfstedt and his school, students of ancient religion like Martin Nilsson (1874-1967) and Sam Eitrem (1872-1966); in another place he seems to have in mind the valuable contributions to the knowledge of religion in the imperial period of the Belgians F. Cumont and J. Bidez. Spain

[46] See the memoirs by B. Ashmole, *PBA* 56, 1970, 443f. and C.M. Robertson, *Gnomon* 43, 1971, 429f.
[47] See my inaugural lecture *Greek Studies in Modern Oxford*, 1961, 14f. = *BG*, ch. 1.
[48] See W. Theiler, *Gnomon* 32, 1960, 387f.
[49] See my obituary notice in *Gnomon* 43, 1971, 634f. = *BG*, ch. 21.

is mentioned in his later pages as the scene of new archaeological discoveries. Now the literary study of classical authors in that country has been revived. The main contribution of modern Greece has been in the field of archaeology; the same is true of Turkey and of Rumania and Bulgaria. Classical studies in Poland, despite all vicissitudes, have kept alive, and in the Soviet Union itself activity, especially in ancient history, seems to be increasing.

Wilamowitz, writing in 1921, scarcely mentions the United States; he thinks it singular that now 'even America' should be building museums; he does not mention the doyen of American scholarship in his day, B.L. Gildersleeve (1831-1924), editor of Pindar's *Olympians* and *Pythians*. The great contribution which that country now makes to classical studies should remind us that the last fifty years have not been a period of unmixed decline. The vast financial resources of America could not by themselves have made this possible. If the Yale excavations at Dura-Europos were directed by a foreigner in Rostovtzev, the Cincinnati excavations at Troy and Pylos were directed by a native American in Carl Blegen (1887-1971); and these great enterprises do not stand alone. American ancient historians may be weaker in Greek and Latin than Europeans, but they are less exposed to the danger of being philologists rather than historians, and they are quick to adopt new techniques from other disciplines. In literary studies, America has produced in Milman Parry (1902-1935)[50] a scholar whose achievement in having altered our approach to the Homeric question, besides having thrown light on oral poetry in many languages, is now recognised even on the Continent. In America students often have to start Greek and Latin only at the university; but many of them make up for this disadvantage by hard work and by a fresher and more imaginative approach than that of many of their European contemporaries. Since European scholars will soon have to deal with pupils who reach the university with no previous knowledge of the ancient languages, they should

[50] See Milman Parry, *The Making of Homeric Verse*, Oxford 1971. The volume has a brilliant introduction by Parry's son, Adam Milman Parry (1928-71), who had he not died in an accident, like his father, at an early age, might have proved himself scarcely less gifted.

study the American scene with special interest. Also, the special mark of the best recent American work on ancient poetry is a literary sensibility which Europeans might with profit try to emulate.

Let us return to the modern debate over the questions raised by Nietzsche, which has continued among scholars since his day, but with increasing anxiety since the First World War. Some scholars, including many good ones, were content to carry on their detailed work without worrying about their credentials; others tried in various ways to overcome the problem. Wilamowitz was succeeded in his chair in Berlin by Werner Jaeger (1888-1961), a learned scholar who made his reputation with an account of Aristotle's philosophical development which for a time appeared essentially correct. Jaeger tried to deal with the crisis along institutional lines. He preached the need for a 'Third Humanism', which was to follow the humanism of the Renaissance and the humanism of the age of Goethe. Philology was to be solemnly divorced from its partnership with history, and was to remind itself at frequent intervals to reflect on its true nature. But this did not help much; the difficulty lay deeper. The noble concept of the unity of *Altertumswissenschaft* could hardly be abandoned, for without it philology would sink into mere *belles-lettres*; at the same time philology in the old sense could hardly be maintained without some new impetus proceeding from the modern situation. National Socialist Germany did not offer the ideal setting for a third humanism; the accident of having a non-Aryan wife compelled its chief proponent to leave for the United States, where he devoted three volumes to a dull history of Greek civilisation seen from the scholastic standpoint before moving on to the study of the Christian Fathers.

Other scholars of Jaeger's generation come to grips with the problem on different lines. Karl Reinhardt (1886-1958)[51] was a pupil of Wilamowitz, whom he much admired, but had been since his early years in contact with the ideas of Nietzsche and

---

[51] See Pfeiffer, *Jahrbuch der Bayerischen Akademie*, 1959, 147f.; U. Hölscher, op.cit. (in n.9 above), 31f.; L.E. Rossi, *ASNP* serie 3, 5, 373f. I have contributed an introduction to a translation of Reinhardt's book on Sophocles (1979) = *BG*, ch. 20.

with those of the circle around the poet Stefan George. His
main interests were literary, artistic and philosophical, and he
lacked all pedantry, and even the innocent delight in the
accumulation of learning for its own sake. His brilliant study
of Parmenides and his three books on Poseidonius are works of
art in which masterly scholarship is among the artist's tools;
later in his article about Poseidonius for the great
encyclopaedia called Pauly-Wissowa he showed complete
command of the technical apparatus needed for the work. His
two books on Sophocles (1933; 3rd edn. 1947) and Aeschylus
(1949) stand without an equal among modern literary studies
of Greek poetry; though they are beautifully written, they are
unfortunately not easily understood without a good grasp of
German. When Jaeger organised a congress to discuss 'the
problem of the classical', Reinhardt wrote an article that
described the crisis of philology with perfect clarity and
sardonic wit and finished with a brilliant analysis, taking one
example from Sophocles and another from Goethe, of the
meaning of the term 'classical' as it is applied to literature.[52]
Reinhardt distrusted programmes for new sorts of humanism,
as he distrusted many general notions. As in dealing with the
problems of the study of antiquity his method was often to
juxtapose the various possibilities, so in dealing with the crisis
of philology he stated the difficulty, and gave his answer by
the example of his own performance. Reinhardt laid no stress
on the value of the tradition linking us through the middle
ages with the ancient world; following Goethe and Nietzsche,
he set out to show how ancient literature, art and philosophy
could enrich modern life. But the maintenance of the
continuous tradition was of primary importance to another
great scholar who looked coolly upon Jaeger's attempt to
promote an institutional new humanism. This was Rudolf
Pfeiffer (1889-1979), whose attitude was profoundly
influenced by his Catholic faith and his education in the
famous Benedictine school of St Stephan, near Augsburg. His
Catholicism was a modern version of that *philosophia Christi*
which is associated with the name of Erasmus, whom Pfeiffer

---

[52] 'Die klassische Philologie und das Klassische', in *Vermächtnis der Antike*,
2nd edn. 1966, 334f.

made one of the central objects of his study. Like Reinhardt, Pfeiffer was an admiring pupil of Wilamowitz; but through his teacher in Munich, Otto Crusius, he inherited also the tradition of Rohde, and this together with his Erasmian philosophy saved him from acquiring any admixture of nineteenth-century positivism and historicism. Even before the thirteen years of exile which he spent in England (1938-1951), his conception of scholarship was not German, but European. Pfeiffer's first great work was an edition of Callimachus, the most representative figure of that Hellenistic age in which poets created philology in order to preserve the achievements of the past; in the great history of classical scholarship which is his second he described the results of their invention, and how it was applied to religious texts as well as secular. His Catholic point of view affords a useful contrast to the standpoint of Wilamowitz.[53]

Germany was the first country in which the crisis of classical studies began to be debated; but now the debate has spread to every western country. In America, some professors contend that the degree of Ph.D. should be abolished; those among them who are concerned with classical studies feel that technique has been over-emphasised and literary appreciation neglected. Even in England, where classical studies have retained a humanistic character, scholars are sometimes criticised for over-concentration upon textual and linguistic studies. The critics are not altogether without justification, but they should remember that without a certain number of people who know Greek and Latin really well classical studies will perish; study of classical literature in translation is better than nothing, but it is a miserable substitute for the real thing. Also, the critics should learn not to confuse the nineteenth-century German tradition of philology with the eighteenth-century tradition of exclusively textual interpretation kept alive by Housman and still adhered to by a tiny handful of heroic Housmanites.

The fundamental causes of the crisis are rooted in the social

---

[53] It is developed in his great *History of Classical Scholarship* (see n.2 above) and in many articles printed or listed in his *Ausgewählte Schriften*, 1960; see also the lecture *Philologia Perennis* (SB Munich, 1961).

situation. The rapid movement of the western world towards the kind of industrial civilisation whose best example can be seen in the United States was bound to affect the whole pattern of education. The threat to the independent schools and the pressure in favour of vocational training in schools of all kinds means that each year fewer people start to learn Greek and Latin at the age at which the memory is best; indeed, the activity of so-called educational experts means that during these years fewer and fewer people are learning anything at all. In all western countries, that is the main problem now confronting the study of antiquity.

This general problem must be distinguished from the problem of the general relation between classical studies and Marxism, although in certain contexts the two problems converge. There is a set of left-wing extremists who believe that all history before the nineteenth century is 'irrelevant' to an age disposing of a modern technology and having a knowledge of their version of Marxism and of the kind of psychology that accompanies it. Educated Marxists, who include some distinguished students of antiquity, are very far from sharing this attitude; they agree with Marx himself that the study of the ancient world is not less valuable than other historical studies, and their particular approach has in several cases led to valuable new lines of investigation.[54] Of course the Hegelian Marxism of the western world is far less philistine than the cruder Marxism of Russia; yet even in Russia, and also in other countries behind the Iron Curtain, signs of a mild revival of the study of antiquity may be discerned.

Marxism is essentially a dogma; and one may question whether the adherents of a dogma are capable of maintaining the critical attitude which in the past has seemed necessary to keep independent scholarship alive. It may be retorted that Christianity also was a dogma, and that the early Christian fathers established a *modus vivendi* with the study of antiquity that on the whole has lasted over the centuries. Pfeiffer's great history, written as it is from the standpoint of an enlightened and Erasmian Catholicism, might be cited as providing

[54] See the special volume of *Arethusa* entitled *Marxism and the Classics* (n.8, 1, spring, 1975); V. di Benedetto and A. Lami, *Filologia e Marxismo: contro le mistificazioni*, 1981.

evidence. Wilamowitz would reply that classical scholarship
was able to apply the severest critical standards only after the
grip of the Catholic Church upon European culture had been
relaxed. Despite Erasmus and the great French Benedictines,
he would remind us, few of the leading classical scholars since
the Counter-Reformation have been Roman Catholics. One
can, I think, foresee some future for classical studies under
Marxism; but it would be too optimistic to imagine that they
are likely in the foreseeable future to flourish in any Marxian
society as they flourished in Wilhelmine Germany, or even in
Victorian England.

Uvo Hölscher in one of the most perceptive treatments of
the crisis[55] has argued that ancient literature and philosophy
presuppose the concept of the human personality, and that
this concept is called in question by the prevailing attitude to
life today. That attitude is by no means an inevitable
consequence of the acceptance of Marxism, or of Freudianism,
although elements of both doctrines have contributed to its
making; many intelligent Marxists and Freudians detest it. A
more important constituent of it is the influence of Rousseau,
tending to undermine the belief that human beings are
responsible for what they do; the whole mish-mash could not
have come into being without the existence of Christianity, of
which it is in the last resort a crude residual version; no
Christian who understands his religion could countenance it
for a moment, though it is widely held among that now
numerous class of stupid, ignorant or dishonest clergymen
whom Dean Inge used to call 'the court chaplains of King
Demos'. Its prevalence supplies one of the best reasons for
thinking that classical studies have seldom been more
necessary than they are today.[56]

The monuments of ancient literature and art are such as to
appeal powerfully to some people in every generation,
whatever the prevailing fashion; and so long as historical
studies of any kind continue, the history of the world of

[55] See n.9 above.
[56] For an excellent exposition of their relevance in one important branch
of study, see Kurt von Fritz, *The Relevance of Ancient Social and Political
Philosophy for our own Times*, Berlin 1974.

classical antiquity, the direct ancestor of our own, can hardly suffer a complete neglect. Scholars cannot give up the noble conception of the study of the ancient world as a whole. They must guard perpetually against the danger of dryness, both the dryness that comes from an excessive concentration on technique and the dryness that comes from the adoption of too narrowly historical a standpoint. They do not maintain that the classics offer an ideal pattern for imitation. Nor indeed can the classicists of the Renaissance or the age of Goethe justly be reproached with this; the idea of imitation of an ideal pattern hardly suffices to explain the relation of a Michelangelo or of a Goethe to the ancient artists from whom they drew inspiration. The study of ancient civilisation presents us not with patterns to be copied but with working models of possible beliefs and methods, which if intelligently and unsentimentally presented can save us from the provincialism of those who know only their own period. The ancients saw no reason to suppose that human nature was likely to change much, whatever social and historical circumstances might prevail; their art and literature dealt with what is constant rather than with what is ephemeral; and that makes their literature, art and history particularly likely to provide experience that may be useful, together with other experiences, in our own practice. The value of that experience, over and above whatever value may be assigned to the maintenance of the tradition that links us with antiquity, must be held to justify the continuance of these studies, so long as any historical and literary studies are thought justified.

U. von Wilamowitz-Moellendorff

# History of Classical Scholarship

The nature of classical scholarship[1] – as it is still called,
thought it no longer claims the primacy the epithet implies – is
defined by its subject-matter: Graeco-Roman civilisation in its
essence and in every facet of its existence. This civilisation is a
unity, though we are unable to state precisely when it began
and ended; and the task of scholarship is to bring that dead
world to life by the power of science – to recreate the poet's
song, the thought of the philosopher and the lawgiver, the
sanctity of the temple and the feelings of believers and
unbelievers, the bustling life of market and port, the physical
appearance of land and sea, mankind at work and play. In this
as in every department of knowledge – or to put it in the Greek
way, in all *philosophy* – a feeling of wonder in the presence of
something we do not understand is the starting-point, the goal
was pure, beatific contemplation of something we have come
to understand in all its truth and beauty. Because the life we
strive to fathom is a single whole, our science too is a single
whole. Its division into the separate disciplines of language
and literature, archaeology, ancient history, epigraphy,
numismatics and, latterly, papyrology can be justified only as
a concession to the limitations of human capacity and must
not be allowed to stifle awareness of the whole, even in the
specialist.

The business of the history of scholarship is to show how the
science, which now is aware of its true nature and function,
developed out of the *grammatikē*[2] of the Greeks which, though

---

[1] Classical scholarship: see above, Introduction, p.vii.

[2] He means *grammatikē* in the sense of the elementary teaching of
literature, not in that of grammar in the technical sense; see H.I. Marrou,
*Histoire de l'Education dans l'Antiquité*, 1948, 224, 340.

scientific, was not yet a historical science but lived on in Rome and Byzantium, in however atrophied a form. This development has kept in step with the modern march of mind, on which the assimilation of the cultural heritage of antiquity has had a powerful influence – beneficial, but also at times inhibiting. Modern thought in its turn has reacted upon scholarship; but to pursue that reaction, interesting as it is, would be beyond the scope of this book, though the reader should always allow for it.

What Europe took over from the 'grammar' of the ancients was, in the first place, intended only to serve the purposes of language-teaching, since Latin, as the language of the universal church, kept its place in practical life. The literary forms of utterance – poetry and prose – were taken over along with the language, and so there grew up a new Latin literature which achieved a splendid flowering that even now is not quite extinct. Imitation – the revival of the ancient arts, including the visual – has at various times and in various ways been the grand object, along with the naturalisation of the old literary forms and styles in modern languages. For long it was customary to treat this activity as part of classical scholarship; but it is irrelevant to the science whose growth we have set out to trace, and we should no more expect the Latin verses of Bembo[3] and Johannes Secundus[4] to be mentioned in these pages than look for a discussion of Palladio and Klenze,[5] Thorwaldsen or Flaxman.[6] Nor do we care whether certain writings of Muretus or Ruhnken[7] were models of classical Latin or not. This should be sufficiently obvious from the fact that nobody regards the composition of Greek verses as a

[3] Cardinal Pietro Bembo (1470-1547): Sandys ii 112; Weiss, *RDCA* 200; Pfeiffer ii 135. See A. Perosa and J. Sparrow, *Renaissance Latin Verse*, 1979, 167f.

[4] Johannes Secundus (1511-1536; Sandys ii 216), of the Hague, wrote a famous book of love-poems called *Basia*. See Perosa and Sparrow, op.cit., 479f.

[5] Andrea Palladio (1518-1580), of Vicenza, a great architect who designed famous buildings in Venice and Vicenza and villas in the Veneto. Leo von Klenze (1784-1864), a classicising Munich architect who designed the Glyptothek and the Propylaeon in that city; see H.R. Hitchcock, *Architecture: Nineteenth and Twentieth Centuries* (Pelican History of Art), 23f.

[6] Bertil Thorwaldsen (1770-1844) and John Flaxman (1755-1826): classicising sculptors.

[7] Muretus or Ruhnken: see below, nn. 234 and 356.

branch of scholarship. (Such verses incidentally lacked style until the nineteenth century, but today fine ones are produced, particularly in England.)[8] And yet it is impossible to overrate the usefulness of such exercises to a scholar, and the pleasure that attends success is all the greater because it is within the reach of a small minority only.

School and university education also has its own separate history. This is not the place for an account of it,[9] important though it is, indirectly, for the business of scholarship, and unjust though it may seem that we should ignore men who, by confining themselves to the role of instructor and mentor of youth, often acquired far greater merit than many a scholar who contributed his mite to the sum total of learning. Vittorino de Feltre and Guarino da Verona[10] are examples in the fifteenth century of this admirable breed of men, and there has been no lack of them since, down to the present day. The translators also must generally be excluded, though they have contributed much to the dissemination of ancient ideas. As an example we need only recall Amyot's Plutarch.[11] The part played by that book in infusing the spirit of Hellenism into modern culture is infinitely more important than most scholars' work, but scholarship it is not.

By thus limiting the field we can sketch the evolution of scholarship in broad outline without naming many of its representatives, for the pioneers in every age are few. Space too is a limiting factor; but convention demands that the foreground be filled with personalities, including some whose short-lived triumphs soon faded from memory – and such piety has its value. Hence J.E. Sandys's *History of Classical Scholarship*[12] is the only book on its subject worth mentioning,

[8] Very few nowadays, unfortunately, since the Second World War.

[9] See Marrou, op.cit. (n.2).

[10] Vittorino da Feltre (1378-1446; Sandys ii 53) was a famous humanist who taught in Mantua; Guarino (1374-1460; Sandys ii 49) taught in Ferrara under the patronage of the House of Este. For the English pupils of both, see R. Weiss, *HE*, index s.v. Guarino's *Regulae Grammaticae* (1418) was the first modern grammar.

[11] Jacques Amyot (1513-1593; Sandys ii 195); see D.A. Russell, *Plutarch*, 150f.); he published translations of the *Lives* in 1559 and of the *Moralia* in 1572; Sir Thomas North's version, used by Shakespeare, depended upon his.

[12] See Introduction, p.v.

and is a work of solid learning; it is indispensable, and I gratefully acknowledge my debt to it. Another standby has been a transcript I made of the lectures on the same subject given in 1868 by Otto Jahn[13] which has helped me all my life. This would have been a book in a thousand if the opportunity had been taken to publish it immediately after his death from his notebooks and the shorthand record. Jahn's erudition was boundless, and yet he was more than a mere *polyhistor* and never hesitated to express opinions.

It would be inappropriate to begin a history of classical scholarship with the Renaissance, for the revival of ancient learning started long before then. The tradition was never completely interrupted in the schools; and it is precisely the earlier centuries that were decisive for the preservation of ancient literature. As a result of the division of the Roman Empire into eastern and western halves and the loss of the western half, where in the Germanic states the church alone preserved a single culture, we must trace two separate streams until their reunion after the fall of Constantinople. They have a common source in that Hellenistic discipline of *grammatikē* which, in the field of etymology and in the doctrine of the parts of speech, dates back to the Sophists[14] – or even further, insofar as it dealt with the elucidation of the poets – and which reached its perfection in the hands of philosophers and 'critics' or 'grammarians', as they were now styled: Eratosthenes[15] (who was modest to call himself a *philologos*, because his interests were of the widest), Aristophanes of Byzantium[16] and

[13] Jahn: see below, pp. 134, 151. His article 'Bedeutung und Stelle der Altertumsstudien in Deutschland' *was* published in *Aus der Altertumswissenschaft*, 1868, 1f.

[14] Grammar in the technical sense has its beginnings in the age of the sophists (see Pfeiffer, *HCS* i ch.2), although in its refined sense 'technical grammar is the latest achievement of Hellenistic scholarship' (Pfeiffer, *HCS* i 272). 'Grammar' in the sense of the interpretation of literature is much earlier; see above, n.2.

[15] Eratosthenes (*c.*285-205 B.C.): see Pfeiffer, *HCS* i 152f. and P.M. Fraser, *PBA* 56, 1970, 175f. and *PA* i 456f.

[16] Aristophanes of Byzantium (*c.*260-185 B.C.); Pfeiffer, *HCS* i 172f; Fraser, *PA* i 459f.

Aristarchus.[17] The little book of Dionysius Thrax[18] and the doctrine of Asclepiades of Myrlea,[19] which we can safely reconstitute, afford at least a glimmering of what was expected of 'grammar' in those days. Philoxenus[20] advanced a step further in the science of language – perhaps because he realised the relevance of Latin – when he arrived at the notion of monosyllabic roots; Buttmann[21] learned from him. In the succeeding age the triumph of classicism depreciated the role of the 'grammarian', since the demand was now for practical instruction in the written and literary language. The aim was to turn the clock back three hundred years – an ambition finally realised in the age of the Antonines, when some people even went back to writing in Ionic. Higher education was centred entirely on the study of rhetoric, but that required preliminary training in the use of language by a 'grammarian'. As early as the reign of Augustus, Tryphon[22] compiled the first *onomastikon*, or vocabulary of the written language, and was also the first writer on syntax. Two hundred years later Herodian[23] finally fixed orthography and 'prosody', both on strict classical principles. Innumerable manuals gave the classical vocabulary, and in time pasticheurs like Aristides became models of style in their own right. On the other hand, scholarly elucidation was reserved for an ever-diminishing range of poetical literature, and scholarship itself sank to the level of pure compilation. We might expect the church, which had sprung from the lower classes, to have paid more regard to the realities of life; but it capitulated to the prevailing rhetoric, and even after it had produced great masters in that style, attempts failed to replace the old school textbooks with the works of Clement, Gregory and Cyril.[24] Homer and Euripides had never been abandoned,

[17] Aristarchus (216-144 B.C.): Pfeiffer, *HSC* i 210f. Fraser, *PA* i 462f.
[18] Dionysius Thrax (active *c*.130 B.C.): Pfeiffer, *HCS* i 266f.
[19] Asclepiades of Myrlea (active *c*.65 B.C.): Pfeiffer, *HCS* i 272f.)
[20] Philoxenus (first half of first century B.C.): Pfeiffer, *HCS* i 273f.
[21] Buttmann; see below, n.444.
[22] Tryphon: Sandys i, 142f.
[23] Herodian: Sandys i 314. The first nineteen books of his 'general prosody' dealt with accentuation in general, the twentieth with quantities and breathings and the last with enclitics, etc. See below, p.144.
[24] Clement of Alexandria (160-215 A.D.): Sandys i 323; see Chadwick,

and so the old system ground on, becoming more and more uninspired, as is amply proved by the writings of Georgius Choeroboscus,[25] the most influential teacher of the sixth century. The cleavage between the literary language and the language of real life grew ever wider, and the upper echelons of society at home in that language grew ever thinner; but the break was never complete, and most of the old books were still available in some libraries, even if few people read them. The collapse did not come until Islam destroyed the ancient seats of culture in Spain, Palestine and Egypt, and with the Iconoclast controversy[26] the end seemed imminent.

Yet a few generations later the study of the old literature was resumed under the great Patriarch Photius,[27] who concerned himself only with prose, in which he shows a surprisingly sure feeling for style. The same applies to Arethas of Patrae,[28] who ended his career as Archbishop of Caesarea in Cappadocia and by his devoted care ensured the preservation of unique or important manuscripts of many of the chief prose writers, including Plato, Aelius Aristides, Lucian, Cassius Dio, Philostratus, Euclid, Pollux, Pausanias, Clement and the Apologists. We need comprehensive research on Photius; Socrates Kugeas has made a start with a valuable monograph. Arethas and other clerics filled the margins of their working copies with explanatory notes, quotations and

---

*EC* 94f. (also his *Early Christian Thought and the Classical Tradition*, 1966, 31f.). Gregory: either Gregory of Nazianzus (330-390) or Gregory of Nyssa (see Chadwick, *EC* 148 and W. Jaeger, *Early Christianity and Greek Paideia*, 1961, Index, svv.). Cyril of Alexandria (412-444): Chadwick, *EC* 194f. Chadwick calls him 'a distinguished and thoughtful theologian'; he was also a fanatical inciter to murder (see Gibbon, *Decline and Fall of the Roman Empire*, ch.47).

[25] Choeroboscus: Sandys i 313, 381. He was active between 750 and 825 (see W. Bühler and C. Theodoridis, *BZ* 69, 1976, 397f.).

[26] The controversy over the use of images in worship lasted from the seventh to the ninth century. As to Islam, contrast p.11; yet both statements are correct.

[27] Photius (*c.*810-891): Sandys i 388; *SS*² 54f.; *ABP* 40; Browning, *BS* 8; Wilson 'The composition of Photius' Bibliotheca', *GRBS* 9, 1968, 451.

[28] Arethas: Sandys i 395; *SS*² 57; Teubner edition of his writings by L.G. Westerink; Browning, *BS* 11. Wilamowitz refers to S.B. Kougeas, Ὁ Καισαρείας Ἀρέθας καὶ τὸ ἔργον αὐτοῦ, Athens, 1913.

conjectural readings, and no doubt altered the text in places where we now complain of interpolation. Such is the origin of the scholia on Plato, Clement and Lucian, most of which have come down to us from antiquity only indirectly. The manuscripts were now arranged in the beautiful new minuscule; word division and 'prosodic' marks were also introduced, presupposing a high level of scholarly activity in the scribes. As aids to the acquisition of the necessary grammar, and also of the artificial literary language, there were compilations both large and small, many anonymous or pseudonymous: etymologies, selections from Herodian, the lexicon of Photius and the lexicons edited by Bekker,[29] many of which can still be read in manuscripts of the period. The vast lexicon of Suidas[30] (of whom nothing personally is known) also belongs to this age and could not have been produced without the extensive collections of excerpts from the historians commissioned by Constantine Porphyrogenitus.[31] Such collections were common: Photius' *Bibliotheca* is an example, as, in the domain of poetry, is the Anthology of Constantine Cephalas,[32] whose sources even include a series of metrical inscriptions – about the only trace of contemporary interest in the stones that must have met the eye at every turn. Of scholarly work on the poets at this time we have no positive evidence; but it was then that the texts and scholia took on the form in which we have them today, which implies a respectable standard of linguistic study. Certainly they can have found readers only within a narrow circle; but this is more or less true of everything, including what was written in the artificial Attic which the scholars continued to handle with great virtuosity – especially in well-turned, but mostly meaningless, epistles after the fashion of

[29] Bekker: see below, n.446.

[30] Suidas: it is nowadays fashionable to suppose that there was no person called 'Suidas', but that the lexicon was called by a medieval word 'Suda' meaning 'fortress'. The whole question of the title is complicated, and it may have originated from a corruption of the Italian word 'guida'; see Cardinal Mercati, *Byzantion* 27, 1957, 173f.

[31] Constantine Porphyrogenitus (905-959); *SS*[2] 58, *ABP* 53; n.122 below.

[32] Constantine Cephalas (active 917 A.D.) compiled an anthology on which much of our Greek Anthology depends. See Gow and Page, *The Greek Anthology: Hellenistic Epigrams* i, 1965, xvii.

the later rhetoric – right down to the fall of Constantinople.

The revival of the Platonic philosophy (banned by the Church) by the influential Michael Psellus[33] was of incomparably greater consequence. Of course this Platonism contained an admixture of impurities, because Psellus' sources include the *Poimandres*, an invaluable work for the student of mystical religion in late antiquity which, as the number of surviving copies of Psellus' manuscripts shows, had many readers from the fourteenth to the sixteenth century and was translated, along with Plato, by Ficino,[34] only to remain completely dead until recent times. A new edition is required in the interests of learning, since it is a prime example, like astrology, of the rot that gradually destroyed the tree of true Hellenism.[35] The study of Aristotle never lapsed, and we must find a place in our academic museum for Byzantine commentaries.[36] John Tzetzes,[37] that most unpleasant man, pretended to wider reading than he possessed and was a complete failure as a critic; but he had some advantages that we have not. The three princes of the church, Eustathius of Thessalonica, Michael Choniates of Athens and Gregory of Corinth (*c.* 1200),[38] rank much higher. From Acominatus we learn that, apart from the Acropolis, the ancient monuments of Athens were already in his day as ruined, and her ancient traditions as forgotten, as when exploration began in the seventeenth century. The amount of material on Homer amassed by Eustathius is astounding, and his commentary, one of the first printed books, dominated Homeric studies for

---

[33] Psellus (1018-1096/7?): Sandys i 401; *SS*² 60; Wilson, *ABP* 68.

[34] Ficino: see below, n.110.

[35] The *Poimandres* is the first tractate of the Hermetic Corpus; see vol. 1 of the edition by A.D. Nock and A.J. Festugière, 1945, and cf. the latter's *La Révélation d'Hermès Trismégiste*, 4 vols, 1950-4.

[36] On Aristotelian scholarship in the twelfth century, see R. Browning, *PCPS* 188, 1962, 6f.

[37] John Tzetzes (*c.*1110-1180): Sandys i 408, *SS*² 62; Browning, *BS* 14.

[38] Eustathius (active *c.*1160-1195), Archbishop of Thessalonica; Sandys i 410; *SS*² 61; Wilson, *ABP* 98; Browning, *BS* 14f. Michael Choniates (incorrectly called Acominatus) (*c.*1138-*c.*1222); Sandys i 411; *SS*² 63; Wilson, *ABP* 108. Gregory of Corinth was shown by P. Maas (*Kl. Schr.* 492f.) to have been active during the tenth or the eleventh century; cf. R. Browning, *Byzantion* 33, 1963, 19.

years; we possess it in the author's own hand. At home it would not have found a public, even if the disastrous Fourth Crusade[39] had not brought about a general decline and made havoc of the still ample heritage of ancient literature.

The damage was irreparable. Henceforth it was only small groups, mostly in monasteries, who exerted themselves to save the last remains. We should be especially grateful to Maximus Planudes[40] for what he did, which included the gathering of all the Plutarch we still possess, the making of excerpts and teaching; curiously enough he translated a number of popular Latin books. The return to the classical poets, by Moschopulus, Thomas Magister and Triclinius,[41] is a remarkable phenomenon. Triclinius is comparable with the humanists whose emendations and interpolations we lump together as the work of the *Itali*, but he is really superior to them, since he carefully distinguishes between his own and the ancient scholia, and when he resorts to conjecture admits it. The truth is that Constantinople still boasted a culture and an art that could challenge the Italians, as anyone must agree who has read the works of Theodorus Metochites[42] and visited the church endowed by him, now known as the Mosque of Kariyeh. This brings us to the fourteenth century, in which the Italian demand for Greek books led to the mass-production of copies, some good, others rank bad, in the ugly cursive of the period. 'Books' is not really the right word, since there was no such thing as the distribution of identical copies

[39] The Crusaders under Venetian leadership sacked Constantinople in 1204.

[40] Planudes (*c.*1255-*c.*1305): Sandys i 417; *SS*² 65, Wilson, *ABP* 126; A. Turyn, *The Manuscript Tradition of Euripides*, 1957, 53, n.88. A. Turyn, *The Manuscript Tradition of the Tragedies of Aeschylus*, 1943, 104, n.89. On his work on Plutarch, see D.A. Russell, *Plutarch*, 147; on his translation of Ovid, see P.E. Easterling and E.J. Kenney, *Proc. Cambridge Phil. Soc.*, suppl. 1, 1965.

[41] Manuel Moschopoulos (active *c.*1300 A.D.): Sandys i 419; Turyn, loc. cit. Thomas Magistros (*c.*1280-1350): Sandys i 419; Turyn, loc. cit. Demetrius Triclinius (*c.*1280-1340): Sandys i 420; *SS*² 66; Turyn, *The Manuscript Tradition of Aeschylus*, p.103, n.89; on his work as a critic, see G. Zuntz, *An Inquiry into the Transmission of the Plays of Euripides*, 1965, 193.

[42] Theodore Metochites (*c.*1260-1331): Sandys i 421; Wilson and Reynolds, *SS*² 131.

through the book trade. Teachers of Greek also began to make
their way to the west at this time and a number achieved
celebrity; but, as scholars, even Chrysoloras and
Chalcondyles[43] were of no account. It was only after the fall of
Constantinople[44] that learning fled her homeland; and all
higher education ceased there for centuries to come.

This makes the achievements of Adamantios Koraës, a
native of Chios (1748-1833), all the greater. Koraës deserves to
be honoured not only by his countrymen, as the restorer of
their language, but by everyone who has a feeling for
patriotism of the noblest kind. The lesson of his career is that
the spirit is immortal, and that the fathers' blessing can give
posterity the strength, centuries later, to build its house anew;
for, by his devotion to ancient Greece and his learned labours,
Koraës paved the way for the political and spiritual rebirth of
his people, as a result of which the *Romaioi* became *Hellēnes*
once more. His scholarly method is astonishing, considering
that he could never have acquired the linguistic knowledge
which his numerous editions attest, either at Montpellier,
where he studied medicine, or even in Paris, where
subsequently he lived a quiet scholar's life; yet his
emendations to Strabo have a felicity that few have equalled.
In the historical investigation of the transition from ancient
Greek, including its dialects, to the living language, which the
scholar can no more afford to ignore than he can Italian,
Koraës broke entirely new ground, and the world had to wait
a long while for his successor. Today native scholars are our
leading authorities in this field. Thereianos has depicted
Koraës's career against a broadly painted background in a
biography that is an outstanding work of art and deserves to
be more widely read.[45]

While on the subject of the Byzantine empire, we must not

[43] Manuel Chrysoloras (*c.*1353-1413): Sandys i 432; *SS* 131; he lectured in
Florence, invited by Salutati, in 1397, and wrote the first Greek grammar
used in the west. Demetrius Chalcondyles (1424-1511): Sandys ii 64; he came
to Italy in 1447, taught Greek in several Italian cities, and brought out the
first printed text of Homer in 1488.

[44] 1453.

[45] Koraës: Sandys iii 361; Dionysios Thereianos (Sandys iii 371)
published his *Adamantios Koraes* in 1889. His library is preserved in Chios,
and his statue stands outside it.

forget how much of the legacy of Greece survived in the provinces which fell a prey to Islam and thus were lost to the Greek-speaking world. A vernacular literature, which preserved Greek works in translation and carried on the Greek tradition in several branches of knowledge, had existed in Syria since the second century.[46] The Arabs became the apt pupils of these Syrians and took with them to Spain whatever learning they had absorbed or evolved for themselves. On the other hand, various kinds of literature – almost exclusively Christian of course – which would otherwise have been lost to us, found their way from Syria, or even directly from the Greek world, to Armenia and Georgia. One example is the Chronicle of Eusebius,[47] the main part of which Jerome left untranslated because it was too learned for the Latins; important writings of Philo Judaeus,[48] whom the church reckoned among its sons, are another example. A fair amount of ecclesiastical literature has also been preserved in Coptic. For linguistic reasons, it has only become possible lately to exploit these sources fully; but a great deal of Greek thought passed into mediaeval science, medicine and philosophy by way of Spain, often through Jewish intermediaries. The whole culture of the east is steeped in Hellenism to a much greater extent than is commonly supposed. On the other hand, we are realising more and more clearly every day how much its Christian neighbours owed to the altogether superior civilisation of Moorish Spain.

[46] See R. Walzer, *Über die syrische und asiatische Galen-Übersetzungen*, 1925. See *SS*² 48f.

[47] The fifth-century Armenian version of Book I of Eusebius' *Chronica* was first published in 1818; see Mark Pattison, *Essays* i 169; E. Schwartz, *RE* vi 1376f. = *Griechische Geschichtsschreiber* 504; Pfeiffer ii 118. Eusebius (265-340 A.D.) is important as a chronographer, and when Scaliger (see below, p.49) was laying the foundation of our knowledge of ancient chronology, he made a reconstruction of the then missing first book which the new discovery to a great extent confirmed. The *Chronica* were translated by St. Jerome (347-419): Sandys i 219; Chadwick, *EC*, 214; J.N.D. Kelly, *Jerome: His Life, Writings and Controversies*, 1975.

[48] Philo, 30 B.C.-A.D. 45, an important intermediary between Judaism and Greek philosophy; his *De providentia* exists complete only in an Armenian version. See E.R. Goodenough, *An Introduction to Philo Judaeus*, 1962.

In Rome, a rudimentary sort of *grammatikē* based on Greek models had grown up among the dilettanti of the age of the Gracchi. Varro's attempt to systematise it was not a success; but what this great worker and noble patriot accomplished single-handed for the old Rome stands comparison with the labours of the army of compilers who searched through all the treasures of the Alexandrian library at the behest of Callimachus. Varro[49] had first-hand knowledge of the life that was destroyed by the civil war, and felt even further out of his element under the make-believe Augustan restoration. Without Varro we should have no real knowledge of the old Romans and their way of life, for anything that later authorities have to say on the subject tends to be traceable to him. Varro has also preserved precious information about their language.[50] The formal scheme on which his grammatical work was based is of course valueless except as a source of indirect information about the Greek theorists. Grammar as a distinct discipline had yet to be created, and this occurred in the early days of the empire, when the Greek grammarians flocked to Rome along with the rhetoricians. Remmius Palaemon[51] produced a Latin adaptation of the primer of Dionysius Thrax; Valerius Probus[52] from Berytus may be compared as an editor with the Alexandrians, and his commentary on Virgil equalled the work of his model, Theon,[53] on the Hellenistic poets. Quintilian[54] gathered together in one great book everything the rhetorical curriculum had to offer. It might with justice have been criticised by the Greek system-builders for its lack of logical structure, but in richness of content and elegance of form Quintilian was supreme. Suetonius[55] was typical of his age in being equally at home in Greek and Latin scholarship. True,

[49] M. Terentius Varro (116-27 B.C.): Sandys i 173; *SS*² 21.

[50] In his *De lingua latina* (ed. R.G. Kent, Loeb Classical Library, 1938).

[51] Q. Remmius Palaemon (c.35-70 A.D.): Sandys i 188.

[52] M. Valerius Probus (*c.*20-105 A.D.): Sandys i 192; *SS*² 25, 217.

[53] Theon of Alexandria lived under Tiberius; see C. Wendel in *RE* s.v. P. Oxy. 2536 is a fragment of his commentary on Pindar's Twelfth Pythian Ode.

[54] Quintilian (*c.* A.D. 35-95).

[55] Suetonius (*c.*A.D. 75-160).

he was only a compiler; but in that capacity he surpassed both his Greek-speaking and his Latin-speaking contemporaries. Thereafter the Latin effort diminished in this department also, for the archaism which set in there too diverted attention from the classics without producing anything of permanent value by way of imitation, and even failed to preserve Lucilius and Ennius. Things rapidly deteriorated, and before long falling standards of culture compelled education to concentrate on the preservation of the literary language. The voluminous later text-books of grammar, metric and rhetoric which we still possess are pretty dreary, and an analysis of them nowhere shows a mind of the calibre of Herodian's. Aelius Donatus[56] certainly did not possess any such, and Servius[57] is merely the old learning and water. Priscian's[58] eleventh-hour contribution was the most important, but only because he stumbled upon the works of Apollonius Dyscolus in Constantinople during the reign of Anastasius. In that age the New Rome diligently cultivated the language of the Old, as the codification of the law under Justinian shows.

As early as the fourth century the best Romans saw a threat to Latin culture in the decay of Greek in the west, and tried to ward it off by means of translations. Augustine[59] himself was scarcely capable of really studying a Greek book, and if there were still professors who lectured on Menander[60] in Bordeaux, one of the principal seats of learning in fourth-century Gaul, precious little came of it. Yet it can only have been from there that a certain knowledge of Greek penetrated to free Ireland; there it survived longer than on the Continent, to which it returned in the Carolingian age. Greek books do not seem to

[56] Aelius Donatus (4th century A.D.; Sandys i 218) wrote a grammar and a commentary on Virgil; a variorum commentary on Terence bears his name.

[57] Servius (second half of fourth century; Sandys i 218) wrote a vast commentary on Virgil.

[58] Priscian (active in Constantinople early in the sixth century); author of a large Latin Grammar.

[59] Augustine (354-430): Sandys i 222; Chadwick, *EC* 216; see Peter Brown, *Augustine of Hippo*, 1967 (paperback 1969).

[60] Wilamowitz has in mind Ausonius 322 *ad nep.* (p.263 Peiper), 45-7: *perlege quodcumque est memorabile. prima, monebo, conditor Iliados et amabilis orsa Menandri evolvenda tibi.*

have reached Ireland, however, and the whole episode is only
a curiosity. To enable Greek-speakers and Latin-speakers to
understand one another there were dictionaries and little
phrase-books exactly of the sort we see today, remnants of
which have survived for the simple reason that they were
widely used – a source of colloquial idiom that is still waiting
to be tapped. The schools' struggle with the vernacular,
reflected in the grammatical works of the final period, is
important mainly for its bearing on the Romance languages,
which developed out of vulgar Latin; and the same applies to
such writings in vulgar Latin as those of Gregory of Tours,[61]
whom Max Bonnet uses in exemplary fashion to illustrate the
process. Translations from the Greek, like the *Mulomedicina* of
Pelagonius,[62] the medical writings of Soranus[63] and the
chronicle known as the Barbarus Scaligeri[64] (though it is in all
essentials the work of Hippolytus), belong to the same type.
Many books became quite incomprehensible in their
barbarous translations, for example the *Aratus Latinus*,[65] the
incomprehensibility of such works as the *Hisperica Famina*,[66]
which passed for elegant Latin in the last phase of ancient
British scholarship, is due to other causes.

Clearly, the old language and the old culture would have
disappeared completely, had not the church decided in favour
of the literary language, as it did in the east, thereby ensuring
the survival of grammar and rhetoric in the Christian schools,
along with a remnant of the old 'encyclopaedic' learning in the
shape of the Seven Liberal Arts. The authors who had been

[61] Max Bonnet, *Le Latin de Grégoire de Tours*, 1891.

[62] Pelagonius (4th century) translated a Greek veterinary work in 35
chapters; *SS²* 129.

[63] Soranus of Ephesus wrote under Trajan or Hadrian; several of his
works exist only in Latin versions.

[64] 'Barbarus Scaligeri' is the name given to the author of the 'Excerpta
Barbari', an eighth-century Latin version of an Alexandrian chronicle of the
early fifth century A.D. published from a Paris manuscript by J.J. Scaliger
(see below, n.206) in 1606; on the work and its relation to Hippolytus, see F.
Jacoby, *RE* vi 1566f. (= *Griechische Historiker*, 1956, 157f.).

[65] The *Aratus Latinus* is a seventh-century Latin version of Aratus'
*Phaenomena* in barbarous Latin, not to be confused with the renderings of the
same work by Cicero, Germanicus and Avienus.

[66] *Hisperica Famina* is a seventh-century work by an Irish monk (Sandys i
438); see the new critical edition by M.W. Herren (vol. i, Leiden, 1974).

studied in the final period – Virgil, Lucan, Cicero in his rhetorical works – kept their places in the curriculum. It did not amount to much; but the senatorial families of Rome, even after they had made their submission to the new religion, were concerned for the preservation of the old literature and, as the 'subscriptions' of many manuscripts show, took pains to procure the best possible texts for the *antiquarii* to copy and distribute. Needless to say, we must be on our guard against thinking of these texts as the product of scholarly recension, of which the *grammatici* of the time understood little and the nobility even less. Boethius'[67] translations, coming as late as they did, had an enormous influence on mediaeval learning, because they preserved in time certain standard works in several of the Liberal Arts. But there is one name that dwarfs all others, that of Cassiodorus.[68] On his retirement from the Ostrogothic public service, Cassiodorus founded a monastery on his estate of Vivarium near Squillace which was also to be a seat of learning; he equipped it with a library, and in the *Institutiones divinarum et humanarum litterarum* he laid down for it, and through it for posterity, a programme of duties and employments which included the copying of ancient books. Cassiodorus was in touch with the centres of culture in the east; and since Greek had not yet completely died out in southern Italy, there were also Greek books available in the library, even though no classics. Certainly, neither the library nor Vivarium itself survived the age of the Lombards, but many of the books seem to have found their way to Bobbio[69] and probably also to the chapter library at Verona – perhaps in the form of palimpsests. The spirit of Cassiodorus and his foundation lived on, thanks to the monks of St Benedict, who held to the *Institutiones*. The founder of Monte Cassino[70]

[67] Boethius (*c*.480-524): Sandys i 237; *SS*², index s.v. See H. Chadwick, *Boethius*, 1981.

[68] Cassiodorus (*c*.485-580): Sandys i 244; *SS*² 72; A. Momigliano, 'Cassiodorus and the Italian culture of his time', *PBA* 41, 1955 (= *SC* 191f. = *SH* 181f.).

[69] It is not now believed that the books of Vivarium passed to Bobbio; most seem to have got to Rome and there to have been dispersed; see *SS*² 73-4.

[70] Monte Cassino was founded by St Benedict about 529; St. Gallen was founded about 613; Fulda in 744.

himself never fostered learning, and it was pursued only on a modest scale in the parent monastery, which in the fourteenth century was as devoid of culture as St Gallen and Fulda. On the other hand, in the Frankish kingdom the Benedictine monasteries soon became the principal seats of learning. It was there that the few survivors of the Arab conquest of Spain sought refuge; in Spain the Roman tradition had held its own as long as the Visigothic kingdom continued, and Isidore of Seville[71] had collected all that remained of ancient learning in his encyclopaedia. This literature now crossed the border into France and exercised a strong and enduring influence there, as well as saving from destruction many works of African origin, such as the Latin Anthology. What was incomparably more important was that Irishmen and Anglo-Saxons brought their learning and their books over with them and founded new monasteries, some on territory which they had first had to win for Christianity themselves, such as Luxueil in the Vosges, Bobbio on the Trebbia, St Gallen, Reichenau and Fulda.[72] Columba, Gallus and Boniface[73] are the most illustrious names; but it was the diligent copyists among the disciples who followed in their train, and scholars who remained outside the monasteries, who actually did the most valuable work. And so it happened that the terrible relapse into barbarism under the Merovingians gave place to the revival of ancient culture which is named after Charlemagne. In fact Charles,[74] who in his own person brought back the title of Roman Emperor, took the lead in every branch of the revival – a true monarch, beside whom even his advisers, led by Alcuin,[75] are no more than the instruments of a master will. Both poetry and prose turned once more to the classical models, new textbooks of grammar and rhetoric showing the way. Speech and writing took on a fresh elegance. The extant remains of the old literature were tracked down and preserved in careful copies. Fortunately quite a few of these Carolingian

[71] Isidore (c.570-636): Sandys i 442; *SS*[2] 74, 226.

[72] Luxeuil was founded about 590, Bobbio about 614, Reichenau in 724.

[73] Columban (c.560-615); Gallus (died c.645); Boniface (c.675-754); see *SS*[2] 77f.

[74] Charlemagne was crowned at Aachen in 800, see *SS*[2] 80f.

[75] Alcuin (c.735-804): Sandys i 455; *SS*[2] 83f.; P. Godman's edition of his poems (forthcoming).

manuscripts have survived, and where we only possess later copies these can usually be traced to a Carolingian archetype and a Frankish monastery. In this business of copying, a technique was developed that deserves the epithet scholarly; the emperor Charles himself enunciated a principle incumbent on us all when he settled a dispute about the genuine antiphonar with the question: 'Where do we get purer water, from the spring or from the brook?' In discussing the Rule of St Benedict Ludwig Traube[76] has given a classic demonstration of how, in its struggle with lazy adherence to the *textus receptus* on the one hand and would-be elegant modernisation on the other, the conscious effort to get back to the authentic text finally lost the day. It would be easy to cite parallels from other periods in the textual history of many Latin poets. Suetonius also provides us with a splendid example of the methods of Servatus Lupus[77] of Ferrières. The central figure in this scholarly movement, Servatus procured ancient manuscripts, collated them and made excerpts – mostly to the benefit of the texts concerned, though he is sometimes guilty of the recklessness we found in Arethas;[78] indeed the whole Carolingian renaissance bears a surprising resemblance to the age of Photius.[79] The Caroline hand is the exact counterpart of the old Greek minuscule, and just as the ancestry of manuscripts in that hand can usually be traced to a single surviving copy of an ancient book, so can the ancestry of the Carolingian archetypes, which it is our prime business to restore. Palaeography, handled with the historical awareness of a Traube, has become a key to the whole world of learning in the age that was decisive for the textual history of Latin literature. As regards Greek, however, the essential work remains to be done.

To consider only its literature would be a grossly one-sided approach to the Carolingian renaissance. The cathedral at Aachen, the imperial palaces, the miniatures and carved ivories are as clearly modelled on Roman buildings as on

[76] L. Traube (1861-1907): Sandys iii 195; 'Textgeschichte der Regula Sancti Benedicti', *SB Munich*, III Cl., XXI Bd.3, 1898, 599f.
[77] Servatus Lupus (*c*.805-862); *SS²* 92.
[78] Arethas: see above, n.28.
[79] Photius: see above, n.27.

works of art from the east. The west was quite capable of developing further what came to it from outside; but this new world, bursting with the energy of youth, was not about to deliver itself completely into the hands of the old. On the contrary, the Teutonic and Latin races now became conscious of their individuality and soon began to write in their native languages, which Latin had helped them to perfect. Romanesque architecture, sculpture and painting breathed a new air, and the same spirit of change inspired the Latin poetry of the time with steadily increasing force until it reached its full power in the vernacular. The west differed in this respect from the east; there classicism had no appeal to the masses and therefore could not give rise to a new, dynamic culture; the difference also determined different attitudes to the legacy of the ancient world. The Carolingian study of classical literature, which can be described as truly scholarly, was not carried on by the next generation. Latin continued to be taught, no doubt, and Wackernagel[80] even claims that some progress was made in grammatical knowledge. It is also true that a school of historical writing was born based on Roman models; but in that field Einhard and the Lombard Paulus[81] (who possessed learning enough to read the lexicon of Festus and preserve it in an epitome) did better work than their successors. The poets too were studied diligently, and men learnt to imitate them with brilliant skill, especially when Ovid was taken as the pre-eminent model; but the greatest heights in poetry were reached only after it had achieved, in the new rhythmical forms, a richness never possessed by the Romans. The Latin in which these poems are written is better than imitation, and only a pedant would despise the neologisms of the schoolmen, considering how many of these survive in our scientific terminology. Anything to do with ancient learning found a ready market, and there was a steady influx of such material even before the Crusades brought the west into direct contact with the Greeks. Southern Italy had never completely lost its Greek character even under the

[80] J. Wackernagel, *Vorlesungen über Syntax* i, 1926, 22f.
[81] Einhard (*c*.770-840; Sandys i 463) wrote the Life of Charlemagne, modelled on Suetonius. Paulus Diaconus (*c*.725-797): Sandys i 456.

Lombard dukes. Here, and in Sicily, geography and the continual change of rulers led to an intermingling of Latin, Greek and Arab influences, and the almost modern look of the Norman princes and their Hohenstaufen successors, Frederick II and Manfred,[82] comes from their identification with the resulting culture. Numerous Greek works of philosophy, natural science and medicine were translated either from the original or from Arabic, and the medical school of Salerno owes its renown to the knowledge thus acquired. These writings, like many from Moorish Spain, also spread to the north. A different Aristotle emerged from Aristotle the logician, who alone so far was familiar, and was received in some quarters with enthusiasm, in others with misgiving. The effect was remarkable, particularly in England. John of Salisbury, Robert Grosseteste and above all Roger Bacon[83] were men of surprisingly wide knowledge; Bacon in particular was inspired with daringly original ideas. The church was not yet ready to tolerate this development, however, and was still able to subordinate everything to its own system, which was authoritatively defined for orthodox Catholicism by Thomas Aquinas.[84] What chiefly concerns us here is that no study of the Greek language, nor indeed anything that so much as prepared the ground for an interest in history or scholarship, emerged from it all. The trouble was lack of contact with the originals, and in the specialist literature not a glimmer of the specifically Hellenic quality – in other words, of the nobility of beauty and art – was to be seen.

On the other hand, the spontaneous productions of the high middle ages do evince this quality; nor were the schoolmen lacking in the power of original thought. The age which, in

[82] Frederick II (1194-1250); Manfred (1232-1266).

[83] John of Salisbury (1110-1180): Sandys i 517; *SS*² 99. Robert Grosseteste (*c*.1168-1253): Sandys i 552; *SS*² 106. Grosseteste was Bishop of Lincoln and Chancellor of Oxford University; a few years ago, there was found in the Bodleian Library a manuscript of the treatise attributed to Dionysius the Areopagite written in Greek at his order by a scribe evidently unfamiliar with that language (R. Barbour, *Bodleian Library Record* 6, 1958, 401f). Roger Bacon (*c*.1214-1294): Sandys i 567; Bacon actually wrote a Greek grammar, and tried, apparently without success, to persuade people to read Greek texts in the original.

[84] Thomas Aquinas (*c*. 1225/7-1274).

Gothic, evolved a style that perfectly expressed every aspect of its genius, could hardly be aware of the possibility of a different style and a different spirit. The monasteries, of course, were in a state of decay; life had deserted them for the towns and princely courts. No wonder the old parchments lay buried in forgotten monastic cupboards; they would all have perished had not a new spirit come from the outer world and discovered them – a spirit which, as it gathered strength, was destined to sweep away Gothic art and scholasticism and usher in a new age with new ideals and new modes of life.

This new spirit was born of the vague longings which caused Italian national sentiment to take hopeful refuge from the miseries of the present in the memory of the greatness of the Roman republic. The supremacy of Gothic did not extend as far as Italy, whose ubiquitous ruins recalled the splendours of a vanished age. True, in Dante[85] Italy possessed a poet such as no other nation could boast, and it was from him that the vernacular received its classic impress; but Dante for his guide chose Virgil, and though he may have glorified the mediaeval outlook and Catholic metaphysics, this did not prevent him from rebuking the church for its misdeeds. The new piety of the mendicant orders soon ceased to seem a panacea, the Ghibelline dream had been shattered and the pope languished in Avignon bereft of both liberty and dignity.[86] Weighed down by the intolerable burden of their world, men were casting about for a fresh start, as the tide of national feeling rose. Cola di Rienzi[87] instructed the Roman people in their sovereign rights by quoting the *Lex de imperio Vespasiani*, and Petrarch was invested on the Capitol with the poet's laurel crown, while the vision of Rome's ancient greatness shone like a distant beacon through the night of her desolation. The prime object of Petrarch, the first humanist,[88] was to bring back to life the

[85] Dante (1265-1321). For his classical attainments and attitude to the classics, see E.R. Curtius, *European Literature and the Latin Middle Ages*, English version 1953 (German original, 1948).

[86] The Great Schism lasted from 1309 to 1377.

[87] Cola di Rienzi (*c*.1313-1354); on his enthusiasm for antiquity, see Weiss, *RDCA* 38f.

[88] Modern research, particularly that of Giuseppe Billanovich, has

beauty of Roman poetry and oratory, and a hunt was instituted for the forgotten works of the Romans on which the new Roman spirit was to be nurtured.

We shall do well not to forget this historical background to the great movement that we call the Renaissance. We all know what came of it – how gradually, all over Europe, it transformed thought and feeling and the assumptions, conventions and aims that governed the whole of life. There is no need to treat of these things here; what matters to us is the negative point that no concern with history or scholarship played any part either in the search for the old literature or in its dissemination. The humanists would long remain men of letters, publicists, teachers, but in no way did they become scholars. The figure of Petrarch fascinates us by its charm; the Florentine collectors of manuscripts – Coluccio Salutati, Niccolò Niccoli[89] and the rest – are sympathetic in themselves; and the more or less wandering *literati*, of whom we may take Poggio[90] as an example, are such singular specimens of humanity, in both their good qualities and their bad, that we follow their careers and their alternations between flattery and abuse with more sympathy than they perhaps deserved. Who can resist the exuberant vitality and bewildering variety of the *Quattrocento*? The general impression remains a blur until we

shown that a fair amount of humanistic activity went on during the thirteenth century. In Padua, Lovato Lovati (1241-1309) and Alberto Mussato (1262-1329) had obtained a number of manuscripts from the monastery of Pomposa, including probably the famous Codex Etruscus of Seneca (Giuseppe Billanovich, 'I primi umanisti e le tradizioni dei classici Latini', 1953, and *CIEC* i 57f.). See Weiss, *RDCA*, ch.2 ('The forerunners of Petrarch'), and *SS*[2] 110. Francesco Petrarca (1304-1374): Petrarch's scholarly activity has been shown by modern research to have been even more important than was realised fifty years ago; see Pfeiffer ii ch.1. See in particular Giuseppe Billanovich's brilliant paper 'Petrarch and the textual tradition of Livy', in the *Journal of the Warburg and Courtauld Institutes* 14, 1951, 137f.; cf. E.H. Wilkins, *Life of Petrarch*, 1961; Weiss, *RDCA*, ch.2, 'The age of Petrarch'; *SS*[2] 113; Pfeiffer ii 4.

[89] Coluccio Salutati (1330-1406): Sandys ii 17; *SS*[2] 119; Weiss, *RDCA* 54; see B.L. Ullman, *The Humanism of Coluccio Salutati*, 1963; Pfeiffer ii 25. Niccolò Niccoli (1363-1437): Sandys ii 43; Weiss, *RDCA*, Index, s.v. Pfeiffer ii 30-1.

[90] Poggio Bracciolini (1380-1459): Sandys ii 25; *SS*[2] 120; Weiss, *RDCA*, Index, s.v., Pfeiffer, *HCS* ii 31f.

focus on each of the separate centres of culture – Rome and Florence, Milan and Naples, Ferrara and Rimini – in turn. Each had its own circle of humanists, though the membership was constantly changing, and many brilliant coteries emerged from the flux; but no account of them is to be looked for in this book. The history of scholarship is concerned with these men only as discoverers and disseminators of the works of ancient authors. We are touched when we read how Cicero's letters to Atticus opened Petrarch's eyes to the painful truth that he could no longer admire Cicero the man as unreservedly as he did Cicero the orator.[91] We share the joy of the people of Verona over the discovery of their fellow-townsman Catullus;[92] we admire Boccaccio[93] for abstracting Tacitus' *Histories* from Monte Cassino, no matter the means by which he did it; in imagination we follow Poggio on his journeys to St Gallen, to the French monasteries and even to England (where there was nothing to be had); we accompany Enoch of Ascoli,[94] in his search at the Pope's behest for a complete Livy, and his return home, if not with Livy, at least with the minor works of Tacitus. We can understand the general excitement over the Lodi codex,[95] which contained all the rhetorical writings of Cicero that had been missing till then, and the repeated efforts made to procure the *Annals* of Tacitus from Corvey, until success came at last in 1508. But we cannot possibly go into the details of all this here and must refer the reader to the *Scoperte dei codici greci e latini* of Remigio Sabbadini.[96] If an ancient manuscript has perished, the next best thing is an immediate transcript by its discoverer, who at that stage would have had no time to think of anything but his

[91] See W. Rüegg, 'Cicero und der Humanismus Petrarcas', in *Das neue Cicerobild* (*Wege der Forschung* XXVII), 65f., cf. Pfeiffer ii p.5, n.1.

[92] One of them, Benvenuto Campesani (1255-1323) celebrated it in an epigram (see *Catullus*, ed. R.A.B. Mynors, 1958, p.105). On Boccaccio, see Pfeiffer, *HCS* ii 20f.

[93] Billanovich (op.cit. in n.88 above) has shown that it was not Boccaccio, but Zanobi da Strada who had the advantage of going there as the bishop's vicar-general.

[94] Enoch of Ascoli; see Sandys ii 33 and 35; he found the manuscript in 1455.

[95] Gerard Landriani found the codex in 1421; Sandys ii 31.

[96] *Le Scoperte dei Codici Greci nei Secoli XIV-V*, 1905-14; new edn., 1967.

copying. It was therefore a relief to scholars when Poggio's[97] faithful transcripts of Manilius, the *Silvae* of Statius and Asconius came to light, for the later copyists made their own alterations – and bewilderingly arbitrary they were – which render the task of recension painfully difficult. In other words, we must not expect *scholarship* of the humanists. The text of Propertius, for instance, undoubtedly goes back to a single manuscript; but we shall never succeed in reconstructing it with any certainty, and in the case of the Lodi Cicero we have so far failed.

Petrarch was already hankering after the great Greek models to which the Romans themselves had directed his attention, and he treasured a Homer he had acquired; but Greek remained a promised land from which he was excluded, for a Greek monk from Southern Italy proved unable to make him free of it. The Basilians there did indeed possess many Greek manuscripts. But these manuscripts were nearly all of a religious cast, and the monks had lost all contact with Byzantine circles that knew the classics. It is true that a number of Greeks in the fourteenth century came over to Italy from the east, but the study of the language made little headway. Great is the fame of Chrysoloras,[98] who taught mainly in Florence, travelled widely as a diplomat and found his last resting-place in Constance – besides writing his *Erotēmata*, the first Greek grammar for foreigners. But only a few, such as Leonardo Bruni,[99] who died as Chancellor of the Florentine Republic in 1444, benefited enough from his teaching to be able to translate competently a serious book. Anyone who really wanted to learn ancient Greek had first to go to Constantinople, and really good manuscripts were only to be obtained from the east. Accordingly, it was in

[97] Only a few years ago A. Campana much simplified the textual criticism of eight of Cicero's speeches by finding in the Vatican Library Poggio's autograph copy of a manuscript found by him in Germany (see R.G.M. Nisbet, *M. Tulli Ciceronis in L. Pisonem Oratio*, Oxford, 1960, xxv. Cf. Kenney 18 and Pfeiffer ii 32.

[98] Chrysoloras: see above, n.43.

[99] Leonardo Bruni (1369-1444): Sandys ii 45; Pfeiffer, *HCS* ii 27. He originally planned to dedicate his version of Aristotle's *Politics* to Humphrey, Duke of Gloucester (Weiss, *HE*, 46f.).

Constantinople that Guarino da Verona[100] learnt the Greek which he later passed on so successfully to his pupils.

Two young humanists, Francesco Filelfo and Johannes Aurispa,[101] who had gone in search of manuscripts came home with an exceptionally rich haul. Aurispa in particular unearthed a cache of the most ancient manuscripts – where, unfortunately, is not known – and thereby preserved for posterity the works of authors such as Athenaeus whom the Byzantines had lost sight of centuries before. As a scholar, Aurispa was of no account; and Filelfo, though he made a great noise for several decades with his violent quarrels, produced hardly anything of lasting value. Translations were still the only medium through which the Greek genius could make itself felt; and that ruled out poetry. Even so, its influence was tremendous. Ptolemy's geography[102] introduced men to the notion of a round earth, which showed the Genoese Columbus his way to India. Greek mathematical and technical writings gave impetus to further study; Leonardo, for instance, could learn from the *Automata* of Hero.[103] Bruni had already made accessible the *Ethics* and *Politics* of Aristotle; in Raphael's *School of Athens*, it is a copy of the *Ethics*, not of the *Organon*, that Aristotle carries. Pope Nicholas V,[104] himself a finished humanist from the circle of Cosimo dei Medici, promoted an important translation of the Greek historians which awakened the power of historical thought in men like Machiavelli, who could only acquire it thus from the Greeks. Herodotus and Thucydides were allotted to Lorenzo Valla,[105] whom we should hail as a man of a totally different stamp from his deadly enemy Poggio and most of his contemporaries

[100] Guarino: see n.10 above.

[101] Filelfo (1398-1481); Sandys ii 55; Pfeiffer, *HCS* ii 48. Aurispa (d.1459): Sandys ii 36; Pfeiffer, op.cit. In 1423 he brought 238 Greek books to Italy.

[102] A Latin version of Ptolemy was published at Rome in 1462.

[103] Heron of Alexandria lived during the second half of the first century A.D.; for extracts, see Wilamowitz, *Griechisches Lesebuch*, 1902.

[104] Nicholas V (1397-1455): Sandys ii 65.

[105] Valla (1407-57): Sandys ii 66; *SS*[2] 125. Pfeiffer, *AKS* 164 points out that Valla's work on Thucydides came at the *end* of his career, so that he cannot have learned method from him. See S.I. Camporeale, *Lorenzo Valla: Umanesimo e Teologia*, 1972; *CIEC* ii, Index s.v. (especially L. Jardine on his dialectic, p.141f.); Pfeiffer *HCS* ii, ch.3.

– in fact as a true critic. His translation of Thucydides is the work of a genuine scholar; at the same time the task was good training for a historian, as his account of king Alfonso of Naples shows. The king had to protect him more than once from the Inquisition, for battle was now joined between historical truth and the authority of the church. Valla could hold his own in Rome only as long as he was shielded by Nicholas V. His exposure of the forged Donation of Constantine was suppressed and did not see the light until Ulrich von Hutten had the courage to print it, with a dedication to Leo X, as part of his campaign against papal pretensions. That a mere scholar like Valla should sit in judgment on the text and style of the Vulgate seemed no less outrageous; but the blind Livy-worshippers were equally indignant when he demonstrated that Tarquinius Superbus could not possibly have been the son of Tarquinius Priscus. (Certain of his emendations, incidentally, still survive in modern texts of Livy.) In his *Elegantiae linguae Latinae* Valla gave proof of the same historical sense in the linguistic sphere by showing how to distinguish the various periods and styles of Latin and waging war, not only on current barbarisms, but also on the practice of mixing words and phrases from entirely different departments of Latin literature – though of course adherence to the best models was bound to end in Ciceronianism, and the case for greater latitude, as advocated by Politian, had its points. Finally, Valla's philosophical writings, in which he tried to do justice even to Epicurus, were equally bold and equally characteristic of the outstanding acuteness and independence of his mind. If we look deeper, we cannot avoid the conclusion that it was Valla's contact with the Hellenic genius that lent wings to his soul, and that the advance from humanism to scholarship was entirely due to the influence of Greek literature, which alone could put new life into philosophy and natural science.

In this respect the influx of real men of learning from Byzantium, which had begun somewhat earlier, had momentous consequences. Theodore Gaza and the less attractive George of Trapezus[106] brought with them the

[106] Theodore Gaza (*c.* 1400-1475): Sandys ii 62. George of Trapezus (1395-1484): Sandys ii 63.

Byzantine conception of the Aristotelian philosophy. The Council of Florence, which met in the vain hope of reuniting the Orthodox and Roman churches, brought the aged philosopher Gemistus Pletho[107] to that city as the reluctant representative of one brand of orthodoxy – for which he had as little use as he had for the other, being an avowed Neoplatonist who had no scruples about allotting a place in the spiritual hierarchy to Zeus. Considering the century in which he lived and the benighted state of the Peloponnese which was his home, Pletho is certainly an impressive figure, and his bold speculations, though often they had to be kept dark, continued to influence opinion in a quiet way. Nor is there any doubt that the fires of Neoplatonism had continued to smoulder beneath the ashes; a hundred years after Pletho they flared again in the person of Giordano Bruno. One of the pupils who accompanied Pletho was Bessarion[108] from Trapezus, for whom Neoplatonism smoothed the way into the church of Rome. Once there, Bessarion took the intelligentsia, including the Platonists, under his wing, was made a cardinal and left his magnificent library not to the Vatican but to the Venetian republic – where freedom of thought had taken refuge, as later it did in Holland. The squabbles among the Greeks between the 'Aristotelians' and the 'Platonists', as they called themselves, are best forgotten; not so the ever-memorable foundation of a Platonic academy in the Florence of the Medici and its fruit in the philosophy of Pico della Mirandola,[109] the disciple of Plato and Pletho who, in the beauty of his person and the sublimity of his thoughts and dreams, seemed to his contemporaries almost some blessed spirit whom it had pleased to dwell among them for a season.

[107] George Gemistus Plethon (*c.*1356-1450): Sandys ii 50; *SS²* 125; Pfeiffer, *HCS* ii 57. On the Council of Florence (1438-9), see Geanakoplos, *BELW*, 1966, ch.iii.
[108] Bessarion (1403-1472): Sandys ii 61; *SS²* 133, 239; Geanakoplos, op.cit., and *Greek Scholars in Venice*, 1962, Index, s.v. Unfortunately his great collection of books seem hardly to have been used for many years, as N.G. Wilson has shown. Platonic Academy of Florence: Sandys ii 80; Pfeiffer, *HCS* ii 57.
[109] Pico della Mirandola (1463-1494): Sandys ii 82; E. Wind, *Pagan Mysteries in the Renaissance*, 1958, Index, s.v.

Inspired by the same faith, Marsilio Ficino[110] took upon himself the arduous task of translating Plato and Plotinus, who, thanks to him, have since been loved by thousands.

It was sheer romantic feeling for Rome's past, with no impulse of philosophy, that misled Pomponius Laetus,[111] as Pontifex of a Roman academy founded by himself, into keeping the feast of Pales, holding secret sessions in the Catacombs and indulging in other basically harmless antics – to which category the fanatical republicanism of his colleagues no doubt also belongs. These follies were visited with severe penalties, including a long spell in prison; but in the end Pomponius died with the full honours appropriate to a great Roman. He also took an interest in the ruins, and collected antiques; but nothing came of it, nor of his wild forays into the domain of textual criticism. His only importance as a scholar lies in the quaternions of Festus, which owe their preservation to his copy of the manuscript from which they subsequently disappeared. A person so characteristic of the period could not be omitted from this book.

The Golden Age of Florence – in other words, the reign of Lorenzo dei Medici – will be represented here on its scholarly side by Lorenzo's close friend Angelo Poliziano,[112] whose beautiful Italian poems rank with the Magnifico's. (His Latin poems incidentally are equally good.) Politian learnt his Greek from Chalcondyles, whose chief service to mankind was his success with this pupil, for Politian knew the language so well that he could even translate poetry. He was a real scholar. His many collations prove that he realised the value of a genuine manuscript tradition, and though his death at the age of forty prevented him from producing an edition of any author, his *Miscellanies* worthily inaugurated a literary genre – which, however, so many scholars have found so convenient

[110] Ficino (1433-1499): Sandys ii 82.

[111] Pomponius Laetus (1425-1498): Sandys ii 83; Weiss, *RDCA* s.v. Leto, Pomponio; Pfeiffer ii 51. Weiss shows that Wilamowitz greatly underrates the importance of Pomponius (see p.76).

[112] Politian (1454-1494): Sandys ii 83; *SS*² 120, 136; Kenney 4f.; Pfeiffer ii, ch.4. The missing second volume of his *Miscellanea*, published by A. Perosa, came to light only a few years ago (see V. Branca and M. Pastore Stocchi, *Angelo Poliziano. Miscellaneorum Centuria Secunda*, 4 vols., 1972).

that they have never progressed beyond detached observations, a practice rightly censured by Scaliger. It was Politian's feeling for individual style, and his reluctance to be content with a fixed vocabulary, that set him against Ciceronianism.

Lorenzo also commissioned a Greek named Janus Lascaris[113] to procure manuscripts for his library. (This man is easily confused with an older kinsman, Constantine Lascaris,[114] who led a poverty-stricken life but was at one point able to present the town of Messina with a valuable collection of books, of which the greater part found its way to Madrid; otherwise his only claim to distinction is that he was the first man to print a Greek grammar.) Janus Lascaris' career took him from Florence to Paris, where he was the foremost representative of his people at the court of Francis I, but he eventually returned to Italy. His fame rests on his *editiones principes* of difficult Greek poets like Apollonius Rhodius and Callimachus and of the Anthology of Planudes. He was equal to the task, and it is no small achievement that he returned to capital letters – in other words, that he realised the barbarousness and unsuitability for print of the contemporary cursive. It was disastrous that the all-powerful printing-house of Aldus Manutius[115] decided to use this cursive for the huge number of type-faces required for its output of handbooks. The *typi regii* employed by the French scholar-printers in the next century led to a reduction in the number, and the process has continued; but we are not yet rid of the Byzantine tradition, and scholars seem to be wedded to it even today, though we have before us the books of Aristarchus' time, which no printed book can surpass in beauty and legibility. What a blessing that for Latin, at least, the humanists fixed on handsome legible types, from which we ought never to have departed!

Printing, which some Germans introduced into Rome as early as the sixties of the fifteenth century, ushered in a new era. It served the interests of every sort of literature, but its

---

[113] Janus Lascaris (1445-1535): Sandys ii 78; Pfeiffer, *HCS* ii, Index s.v.
[114] Constantine Lascaris (1434-1501): Sandys ii 76; Pfeiffer, *HCS* ii 53.
[115] Aldus Manutius (1449-1515): Sandys ii 98; *SS²* 138; Pfeiffer, *HCS* ii 56.

most spectacular achievement was the great series of Aldine
classics, which made Greek literature as a whole accessible.
These were folios and were only to be seen on the tables of
scholars; but the Latin classics were also available in handier
formats – they too in the elegant types which the English call
italic. The time was ripe for them. Many printed books were
simply reproductions of a manuscript; but others were the
result of hard critical work on the part of the publisher. Here
Aldus enlisted the services of a Greek named Marcus
Musurus,[116] who showed marvellous skill in dealing with such
difficult texts as Athenaeus, Hesychius and the Aristophanic
scholia, but also, inevitably, some violence, so that we hear
complaints of interpolation. Other printing-houses sprang up
alongside the Aldine Press – of the Giunta in Florence, for
instance, and Zacharias Callierges[117] in Rome, whose Pindar
remained indispensable till quite recently on account of its
scholia; his edition of the Homeric scholia is indispensable
even now. But no firm could compete with the Aldines.
Strictly speaking, we should use the family name and call
them 'Manutians', for the firm continued after the death
of its founder, the great Aldus, though Aldus' son, Paulus
Manutius,[118] was no longer in charge of the technical side of
the business. Paulus is the most important Latinist of
sixteenth-century Italy, and his name will always remain
linked with that of Cicero. For many of the speeches, but more
especially for the letters, he laid the foundations on which all
later commentators have built. He also played a distinguished
part in contemporary archaeological research. With him we
are already far into the sixteenth century, and there are no
further (Italian) critics or interpreters of the classics of any
importance to be mentioned; for the *Thesaurus Ciceronianus* of
Nizolius,[119] the bible of the orthodox observance, was also

---

[116] Marcus Musurus (1470-1517): Sandys ii 79; *SS*² 139; Geanakoplos
*BELW* 127; Pfeiffer, *HCS* ii, Index s.v.

[117] Callierges (active 1499-1523): Sandys ii 80; Geanakoplos, *GSV* chs 7
and 8; id., *GELW* 126. His edition of the scholia on Pindar was finally
superseded only by that of A.B. Drachmann, 1903-27; the scholia on the
Iliad are now being edited by H. Erbse (vol.i 1969, vol.ii 1971, vol.iii 1974,
vol.iv 1975).

[118] Paulus Manutius (1512-1574): Sandys ii 100.

[119] Nizolius (1498-1576): Sandys ii 146.

published under the title of *Apparatus Latinae locutionis* – an admission that it was intended to serve a practical purpose.

In Rome, however, there remained one man, Fulvius Ursinus,[120] who performed valuable services to learning even under the entirely changed conditions resulting from the Counter-Reformation. The collection of manuscripts he built up as librarian to the Farnese family today forms a special section of the Vatican library and contains many manuscripts of the highest quality. Thanks to his contacts with the princes of the church and his own ample means, Ursinus was in touch with the entire learned world; and he was always ready to make his library and rich collections of antiques, together with his time and knowledge, available to others – to Agostino,[121] for instance, in connection with his *De legibus et senatus consultis*; he received in return a copy of the manuscript of the *Excerpts* of Constantine Porphyrogenitus[122] in the Escorial, of which, among other things, he produced the *editio princeps*. Ursinus realised the need for collections of fragments, and his edition of the *Carmina illustrium feminarum et lyricorum*[123] included new material from hitherto unknown manuscripts. His use of Roman family medals for prosopographical purposes shows a similar turn of mind. Today he is remembered mainly for his *Imagines*, the first iconography, which has preserved much that would otherwise have been lost to us (along with numerous forgeries by Ligorio, of course) and on which he worked until his death in 1600. The portrait of Aristotle has recently been extracted from the original drawings intended for a sequel.[124]

In the domain of Greek studies, Italy produced only one more great figure, Petrus Victorius,[125] who deserves the title primarily for his conscientious editing of the manuscripts put

[120] Fulvius Ursinus (1529-1601): Sandys ii 153; *SS*² 150.

[121] Agostino: see below, n.151; see C. Mitchell in *Italian Renaissance Studies*, ed. E.F. Jacob, 1960.

[122] Constantine Porphyrogenitus: see above, n.31. An important collection of excerpts from Greek historians had been made at his order.

[123] *Carmina novem illustrium feminarum ... et lyricorum Alcmani Stesichori Alcaei Ibyci Anacreontis Simonidis Bacchylidis ... ex bibliotheca Fulvii Vrsini Romani*, Antwerp, 1598. See D.L. Page, *Poetae Melici Graeci*, 1962, v.

[124] See Gisela Richter, *The Portraits of the Greeks* ii, 1968, 172.

[125] Petrus Victorius (1499-1585): Sandys ii 135; *SS*² 149; Pfeiffer, *HCS* ii 135.

at his disposal by the Laurentian Library. His editions of the
*Strōmateis* of Clement of Alexandria, Porphyry's *De abstinentia*
and two rhetorical works by Dionysius of Halicarnassus were
*editiones principes*; he was also the first to print the *Electra* of
Euripides and a complete Aeschylus. His commentaries on
the *Rhetoric* and the *Politics* of Aristotle are equally important,
and Cicero's Letters also benefited from his consistently
judicious criticism. But this list hardly represents the full
extent of his interests; witness his literary remains (now in
Munich), and his *Variae lectiones*. His transcripts of scholia on
Homer, for instance (from the Towneleianus, at that time in
Florence) and Hesiod were used, as late as the nineteenth
century, before the originals. Victorius fully deserved the
reputation he enjoyed during his lifetime. While on the
subject, we may also mention Francesco Robortelli,[126] who
likewise published editions of Aeschylus and Aristotle's *Poetics*
and, as a keen student of aesthetic theory, was justly proud
that it fell to him to produce the *editio princeps* of the treatise *On
the Sublime*. It was his misfortune that in the matter of the *Fasti
consulares* he crossed swords with Sigonius, an opponent for
whom he was no match.

The ancient monuments, especially those which rose in
perennially majestic grandeur from the desolation of the
Campo Vaccino and the Palatine, where the Septizonium[127]
still stood, were from the first a favourite subject with artists,
and the Colosseum already appears in paintings of the
*Trecento*. Nicola Pisano[128] imitated the reliefs on the
sarcophagi; and the great Florentine architects not only
adopted ancient ornamental motifs but created a new style, in
contrast to Gothic, which was based on the surviving ruins, at
a time when the rules of Vitruvius had not yet acquired the
force of law. The art of Mantegna[129] reveals the existence of

[126] Robortelli (1516-1567): Sandys ii 140; A. Carlini, *L'Attività Filologica
di Francesco Robortello*, Udine, 1967; Pfeiffer, ii 136. On his treatise on textual
criticism, see n.158 below.

[127] The Septizonium was the colonnaded front added to the palace of the
Caesars by Septimius Severus, and finally destroyed in 1585; see Rumpf,
Tafel 5a for an illustration.

[128] Nicola Pisano: see Weiss, *RDCA* 14.

[129] Mantegna; see Weiss, op.cit., s.v.

positively archaeological leanings in this great master. The minor arts attracted many collectors; so did statuary, and many drawings were made of the group of the Three Graces which stands in the cathedral museum in Siena.[130] Poggio's miscellaneous collection of ancient objects picked up on his walks among the ruins of Rome and in the Campagna was a touching expression of the feelings aroused by the spectacle of ancient greatness in decay, and these tastes were shared by Pomponius Laetus and his circle. In due course all this became the subject of serious study, and Flavius Blondus,[131] in addition to producing a *Roma instaurata* and an *Italia illustrata*, set out in his *Roma triumphans* to depict the whole life of the ancient Romans at the height of their power. In the golden age of the High Renaissance these ambitions reached such a pitch that the idea was mooted of a systematic exploration of the ancient city, no doubt including excavations, and statues were eagerly sought after. The Apollo Belvedere was brought in from Antium, and the Laocoon[132] from the Baths of Titus; the rapture with which the Laocoon was greeted on its arrival is well-known. Finds like these served for the adornment of gardens and palaces. Portrait-busts of emperors and great writers had long been highly prized; and faith, where necessary, created its own supply by boldly attaching their names to any surviving antique heads. And where, we may ask, would Raphael's *Loggie*[133] have been without the *grottesche*, paintings and plaster-work of certain ruined vaults? Raphael was himself a leading supporter of archaeological projects, along with Andreas Fulvius,[134] who laid the foundations of Roman topography in his *Antiquitates urbis Romae* shortly after

[130] Illustrated by R. Lullies, *Mitteilungen des Deutschen Institutes der Archaeologie in Rom* i, 1948, 45f., pl.6.
[131] Flavius Blondus (1388-1463): Sandys ii 40; Weiss, *RDCA* passim; Pfeiffer, ii 50-1.
[132] Julius II, who became Pope in 1503, placed the Apollo in his garden at San Pietro in Vincoli. Later both it and the Laocoon, discovered in 1506, were placed by him in the Vatican Belvedere which he instituted. See Weiss, *RDCA* 192.
[133] Raphael was active in Rome from 1509 till his death in 1520; see Weiss, op.cit., 94, etc. and N. Dacos, *CIEC* ii 325f.
[134] Andreas Fulvius (*c*.1470-1527): see Weiss, op.cit., 86, etc.

the appearance of Francesco Albertini's[135] *Mirabilia urbis Romae.* But the sack of Rome put an end to these promising activities.

Inevitably the urge to copy inscriptions, which spoke an immediately intelligible language, had been felt earlier; but apart from what was noted down by pilgrims to Rome from the eighth century on (for example the *Anonymus Einsiedlensis*)[136] the collections that have survived in manuscript form can be traced to the beginning of the fifteenth century. The most laborious research in libraries was required to get back, where possible, to the original transcriptions and test the trustworthiness of the witnesses. This prelimary work for our *Corpus*, which was performed by Mommsen, Henzen and De Rossi,[137] was no mean feat of textual criticism. The copyists and collectors varied greatly in their industry and reliability: the engineer Fra Giocondo[138] of Verona was easily the best; Poggio also did well. In later times there were many plans for publication on a grand scale, but they had to wait for Janus Gruter,[139] who carried them through at the instigation of Scaliger.

One extraordinary character calls for mention here on account of his exploration of Greece, namely Cyriac of Ancona,[140] who in addition to his other journeys travelled more or less throughout the country, or at least throughout its coastal regions, where, in the middle of the fifteenth century, he often found his own countrymen still living as feudal lords in their castles. In Athens Cyriac made the first rough sketches of sculptures on the Parthenon, though otherwise he put surprisingly little down on paper. He brought home a

[135] F. Albertini (wrongly called 'Albertinelli' by Wilamowitz) was active 1493-1510: Weiss, op.cit., 84, etc. His book was entitled *Opusculum de mirabilibus novae et veteris urbis Romae*, 1510.
[136] A monk of Einsiedeln who during the eighth or ninth century visited Pavia and Rome, made copies of Latin, and even Greek inscriptions and made a plan of Rome; see Mommsen, *Gesammelte Schriften* viii 64f.
[137] Mommsen, Henzen and de Rossi: see below, pp.156-8.
[138] Fra Giocondo (1443-1515): Sandys ii 121; Weiss, op.cit., 150, etc.
[139] Gruter: see below, n.272.
[140] Cyriac of Ancona (*c.*1391-*c.*1455): Sandys ii 39; Weiss, op.cit., s.v. Ancona; Pfeiffer, *HCS*, ii 51. B. Ashmole, *PBA* 45, 1959, 25f. gives an attractive account of him.

mighty haul nevertheless, particularly of inscriptions. Even if much has been lost, our debt to him is substantial, and it is difficult to believe that nothing more remains tucked away in libraries. We must not take too seriously Cyriac's boundless vanity and occasional dishonesty; they are venial sins by the standards of his day. What is more remarkable is that he should have been so industrious, and on the whole so careful, a copyist. It was long before his like was seen again.

By the time the church recovered its strength, inwardly and outwardly, after the shock of the Reformation, its attitude to antiquity had completely changed. The spirit of humanism was stifled by the Jesuits, who countenanced nothing but formal training in Latin grammar and rhetoric, and used it in their schools with ruthless efficiency to further their own ends. Romantic feeling of any kind was entirely alien to the age of the baroque, when ancient remains were recklessly sacrificed for the sake of ambitious programmes of new building.[141] The famous quip *Quod non fecere barbari fecere Barberini*[142] was just; Sixtus V would have liked nothing better than to rebuild the Colosseum itself to house some new foundation. Antique statues continued to be the favourite form of decoration for halls and gardens, but they were subjected to every sort of indignity to fit them to the purpose. In the circumstances we can be thankful that architects like the two Sangallos[143] made measured drawings of numerous architectural features, as well as recording buildings, and that accurate drawings were also made of sculptures, such as we find for instance in the *Codex Pighianus*[144] in Berlin and the sketch-book in Coburg. The value of the great works of Bellori and Pietro Santo Bartoli,[145] which date from the seventeenth century, lies also

[141] See chapter seven of Weiss, *RDCA*, which is called 'The topography and the destruction of Ancient Rome'.

[142] The words appeared on the Pasquino statue in 1638, when Urban VIII was planning to melt down the brazen doors of the portico of the Pantheon to make cannon for his war against Urbino.

[143] On Giuliano de San Gallo's copies in a Barberini codex, see Rumpf 41.

[144] Stephanus Pighius (1520-1604) was secretary to Cardinal Granvella. The manuscript in question still remains unpublished (Rumpf 49).

[145] Giovanni Pietro Bellori (1615-1696; Sandys ii 179) was librarian to

in their illustrations. But for them, we should have only an imperfect knowledge, in particular, of a fraction of the murals. Christian archaeology dates from the publication by Antonio Bosio[146] of *Roma Sotteranea,* which Giovanni de Rossi was to bring up to date so magnificently. The *Vedute* – by which visitors to Rome kept their impressions alive – are also useful indirectly, right down to the well-known engravings of Piranesi, when we reach the age of Winckelmann. Much was done on the same lines for other parts of Italy, especially Etruria. There were plenty of collectors and occasionally a sharp-eyed observer like Flaminius Vacca,[147] but this is not the place for an account of what after all was no more than raw material for the scientific archaeology of the future; for the use made of it at the time, insofar as it was used at all, was still quite unscientific.

One man must still be mentioned, who investigated the monuments of every period with the greatest diligence and energy but who was also a forger on a grand scale: Pirro Ligorio.[148] His literary remains are contained in numerous folios distributed over many libraries; but he also communicated a great deal to his contemporaries, so that along with the genuine material a mass of forgeries abounded, and errors of long standing have only gradually and laboriously been eliminated. The uncomfortable fact remains that we dare not reject the whole of Ligorio's work out of hand. Inscriptions have been forged on paper in every age; some of these fakes are naive in the extreme, like the Latin letter from the Virgin Mary to the town of Messina (*CIL* x 1042), but there are also some ingenious ones. The spurious items in our *Corpus* number thousands, and even forgeries on stone are not unknown. It may be that no deception whatever was intended when the supposed sitter's name was carved in 'monumental' script on a bust. That happened also to Greek heads, and now and then we come across other Greek

---

Christina of Sweden in Rome, and collaborated with the brothers Pietro Santo and Francesco Bartoli in publishing many Roman monuments.

[146] Antonio Bosio (1575-1629): Sandys iii 247.

[147] The sculptor Flaminius Vacca published his account of the Roman antiquities discovered in his time in 1594.

[148] Pirro Ligorio (1530-1586): Sandys ii 154; Rumpf 50; Speyer 320, n.2.

forgeries on stone which are so crude as to be harmless. On paper, the gentle art has always been practised; its last exponent was probably François Lenormant,[149] who remained a member of the French Academy even after he had been exposed. Having fooled his countrymen, he decided to amuse himself at the expense of the Germans, and for a while succeeded.

The real harm done by Ligorio is that he was relied upon by antiquaries, especially by the Augustinian monk Onuphrius Panvinius.[150] Panvinius was cut off by an early death in the midst of far-reaching plans, leaving behind a mass of material later much used by other scholars which included extensive antiquarian collections as well as a series of inscriptions. Another worker in this field was the Spaniard Antonio Agostino,[151] who died in 1586 as Archbishop of Tarragona; his *Dialogos de las medallas y inscriziones y otras Antiguedadas* were soon translated into Latin and Italian and, like certain of his legal writings, made a deep impression. Several individual Spaniards pursued humanistic studies when they went abroad, and some will engage our attention later. Here we may mention Nunnesius,[152] who produced the *editio princeps* of Phrynichus' Lexicon on which our knowledge of this work is still largely based. On the other hand, the *Minerva, seu de causis linguae Latinae* (1587) of Franciscus Sanctius[153] which long remained influential, continued the grammatical tradition of the Middle Ages. The Italian influence, which is noticeable also in the classical poetry of Spain, dates only from the Counter-Reformation, which clipped the wings of humanism. Greek studies never flourished in Spain,[154] despite all the treasures in Madrid and the Escorial, where a great many of them perished in the fire of 1671.

Only one man – all the more honour to him! – succeeded in

---

[149] F. Lenormant (1837-1883): Sandys iii 165; Speyer 323, 5.

[150] Onuphrius Panvinius (1529-1568): Sandys ii 145; Pfeiffer, *HCS* ii 95.

[151] Antonio Agostino (1517-1586): Sandys ii 160; see above, n.121.

[152] Nunnesius (=Pedro Juan Nunez, d.1602): Sandys ii 159; Pfeiffer, *HCS* ii 65.

[153] Sanctius (=Francisco Sanchez, 1523-1601): Sandys ii 159.

[154] During the twentieth century they have revived; in 1974 the Sixth International Congress of Classical Studies was held in Madrid.

crossing the dividing line between antiquary and historian –
Carolus Sigonius of Modena.[155] Though most of his
numerous writings deal with particular questions connected
with constitutional history and public law, Sigonius was
always capable of seeing the wood for the trees, and was far
above the trivialities that filled the pages of most 'Antiquities'.
Roman themes naturally predominated; but Sigonius was
also the first man to inquire into the Athenian constitution,
and though there was little to be learnt about it in his day, the
sorting out of demes and tribes was the right track to follow.
Sigonius was the first and greatest editor of the *Fasti consulares*,
discovered near the temple of Castor in 1546-7, and by
comparing them with the annalistic narrative of Livy he laid
the foundations of Roman chronology. The obvious next step
was to provide Roman history with a firm framework of the
fullest possible lists of the holders of the various magistracies,
but that had to wait for the *Annales* of the Dutchman
Stephanus Pighius,[156] which have remained indispensable
almost to the present day. Sigonius also embarked on a history
of his own country, but he began only from the end of the
ancient world. Where there is so much light, we would
willingly endure the shadow of unedifying polemics, but in
this case matters are more complicated. It can hardly be
doubted that Sigonius fabricated a *Consolatio*[157] and passed it
off as Cicero's. This is what Riccoboni[158] maintained, and he
seems to have been right. There had been enough forgeries,
not to mention the attribution of modern work to the ancients.
Scholars have sometimes tried to amuse themselves at the
expense of their learned colleagues by hoaxing them with
verses of their own. One instance is worth mentioning just for
the humour of it. A member of one of the first families of
Volterra, the Inghirami,[159] quoted from Etruscan *libri lintei*,

[155] Sigonius (*c.*1524-1584): Sandys ii 143; Pfeiffer, *HCS* ii 136.
[156] Pighius; see above, n.144.
[157] On the *Consolatio* (1583), see Speyer 319, n.1.
[158] Wilamowitz says 'Robortelli', but that is a mistake for Antonio
Riccoboni (1541-1599; Sandys ii 144). See n.126 above, and Carlini, op.cit.,
36, n.71; Kenney 29f.
[159] Curzio Inghirami (1614-1655), in his *Etruscarum antiquitatum fragmenta*
of 1637.

which contained oracles about the Reformation just as the Sibylline Oracles[160] do about Antichrist. Other forgeries, such as the *De progenie Augusti* of Messala[161] and the *De orthographia* of Apuleius,[162] imposed on the world for longer, the *De orthographia* down to the time of Madvig. The practice of referring to fictitious manuscripts remained common right up to the nineteenth century, though ancient handwriting is as difficult to forge as ancient stone carving. And yet in the middle of that century a Greek named Simonides[163] almost succeeded, among similar misdeeds, in imposing upon the pundits of the Berlin Academy with a forged Greek manuscript; and quite recently a leaf from an alleged palimpsest was actually published in facsimile – though this Anonymus Cortesianus[164] was not destined for a long life. Meanwhile a graver charge hangs over Sigonius – of publicly defending the work in question after the fraud had been discovered. But if he was guilty, his importance as a scholar remains; indeed it shines out all the more since he had no successors in Italy.

When the Heidelberg library was carried off to Rome,[165] the Vatican could find nobody to superintend the operation except the Chian, Leo Allatius, who was afterwards librarian at the Barberini Palace and brought out a number of unpublished writings, including certain letters of Socratics and some Neoplatonic material. Apart from him, there was no

[160] The Sibylline Oracles (extant in 14 books) originated in the late Hellenistic and early imperial periods, and contain much material derived from Jewish sources. For a bibliography see Fraser, *PA* ii 989, n.217.

[161] *De progenie Augusti Caesaris*, attributed to the Augustan statesman M. Valerius Messalla Corvinus, is a fifteenth-century forgery; see Teuffel and Schwabe, *Geschichte der römischen Literatur*, i, 5th edn., 477.

[162] This work was accepted as authentic by Cardinal Mai (see below, n.449), but was exposed by Madvig (see below, n.487) in 1829 (Madvig, *Opuscula academica*, 2nd edn. 1887, 1f.).

[163] K. Simonides forged a codex of 72 leaves containing a history of the kings of Egypt supposed to be by Uranius of Alexandria; see Sandys iii 381 and Speyer 323, n.4.

[164] Giacomo Cortese forged fragments of a thirteenth book of the *De viris illustribus* of Cornelius Nepos; see Speyer 323, n.8. Speyer calls it 'a kind of mystification'; Sigonius may not have intended to deceive.

[165] In 1623, after the occupation of Heidelberg by the Imperial troops who had defeated the Elector Palatine at the battle of the White Mountain; see Sandys ii 361, and Pfeiffer, *HCS* ii 138. Allatius (1586-1669).

librarian of any consequence, either there or at the Vatican, except the German Lucas Holstenius,[166] who was educated at Leyden and published little of the abundant material he had collected but did some preparatory work on several subjects – for instance, the lesser Greek geographers, who have remained unlucky to this day. The same is true of the fragments of Porphyry, which he planned to collect. Holstenius did in fact complete a life of Porphyry, an important piece of work for its time and not completely superseded even today.[167] His papers, which are divided between the Vatican and his native Hamburg, have also proved a profitable hunting-ground for grammarians. His interest in geography had been aroused by Philip Cluverius of Danzig,[168] a far more considerable figure than his reputation suggests, whom the greatest authority on the subject has taught us to recognise as the founder of historical geography. Cluverius was an indefatigable traveller who explored the whole of Italy and Sicily on foot and wrote a description which combines acute observation with an intelligent use of the literary sources. On it Christophorus Cellarius[168 a] based the comprehensive work in which, from his study, he surveyed the whole of ancient geography. Though written in the manner of the *polyhistors*, not only is this work learned but it treats the subject in an orderly and logical fashion.

Our survey of the course of humanism down to the point at which it ceased to have any influence on our science in Italy has taken us far, and before completing it we have already found ourselves including certain German names. We must now return to the fourteenth century. All attempts to keep to a chronological sequence are doomed to failure, for the simple reason that the various developments in different countries cannot be fitted into a single framework.

[166] Holstenius (1596-1661): Sandys ii 364. See Aubrey Diller, *The Tradition of the Greek Minor Geographers*, 1952.

[167] Wilamowitz certainly knew the *Vie de Porphyre* (1913) by J. Bidez (1867-1945) p.45. Cluverius (1580-1623): Sandys ii 313.

[168] H. Kiepert: see below, n.585, and cf. Wilamowitz, *Erinnerungen*, 2nd edn. 174.

[168 a] Cellarius (1638-1707): Sandys ii 369.

There is no room to trace the threads that connect the palace of the Luxemburg emperors in Bohemia with the beginnings of the Italian Renaissance, or to describe the Germany which Aeneas Sylvius[169] visited a hundred years later. The founding of the universities, the struggles for recognition of the artists and poets, the worthy Reuchlin[170] and Master Ortvinus Gratius[171] with his Jew Pfefferkorn, the Erfurt circle of poets and men of letters, Hutten and Zwingli and Luther's burning of the bull of excommunication – this whole movement, which prepared a mansion for the new spirit in science and religion, would one day allot a modest corner in it also to scholarship; but at the time we are considering, scholarship has not yet moved in. Regiomontanus[172] deserves a place of honour simply for devising a reform of the calendar and, though an archbishop, thereby falling foul of the Curia; however, it was purely as an astronomer that he produced the *editio princeps* of Manilius.[173] In truth there is no one who need detain us until we come to Erasmus.

Erasmus achieved European status at one bound when Aldus brought out the second edition of his *Adagia*.[174] It is a

[169] Aeneas Silvius Piccolomini, pope as Pius II from 1458 to 1464: Sandys ii 72, Weiss, *RDCA* s.v.; Pfeiffer, *HCS* ii 59f.

[170] Johannes Reuchlin (1455-1522): Sandys ii 156; Pfeiffer, *HCS* ii 86f.

[171] Ortvinus Gratius of Cologne (1491-1541): Sandys ii 257. His polemic against Reuchlin provoked the *Epistolae obscurorum virorum*; the first series (1516) were mainly by the Erfurt humanist Johann Jäger, the second (1517) by Ulrich von Hutten. The leader of the Erfurt group was Conrad Muth (*c*.1471-1526): see Sandys ii 156f., Bursian 119f. Johann Pfefferkorn, a renegade Jew, made a proposal to burn the Jewish sacred books which was opposed by Reuchlin; see Bursian 125 and Pfeiffer *HCS* ii 89.

[172] Regiomontanus: Johann Müller of Königsberg (1436-1476): Sandys ii 252.

[173] Housman says he was 'no critic at all' (*Manilius* i, 2nd edn. 1937, xix) He accompanied Cardinal Bessarion to Rome in 1461 (see Pfeiffer, *HCS* ii 37, n.8).

[174] It is a collection of proverbs and notable sayings, originally inspired by Plutarch. Erasmus (1466-1536): Sandys ii 127; *SS*² 142, Pfeiffer *HCS* ii ch.7. Of the enormous literature about Erasmus one may mention the accounts by P.S. Allen (*Erasmus: Lectures and Wayfaring Sketches*, 1934) and J. Huizinga (*Erasmus of Rotterdam*, 1952) and the essays by R. Pfeiffer ('Erasmus und die Einheit der klassischen und der Christlichen Renaissance', *Historisches Jahrbuch* 74, 1955, 175f. = *AKS*, 1960, 208f.) and H.R. Trevor-Roper,

work of immense erudition, though not of scholarship in the strictest sense of the word; yet the whole personality of the man – the quiet, humorous observer of the ways of mankind – is present in it. How he worked his way up from extreme poverty and, mainly in Paris, acquired his knowledge, in particular of Greek, remains astonishing. In England, where he won appreciation and encouragement, he was one of the first apostles of Greek; but More's *Utopia* too shows unmistakable signs of Erasmus' subtle influence – the two were on friendly terms. He took an active part in the foundation of the *Collegium Trilingue* at Louvain, out of which grew the university, and he was already famous when he visited Italy. We like best to think of him in Basel, the haven of his old age. Holbein's brush has made his delicate features familiar to all the world, and the portrait exactly matches his writings. Many of them – the *Colloquies*, the *Praise of Folly*, the Letters – still find appreciative readers, and no matter where we open Erasmus he is fascinating. As a Dutchman by birth, having close ties with France, Brabant and England, he looked upon himself as a citizen of the great world of humanism, whose language was Latin, and for that very reason refused to be shackled by Ciceronianism. His whole life's work was a protest against the spirit of scholasticism which prevailed in the church, and in fact against the church itself as it then was. Indeed it must have been Erasmus who influenced the Spaniard Juan Vives[175] to abjure and attack scholasticism with such effect. Melanchthon too is quite unthinkable without Erasmus. It was a great blow to the cause of the Reformation that Erasmus, who had exposed the abuses in the Church and prepared the way with his Greek Testament for a return to the Gospel, in the end dissociated himself from it. His attack on Hutten shocks us; but understandably he felt he had no choice, for Hutten in his

---

*Historical Essays*, 1962, 35f. The most celebrated of the three portraits of Erasmus which Holbein painted is in the Louvre. A translation of Erasmus' works in many volumes is in process of publication.

[175] Juan Luis Vives (1492-1540): Sandys ii 214; Pfeiffer, *HCS* ii 96. From 1523 to 1525 he was at Corpus Christi College, Oxford. See C.G. Norena, *Juan Luis Vives*, 1970 and J-C. Margolin in *CIEC* ii 245f.

lifetime was far from wearing the halo that now adorns his image. Besides, Lutheranism could not but disgust the great humanist, because it meant, as Goethe put it, a set-back to quiet culture. Erasmus produced editions, in many folios, of the most prolific of the Fathers – Ambrose, Augustine and Jerome – as well as of sundry Roman prose-writers, though only a few of Greek authors. These books have slumbered undisturbed on their shelves for centuries, but the man himself lives and will continue to live. His influence on his own age was enormous.

Erasmus' name is linked with the Erasmian pronunciation of Greek,[176] with the result that modern Greeks to a man – except for the few trained philologists among them – curse him loud and long. Having learnt the language from books, rather than from the lips of Greeks, he very naturally insisted on the pronunciation that had been current at the time when the script was formed. Nor was he even the first person to do so (as Ingram Bywater demonstrated with rare learning);[177] that was the Spanish humanist Antonius Nebrissensis, and no less a man than Aldus Manutius shared his view. Now that scholars have come to realise that every language in every age sounds differently as spoken by different people, and that in the course of time the accepted pronunciation of the written characters also changes, the dispute has lost its relevance. How we are to pronounce, or try to pronounce, ancient Greek is a purely practical question that admits of no universally valid answer, and the idea of condemning the living language of modern Greece as ugly, because, like ours, it has lost its sonority, is one that no scholar at least should ever entertain.

That the printing-houses which did for the north what their counterparts had done for Italy were located in Basel[178] was

[176] See W.S. Allen, *Vox Graeca*, 2nd edn. 1974, 127f.

[177] I. Bywater, 'The Erasmian pronunciation of Greek and its precursors', OUP, London, 1908 (on Bywater, see below, nn.529-30). On Antonius Nebrissensis (1444-1522) see Sandys ii 157; Pfeiffer, *HCS* ii 65 and the special volume of the Spanish journal *Emerita* brought out in his honour (*Miscellanea Nebrija, Emerita*, 13, 1945).

[178] On the printers of Basle, see Sandys ii 262 and Pfeiffer, *HCS* ii 83 (n.7). Their dates of foundation were as follows: Amorbach 1478, Froben 1491, Cratander 1518, Hervagius 1531. See P.S. Allen, *The Correspondence of an Early Printing-House: the Amorbachs of Basle*, 1932.

enough alone to recommend it to Erasmus as a place of residence. As printers, the Amorbachs, Frobens, Cratanders and Heerwagens had no need to fear comparison with Aldus. It is worth noting that wood-engraving now came into use for reproducing illustrations. Moreover, in accordance with the more scientific methods of the time, the scholars who were responsible for the texts were more careful than the *Itali* and less high-handed as critics. They also availed themselves of such valuable manuscripts as the monasteries still possessed. These, with the exception of the Irish codex containing the remains of the fifth decade of Livy[179] (edited by Grynaeus and now in Vienna), have been lost. Their loss enhances the value of the editions of Velleius Paterculus by Beatus Rhenanus,[180] of the fourth decade of Livy by Rhenanus and Gelenius, of Ammianus Marcellinus, of the letters of Symmachus and Pliny's *Natural History* by Gelenius, and of Cicero's Letters by Cratander.[181] These scholars by no means confined themselves to textual criticism, in which Beatus Rhenanus[182] was particularly proficient, but added useful explanatory

[179] Vienna lat.15; see *SS*² 88, 124; Grynaeus found the manuscript at Lorsch in 1527.

[180] The unique manuscript was found by Beatus Rhenanus at Murbach in 1515; it was last heard of in a sale-room in 1786 (*SS*² 124).

[181] On the fifth-century manuscript of the fourth decade found in the cathedral of Speyer and used for the edition by these two scholars published by Froben in 1535, see *SS*² 96, 115. This, like the Hersfeldensis of Ammianus, was destroyed by being used as a copy for the press. Beatus Rhenanus had a Pliny found at Murbach that is now lost. On Cratander's Basle edition of 1528, see D.R. Shackleton Bailey, *Cicero's Letters to Atticus* i, 1965, 85f.

[182] Beatus Rhenanus (1485-1547): Sandys ii 263; A. Hentschke and U. Muhlack, *Einführung in die Geschichte der Philologie*, 1972, 14f.; Kenney 52, Pfeiffer, *HCS* ii 82f; Glareanus (Heinrich Loriti, 1488-1563): Sandys ii 263, Bursian 154, Pfeiffer, *HCS* ii 85. Sigmund Gelenius (1497-1554): Sandys ii, 263; Bursian 152. Following in the tracks of Conrad Celtis (1459-1508; Sandys ii 259; Bursian 109, Pfeiffer, *HCS* ii 63), Beatus Rhenanus added to this Froben edition of Tacitus' works a glossary of proper names connected with Germany (1519). Rhenanus was a friend of Conrad Peutinger (1465-1547) of Augsburg, who published an account of the monuments of his own district (1505); see Pfeiffer's delightful essay 'Conrad Peutinger und die humanistische Welt' (Munich, 1955, reprinted in *AKS*, 1960, 222f., and see Pfeiffer, *HCS* ii 62-3). Rhenanus planned a *Germania illustrata* on the lines of Blondus' *Italia illustrata* of 1474 (see above, n.131).

notes. Tacitus aroused patriotic feelings in their German breasts, and their anxiety to make him widely known was bound up with their sense of history. Glareanus published a large number of texts, most of them Latin, with notes, and also worked on chronology. Greek books too were published at Basel in large quantities, including a substantial number of *editiones principes*, especially of Neoplatonists; and many reprints of Italian editions were a textual improvement – for example, the Anthology of Planudes.[183]

Humanism now had a firm footing along the upper Rhine valley towards Schlettstadt and Strasburg and as far as Heidelberg, in sharp contrast with Cologne; but it counted for nothing in the Protestant north, except insofar as the Reformed Church pressed it into service in its schools. It was just this policy of founding schools, however, that proved a blessing for posterity because, among other things, it led the Jesuits to found rival schools of their own, in which formal and rhetorical education through the medium of Latin achieved notable successes. These schools remained hostile to the Greek spirit, but the Lutheran schools were equally averse to it. From his chair in Wittenberg Melanchthon,[184] a true *Praeceptor Germaniae*, left his mark on the German educational system, wrote grammars (a revised version of his Greek Grammar remained in use down to the time of Buttmann)[185] and produced aids to the teaching of rhetoric – which, curious as it may seem to us, was cultivated there, and also by Camerarius.[186] Luther throughout his life busied himself with the interpretation of the Scriptures – in a tradition going back to the Fathers, be it said. Nor was he afraid of criticising their content. The theologians followed his example. That was more than would be attempted for the classics for many a long day; but then this practice of the theologians seems never to have influenced classical scholarship. The same is no doubt

[183] Planudean Anthology: ed. princ. by J. Lascaris, Florence, 1491; improved upon by J. Brodaeus, Basle, 1549, with commentary by Gelenius.
[184] Philip Melanchthon (1497-1560): Sandys ii 265; Bursian 173. Pfeiffer, *HCS* ii 91.
[185] Buttmann: see below, n.444.
[186] Joachim Camerarius (1500-1574): Sandys ii 266; Bursian 185; Pfeiffer, *HCS* ii 139. His edition of Plautus appeared in 1552.

true of the great critical work on the history of the ancient Church produced by the Centuriators of Magdeburg[187] under the direction of Flacius Illyricus. It had few successors, alarming orthodox opinion everywhere and eliciting erudite apologies from the Catholic side, which in the long run also benefited learning. Joachim Camerarius[188] of Nuremberg was a faithful pupil and colleague of Melanchthon's and devoted his energies to the production of annotated editions intended mainly, though by no means exclusively, for educational use. The name of Camerarius will remain forever linked with that of Plautus, whose best manuscripts he brought to light.

The Zurich doctor Conrad Gesner[189] is a most unusual figure, for he combined scholarly and medical interests and distinguished himself in both fields. We could wish, however, that he had chosen for his subject some other work of Greek natural history than Aelian's grotesque *Historia animalium*, of which he published the *editio princeps*, as he did also of Stobaeus' *Florilegium*. In both he went to work in an arbitrary fashion, but they remained for long the standard editions; his great compilations, on the other hand, are now forgotten. Classical scholarship and a medical practice often went together in those days, for scientific medicine owed its origin entirely to Greek teaching, and it was therefore natural for doctors to engage in the editing and translation of Greek books. An honoured name among these scholar-doctors is that of Janus Cornarius,[190] who displayed astonishing acumen also as a corrector of the text of Plato. After him came Zwinger and, at the end of the century, Anutius Foesius[191] of Metz with his edition of Hippocrates, indispensable even today for interpreting the Hippocratic writings, which have long been scandalously neglected by scholars. (Looking forward, readers

[187] Centuriators of Magdeburg, 1559-1574.
[188] See above, n.186.
[189] Conrad Gesner (1516-1565): Sandys ii 269; Bursian 216.
[190] Janus Cornarius (1500-1568): Bursian 191. His edition of Hippocrates appeared at Basle in 1538.
[191] Theodor Zwinger (1533-1588) made a vast collection of commonplace excerpts called *Theatrum Humanae Vitae* (1st edn. 1565); see W.J. Ong in *CIEC* ii, 111f. A. Foesius published his edition at Frankfurt in 1595; his *Oeconomia Hippocratis* of 1588 is called by W.H.S. Jones (Loeb edition of Hippocrates ii, 1923, lxviii) 'a perfect mine of medical lore'.

are hereby warned against Chartier's[192] edition, which also includes Galen (latest impression, Paris 1779) and has enjoyed its high reputation far too long, alas! As becomes clearer every day, parts of it are highly suspect, and it contains actual forgeries.)

As the sixteenth century progressed, a number of admirable German scholars also produced editions of Greek authors which were of permanent value – for instance, Hieronymus Wolf's[193] Demosthenes and Isocrates, Leonclavius' Xenophon, Xylander's Plutarch (whose pagination is still used for reference) and Marcus Aurelius (the *editio princeps*), Sylburg's Clement and Dionysius of Halicarnassus, together with his editions of the *Etymologicum magnum* and Apollonius on syntax. Sylburg deserves no small credit for tackling the grammatical literature, which was of interest only to the more austere kind of scholarship and meant nothing to the humanists; he also had the honour of collaborating in the compilation of the *Thesaurus* of Stephanus.[194] In other words, Sylburg belongs already to a different age, in which scholarship had become conscious of its status as a science, thanks to the French renaissance.

Ever since the Carolingian age, northern France[195] had been the intellectual leader of Europe. English rule, so far from putting an end to this supremacy, had strengthened the Latin as opposed to the Saxon element in England itself. Paris had been the stronghold of scholasticism and as such had offered a stubborn resistance to Italian humanism; but the French invasions of Italy opened the door to the new spirit, and once

[192] R. Chartier's edition first appeared at Paris in 1679.

[193] H. Wolf (1516-1580): Sandys ii 168; Bursian 210; Kenney 87; Pfeiffer, *HCS* ii 139. Leonclavius (=Johann Loewenclau, 1533-1593): Bursian 234; he also travelled in Italy and edited Byzantine authors. Xylander (=Wilhelm Holzmann, 1532-1576): Sandys ii 170; Bursian 228; Pfeiffer, *HCS* 140. F. Sylburg (1536-1596): Sandys 270; Bursian 229; Pfeiffer, *HCS* ii 141.

[194] See below, n.221.

[195] On classical studies in France, see E. Egger, *L'Hellénisme en France*, 2 vols, 1869 (lately reprinted). Some people would contend that during the fourteenth and fifteenth centuries the leadership passed to Italy, to return to France after Charles VIII's invasion of 1498.

the all-powerful monarchy had decided to support it the nation surrendered in a body. Francis I invited the great Italian artists to his court, established a centre for Greek studies, collected a library and founded the Collège de France. One need only mention the names of Rabelais, Montaigne and Ronsard[196] to realise how widely and deeply humanism, which was now fully mature, influenced the national literature, bringing with it a new conception of the world, mankind and art. Calvin adopted the reformed religion and remodelled it on Latin lines, with the result that the Calvinists retained a stronger tincture of humanism than the Lutherans. The terrible wars of religion and the conflicts of the nobles among themselves and with the crown only helped the nation to develop its powers to the full, just as the internecine feuds of the Italians had. To this turbulent age belong the great scholars to whom we owe homage as the founding fathers of our science. But before we come to them, we should spare a thought for a proud man who was almost alone in preparing the ground for humanism, the Parisian Budaeus[197] (Guillaume Budé). Budaeus was a practising lawyer and initiated the historical study of Roman law, which remains one of the special glories of French scholarship. Cujacius[198] (Jacques Cujas), who certainly ranks as a founding father, brought to his trade a thorough acquaintance with the tools of scholarship – the famous manuscript of the *Pandects*, which Florence filched from the Pisans, had already been used as such by Politian – and ranks in every way as an equal of the foremost scholars of the age. His successors included Hotomanus and later Gothofredus, whose commentary on the Theodosian Code is still indispensable to historians of the period. From the study of Roman law Budaeus proceeded to occupy himself with the Roman coinage;[199] but he also

[196] See Pierre de Nolhac, *Ronsard et l'Humanisme*, 1921.
[197] Budaeus (1467-1540): Sandys ii 170; *SS*² 154; Pfeiffer, *HCS* ii 101. His portrait is in the National Gallery in London.
[198] Cujacius (1522-1590): Sandys ii 193; Pattison, *Essays*, i 15; Pfeiffer, *HCS* ii Index, s.v. Franciscus Hotomanus (1524-1590): Sandys ii, 193. Jacobus Godofredus (1587-1652): Sandys ii, 193. Wilamowitz has confused him with his father Denys (1549-1621), who edited the *Corpus Juris Civilis*.
[199] See Weiss, *RDCA* 177.

successfully defended the cause of Greek against the deep-rooted suspicions of the Church and the Sorbonne, and played an important part in the foundation of the Collège de France.[200] In his last years he enjoyed a personal prestige comparable to that of Erasmus.

Among the Greeks who were invited to the French Court, the best men, such as Janus Lascaris,[201] came only briefly; but there were also doubtful characters who did their best, after their own fashion, to meet the demand for manuscripts. Slovenly copies by scribes like Darmarius[202] were only too plentiful, and forgeries masquerading under famous names were not unknown. Diassorinus,[203] for instance, fabricated the 'Lexicon of Philemon' and the 'Metrics of Dracon'; the *Historia physica* of Pollux' comes from a workshop of the same kind. All of them imposed for a longer or shorter period, even on their learned readers, none more grossly than the 'Lexicon of Eudocia' vamped up by Constantine Palaeokappa mostly from printed sources.

From the practical point of view the most momentous event in France as elsewhere was the introduction of the printing-press, for which the king had the Greek types cut. The leading printing-house was that of the Estienne family, the head of which doubled the roles of director and learned editor. Robert Stephanus[204] was the first to print the Greek Old Testament, and the numbering of the verses in our Bible goes back to him. His *Thesaurus linguae Latinae* was the model for the Greek *Thesaurus* of his greater son Henri (greater as a printer too), known as 'Henri le Grand' to distinguish him from the rest of his large family. But before we turn to him we must make the

[200] The Corporation of the Royal Readers, founded 1530, later became the Collège de France.

[201] Janus Lascaris, see above, n.113.

[202] Andreas Darmarius; see Pattison, *Isaac Casaubon*, 35.

[203] On Darmarius, Jacob Diassorinus, Constantine Palaeokappa and other sixteenth-century Byzantine forgers, see Speyer 321. The 'Historia Physica' was forged by Darmarius (see Speyer, loc. cit.).

[204] Robertus Stephanus (=Robert Estienne, 1503-1559): Sandys ii 173; Pattison, *Essays* i, 66f.; Pfeiffer, *HCS* ii 66). Elizabeth Armstrong, *Robert Estienne, Royal Printer*, 1954, is occupied mainly with the technicalities of printing.

acquaintance of another father of an illustrious son, Julius Caesar Scaliger,[205] who left his native Riva on Lake Garda and made southern France the scene of his turbulent career. J.C. Scaliger's writings, in which he gave vehement expression to his convictions and feelings, were widely read in his own day, and one cannot help respecting the honesty of this creature of impulse, even when he is guilty of such violent and unjustifiable attacks as those he made on Erasmus. He also possessed no mean talent as a critic, which he displayed in his treatment of the botanical writings of Theophrastus and the pseudo-Aristotle. But his greatest success was achieved in another field. His *Poeticē* long enjoyed canonical authority. It complements contemporary Italian works written with Aristotle and Horace in mind, but does so on a grander scale and with perfect independence of judgment. In it the deep-rooted Latin antipathy to the *spiritus Graiae tenuis Camenae* is frankly expressed. Needless to say, the theoretical framework of his theory of poetry and his doctrine of the figures of speech is derived from the Greeks, and Scaliger is surprisingly knowledgeable about them – indeed he attempts a historical survey – but it is only in his last books, the *Liber criticus* and *Liber hypercriticus*, that he reveals the purpose nearest to his heart; namely, the comparison of the Greek with the Roman poets, in which not only Virgil, but Valerius Flaccus and even Claudian, invariably come off best. Latin poetry, for him, includes the humanist poets on equal terms with the ancients, and his aesthetic sense sits in judgment on them all without respect of persons. Such was the taste of the baroque age, shared by Voltaire and Frederick the Great.

Joseph Justus Scaliger,[206] Julius Caesar's son, firmly believed that he was descended from the princely family of the Della Scalas, Lords of Verona. Whatever the truth of that, he would still be a prince, every inch a prince, even had his

[205] J.C. Scaliger (1484-1558): Sandys ii 177; Pattison, *Essays* i 135f.; *SS²* 155, 242; Pfeiffer, *HCS* ii 113.

[206] J.J. Scaliger (1540-1609): Sandys ii 199; J. Bernays (see below, n.528), *Joseph Justus Scaliger*, 1855; Pattison, 'Joseph Scaliger', *Essays* i 132f. (a review of Bernays, first in *Quarterly Review*, 1860); id. 'Life of Joseph Scaliger', *Essays* i 196f. (unfortunately only a fragment); *SS²* 158; Pfeiffer, *HCS* ii 113-19.

father's origins been as humble as his despicable enemies declared, among whom a renegade German named Caspar Schoppe (Scioppius)[207] played a shameful part. Schoppe is entitled to some credit for his work on the letters of Symmachus, though even there we no longer need him; he was a man of parts ruined by lack of principle. Scaliger's portrait[208] shows us the man of strong character and handsome appearance, conscious that he is born to rule. Scaliger indeed was head and shoulders above Stephanus and Casaubon, the other two responsible for the transition from a potential to an actual science of classical antiquity; and though the scope of this science may still have been limited to the literary remains of the ancient world, owing to the available material, that did not impair the ability of these great scholars to see it whole. They have this in common also, that they were obliged, all three, to leave their country for reasons of religion, a fact which had grave consequences for Greek studies in France. In order of importance, though not of time, Scaliger comes first. The world had recognised his princely rank by 1594, when he was offered a chair in the Protestant university of Leyden – which was proud of its origins in the Dutch war of liberation and aggrieved when Justus Lipsius[209] went over to the old faith and moved to Louvain, now the intellectual capital of Catholic Brabant. Leyden offered the Calvinist Scaliger the most dazzling terms: he was to be free to devote himself exclusively to the pursuit of learning without any obligation to lecture. The expectation that his name alone would attract the young men to Leyden proved correct. Such was the incomparable position in which Scaliger found himself after an adventurous life which had carried him far afield, for as a Calvinist he had no chance of an appointment in France; in fact, the only post he had ever held was in Geneva, where he had lectured briefly. His close relations, however, with a true *grand seigneur*, De la Roche-Pozay, not only enabled him to visit Italy and England but

[207] Scioppius (1576-1649): Sandys ii 362; Kenney 37f.

[208] The oil-painting in the Senate House at Leiden is reproduced as frontispiece by Bernays and opposite p.201 by Sandys.

[209] Lipsius: see below, n.235.

provided him with a refuge that was always open to him. Scaliger was at home in country houses and cultivated the friendship of scholars of the highest distinction such as Cujacius, Auratus and Thuanus,[210] who recognised him as their equal. No doubt his fame would have been assured even if he had written nothing more in the fifteen years of life that remained to him (he died in 1609); but it was only in Leyden that he became the prince of scholars, thanks to his exemption from routine university teaching, and also the first of the academic organisers. The *Scaligerana* noted down by admiring disciples were well worth collecting, for they are comparable, though not quite on a par, with Luther's *Table Talk* and the *Conversations* of Eckermann; (the worthless later '*ana*'[211] are not fit to be mentioned in the same breath). Much learned correspondence was carried on between scholars, and published, in those days. Often these letters are full of matter and contain charming personal touches; many of them, on the other hand, having been written with an eye to future publication, are lacking in substance and meretricious in style. The differences of character between their authors are thus brought out all the more clearly, and here too Scaliger shows his superiority, but not as a creative writer – if one expects poetic feeling in a creative writer – though of course he was capable of *tours de force* which no one has succeeded in imitating. Philosophy was entirely foreign to him, and to enter into a poet's mind and understand his essence was beyond him. So much must be conceded, if only because Scaliger's text of the Roman *Triumviri amoris* for centuries hampered a proper understanding of them.[212] Indeed Scaliger's recensions are in general not particularly remarkable; he produced no edition at all of a Greek author, and the numerous

---

[210] Cujacius: see above, n.198. Auratus: see below, n.232. Thuanus (=Jacques Auguste de Thou, 1553-1617): President of the Parliament of Paris; the great historian; see Pfeiffer, *HCS* ii, Index s.v.

[211] On the 'Ana', see Pattison, *Isaac Casaubon*, 425-6; he quotes the Abbé d'Oliver as calling this genre, in 1743, 'the disgrace of our age'.

[212] D.R. Shackleton Bailey, *Proc. Cambridge Philological Society* 182, 1952-3, 10, speaks of 'the six or seven weeks of convalescence which produced (along with editions of Catullus and Tibullus) the prodigiously transposed *Propertius* of 1577' (cf. M. Haupt, *Opuscula* iii 34-6; Kenney 54-7).

emendations to be found here and there in our texts were the
casual by-products of a lifetime of omnivorous reading. He
took great trouble to procure manuscripts, and there is much
that we owe entirely to his exertions, but he was content to
leave the editing to others. Greek authors were handled by
Stephanus, while Casaubon[213] provided the commentaries; so
what was there left for him to do?

   The answer is something which nobody else was capable of
or had even contemplated: the discovery of early Latin.
Scaliger succeeded in extracting it from Varro and Festus. To
him it was so much a living language that he translated the
Orphic Hymns and Lycophron into it, just for the delight of
using the archaic words. Furthermore he realised that there
can be no history without a firm chronological scaffolding;
and as all chronology was based on Jerome, and Jerome had
translated Eusebius, his next task was the reconstruction of
Eusebius.[214] This he attempted, and later generations were so
completely out of their depth that they took his Ὀλυμπιάδων
ἀναγραφή for an ancient document. The idea of a complete
collection of Latin inscriptions was also Scaliger's. There had
been earlier moves in this direction, as we have seen, and by
now the Dutchmen Martin Smetius and Pighius[215] had made
good copies, so that plenty of material, published and
unpublished, was available; but to carry the scheme through
was an achievement that would require the mobilisation of an
Academy today. In Janus Gruter,[216] Scaliger found an
assistant with the necessary industry and self-abnegation, but
the indexes he made himself. Collections of fragments had also
begun to appear. Henricus Stephanus[217] brought out the
fragments of the Greek lyric poets in a pretty duodecimo
volume. Merula's *Ennius*[218] was not the first in the field and,

---

[213] Casaubon: see below, n.226.

[214] On Scaliger's reconstruction of the first book of Eusebius' *Chronica* and
on Jerome, see above, n.47.

[215] Martin Smetius (d.1578): Sandys ii 145. Pighius: see above, n.144.

[216] Gruter: see below, n.272.

[217] H. Stephanus: see below, n.221.

[218] Paulus Merula (1558-1607: Sandys ii 240) published his *Ennius* at
Leiden in 1595. For the forgeries, see Vahlen's *Ennius*, 2nd. edn. 240f.; S.
Mariotti, *Lezioni su Ennio*, 1951, 43 thinks they may not have been made by
Merula himself.

incidentally, contained some shocking forgeries. Franciscus Dousa's fine Lucilius was a product of the school of Scaliger, and Putschius[219] assembled a mass of dry but indispensable material in his *Grammatici Latini*. What makes Scaliger's own edition of Manilius[220] remarkable is not his wild conjectures but the fact that he took the astrology seriously – not because he believed in it, but as a facet of ancient belief. All these projects were in the nature of first attempts, and few progressed beyond that stage; but that is of small importance compared with the end towards which they were directed: namely, the creation of a single, vast and yet indivisible science. Nobody before Niebuhr rated Scaliger at his true worth.

Henricus Stephanus[221] also led a wandering life, and it may be partly due to his character that he was never free for long from anxiety and distress and died impoverished and alone in the Lyons hospital in 1598. How in such conditions he accomplished such a prodigious amount of work, both as an editor and as a printer, is a mystery. Stephanus brought out a large proportion of the Greek classics in editions that held their own down to the last century, and because Immanuel Bekker[222] referred to his edition of Plato as **ς**, this symbol is often used for the vulgate reading even when it is not his. His massive output included numerous *editiones principes*; among them the greater part of Diodorus, some parts of Appian and the *Anacreontea* – which created the greatest impression of all, for here at last was Greek poetry to which the age could respond, a sure sign that it was no longer truly Greek. Stephanus' treatment of the texts he published varied according to the material immediately available. He gave variant readings, but only as occasional adjuncts, and there were some pure conjectures among them, though that was

[219] Dousa (1577-1606; Sandys ii 301; Pfeiffer, *HCS* ii 119) published his *Lucilius* in 1597. Putschius (Helias van Putschen, 1585-1606): Sandys ii 313.

[220] On Scaliger's *Manilius*, see Housman, *Manilius* i 2nd. edn. 1937, xiii: 'Perhaps no critic has ever effected so great and permanent a change in any author's text as Scaliger in Manilius.'

[221] H. Stephanus (*c.*1528/31-1598): Sandys ii 175; Pattison, *Essays* i 66f.; Pfeiffer, *HCS* ii 109.

[222] Bekker: see below, n.446.

certainly not intentional. He could not afford to spend much time over a text; and yet he completed his *Thesaurus linguae Graecae*, thereby doing his age a service single-handed that all the Hellenists in the world failed to undertake between them, even at a time when scholars still had a sense of common purpose. As far as we know he had little help, so that as he read he must constantly have been alert for anything that might be useful to him as a lexicographer. Obviously he had a special interest in language from this point of view; indeed he wrote admirably in his mother tongue, in which he had an excellent style, an advantage he shares with no scholar before Bentley. Inevitably the effects of a random choice of sources made themselves felt in the *Thesaurus*. For instance, the historian Herodian,[223] an insignificant imitator who had no place there, is quoted frequently; the late author Synesius[224] is another favourite. Clearly discrimination between the various periods and styles could not be expected yet, and the revised edition produced by Hase and the brothers Dindorf[225] does little to remedy the defects, though we have to make do with it.

Stephanus' son-in-law, Isaac Casaubon,[226] complemented the other two giants, whom he regarded as his seniors. By nature an expositor, pre-eminently of subject-matter, he specialised in authors who required the widest learning for their elucidation, and whatever author he tackled the result was decisive. Diogenes Laertius, Strabo, Theophrastus' *Characters*, Athenaeus, the *Scriptores historiae Augustae*, Persius – the list shows clearly where his tastes and abilities lay. The learning is marvellous, but it is not displayed for its own sake, as in many later commentaries. We are all still living on the capital accumulated by the industry of Casaubon and Stephanus; Scaliger is our great exemplar because he showed us the true end of all our labours. The writers treated by

[223] Herodian (3rd century A.D.) wrote a history of the Roman Empire from Marcus Aurelius to the death of Maximin in eight books.
[224] Synesius (born *c.*375), Bishop of Ptolemais, Platonist, author of speeches, letters and hymns; on the hymns, see Wilamowitz, *Kleine Schriften* ii 163f.
[225] Hase and Dindorf: see nn.511 and 534 below.
[226] Casaubon (1559-1614): Sandys ii 204; life by Mark Pattison, 1875, 2nd. edn. 1891; *SS*² 159; Pfeiffer, *HCS* ii 120.

Casaubon, particularly Athenaeus, led him to the study of literary history, and he produced the first critical survey in his *De satyrica Graecorum poesi et Romanorum satira,* which has gone through many editions and can fairly be called a model of its kind. After the murder of Henri IV, Casaubon too, a Protestant, had to leave his country; England gave him a hospitable welcome, and he is buried in Westminster Abbey.

Beside this trinity of stars of the first magnitude there were lesser luminaries who in themselves would suffice to ensure the pre-eminence of French scholarship. The brief notice which is all that they can here receive is less than they deserve, and even so there is room only for a selection. The two Pithoei[227] (Pithou) and the Puteani[228] (Du Puits) were collectors of manuscripts; the Puteanus of Livy commemorates one of these families. Pierre Pithou consulted many manuscripts which have since disappeared, especially of Phaedrus, of whom he produced the *editio princeps.* Josias Mercier's[229] Nonius remained the best edition until recent times. Willem Canter,[230] a Dutchman – mentioned here because of his French education – was the first to track down the metrical responsions in Greek tragic choruses, and his work on Aristides is rated highly by the few scholars who have grappled with the text of this difficult orator. But when all is said and done, none of these men has the importance of Lambinus and Turnebus, whose works are still indispensable today, even if they are consulted only by scholars concerned with the same authors.

Adrianus Turnebus,[231] who died before his time in 1565,

[227] Pierre Pithou (1539-1596): Sandys ii 192) published in 1585 the first important edition of Persius and Juvenal, using the 'Codex Pithoeanus' once at Lorsch and now at Montpellier. François Pithou, Chancellor of the Parliament of Paris, died in 1691.

[228] Pierre du Puits died in 1651; Jacques du Puits, who became historian of the Royal Library in Paris in 1645, died in 1656.

[229] Josias Mercier (d.1626; Sandys ii 210) published his *Nonius* in 1583.

[230] Willem Canter (1542-1575): Sandys ii 216; *SS*² 161. Pfeiffer ii, Index s.v. B. Keil, *Aelii Aristidis Opera Omnia* ii, 1898, vi, called his work 'artis nostrae et scientiae admirabile opus'; cf. Ed. Fraenkel, *Aeschylus, Agamemnon* i, 1950, 35, and M. Mund – Dopchie in *Album Charles Verlinden*, Ghent, 1975, 233f.

[231] Turnebus (= Adrien de Tournebu, 1512-1565): Sandys ii 185; *SS*² 156; Pfeiffer, *HCS* ii 111.

made a deep impression as a teacher in Paris. Montaigne, who hated pedants, sang his praises, and one could wish that Turnebus had edited and expounded more of the classics instead of following the fashion for *Adversaria*. How few men in any age have been equal to emending the text of Aeschylus, and what must it have meant to be such a man in those days! Turnebus' friend Auratus[232] also had some success in this sphere, but it was unjust of Hermann to prefer him to Turnebus. It is true that, relying on Triclinius, Turnebus corrupted the text of Sophocles – damage that was only repaired by Brunck. But this was because he had at his disposal a manuscript of Triclinius' recension which contained many correct readings, and no one at the time could have detected that it was based on the work of Byzantine correctors. His commentary on Cicero's *De legibus* is still the best, because he found the key to it in the Stoic philosophers, from whom he quotes copiously. Which of his contemporaries saw as far as that?

Dionysius Lambinus[233] has been more loudly acclaimed, because he was a Latinist. That he was able to collect manuscript material in Italy was a further advantage, thanks to which, in addition to editing Cicero, he substantially improved the texts of Lucretius and Horace, in particular, and laid the foundations on which the exegesis of these two poets rests; for in Lucretius he was capable of following the philosophical argument, and in Horace he recognised both the imitator dependent on his models and the great original artist, whom one is glad to see thus rescued from the pedants' clutches.

Muretus[234] on the other hand, who was also a Frenchman,

---

[232] Auratus (= Jean Dorat, 1508-1588): Sandys ii 186; Pfeiffer, *HCS* ii 102f. Pfeiffer, in his essay 'Dichter und Philologe im französischen Humanismus', *Antike und Abendland* 7, 1958, 73f., and in his history rightly protests against this inadequate treatment of a scholar and poet who had a profound effect on his contemporaries. G. Hermann thought his the most brilliant of all contributions to the emendation of Aeschylus; see E. Fraenkel, *Aeschylus, Agamemnon*, i 35. Pattison, *Essays* i 206f. was right about Auratus, as Pfeiffer says.
[233] Lambinus (1520-1572): Sandys ii 188; *SS*² 151; Pfeiffer, *HCS* ii 112; H.A.J. Munro, *Lucretius* i 14-15; Kenney 63f.
[234] Marcus Muretus (1526-1585): Sandys ii 148; Pattison, *Essays* ii 124;

had every reason to seek refuge abroad in the bosom of the
Roman church. In Rome he found a safe haven in the
priesthood for his few remaining years, and made a position
for himself. He must have possessed enormous charm to
captivate the most eminent scholars of the day by his wit and
learning, though he had no scruples about decking himself in
borrowed plumes at their expense. His style, Ciceronian
without pedantry, won him a celebrity denied to many greater
scholars and better men. What after all has he to show that
left its mark on the history of scholarship?

Muretus' desertion was no doubt in its way a triumph for
the church; but it was as nothing compared with Lipsius'[235]
resignation from his chair at Leyden and his return to the faith
he had abjured in his youth and even attacked during his short
tenure of a professorship at Jena in his *Wanderjahre*. Lipsius
was a native of Brabant, and at the time he exchanged Leyden
for Louvain the antagonism between the Spaniards and the
free Netherlands overflowed into academic life. He was
regarded as the leading figure in the Catholic camp, and was
undoubtedly the foremost textual critic of his day in the
domain of Latin prose literature. He was the first editor of
Tacitus to make use of the Medicean manuscripts, though he
had not examined them himself in Italy. He excelled in
historical as well as textual criticism – indeed his
professorship was in history – and, in addition to the usual
*Variae lectiones*, he wrote with distinction on the Roman army.
A more important point, no doubt, was that his *Manuductio ad
philosophiam Stoicam* exactly fitted the mood of the age, for to
many people Seneca was now the fount of all wisdom, even
more than he had been to Montaigne. Rubens' picture in the
Pitti Palace of the four friends, with the (supposed) head of

Pfeiffer, *HCS* ii 112. His panegyric on the massacre of St Bartholomew came
near to earning him a cardinal's hat, despite the circumstances in which he
had left France.
[235] Justus Lipsius (1547-1606): Sandys ii 301; *SS*² 162; Kenney 53-4;
Pfeiffer, *HCS* ii 124. It is not true that Lipsius was the first to use the
Medicean manuscripts of Tacitus; see C.O. Brink, *JRS*, 41, 1951, 32f. On
the importance of his commentary and its relation to its successors, see A.
Momigliano, *JRS*, 37, 1947, 91 (= *Contributo* 37f.). Lipsius observed a kinship
between certain Flemish and German words and their Persian equivalents.

Seneca in the background, is a splendid epitome of the age.
Lipsius' command of Greek was amply sufficient for his needs,
but he described his knowledge of it as 'no more than a feather
in a scholar's cap', a saying which the Belgians and the Dutch
took only too much to heart.

France too has had to pay dearly for casting out her most
distinguished sons on grounds of religion, for she has
produced no important critic or expounder of the real Greek
classics since. The sound tradition lasted for another century,
but now it was in the keeping of the great religious orders or
parties, and that determined the field of its activities. Most of
its representatives were drawn from the ranks of the Jesuits or
their pupils. In the most notable of them, Dionysius
Petavius,[236] the desire not merely to correct Scaliger but to
discredit him is unmistakable. Petavius did in fact correct
Scaliger in some important respects in his *Doctrina temporum*,
and may perhaps be pardoned for having forgotten in the
process who it was who had posed the problems and so paved
the way for their solution. In his *Uranologium* he rescued from
oblivion certain writings important for the study of
astronomy, and he also produced successful editions of several
writers of the fourth century A.D., all of which were useful,
none exhaustive; his Synesius held its ground for more than
two hundred years. Henricus Valesius[237] brought out even
better editions, with explanatory notes, of the ecclesiastical
historians from Eusebius to Evagrius, and also of Ammianus,
who gives the general history of a considerable part of the
period. It fell also to Valesius, as the first test of his diligence
and zeal, to follow up the notable preliminary studies by
Grotius and Salmasius[238] with an edition of the important
section of the *Excerpts* of Constantine contained in the
manuscript belonging to the indefatigable collector Peiresc.[239]

Jacques Sirmond,[240] who wielded great influence as the
king's father confessor, was equally admirable as a man and a

---

[236] Petavius (1583-1652; Sandys ii 283; Pfeiffer, *HCS* ii 118, 132)
published his *Doctrina Temporum* in 1627.

[237] H. Valesius (1603-1676): Sandys ii 287.

[238] Grotius: see below, n.279. Salmasius: see below, n.283.

[239] C.F. Peiresc (1580-1637): Sandys ii 185; Pfeiffer, *HCS* ii 133.

[240] Sirmond (1559-1651): Sandys ii 283.

scholar. His familiarity with the age of transition from antiquity to the Middle Ages was unrivalled, and his Sidonius Apollinaris remained the standard edition until recently. François Guyet[241] worked entirely on his own and never published anything, but the conjectures unearthed from his papers, which found their way into the library of the Jesuit College after his death, give the impression – for their boldness and more especially their author's delight in athetising – of being centuries before their time. They show quite outstanding sagacity, and many of them will be accepted in the end. Du Cange's[242] *Glossaria medii aevi*, 1678-88, are still unsurpassed and bear comparison with the *Thesaurus* of Stephanus. For both languages, but particularly for Greek, he remains our sole guide – a wonderfully trustworthy guide – and it is difficult to imagine how he could have acquired his knowledge of vulgar Greek. These works cry out to be brought up to date – a pious hope, no doubt, for years to come. Port Royal produced a counterpart to Du Cange in the person of his contemporary L.S. Lenain de Tillemont,[243] author of the *Mémoires ecclésiastiques* and the *Histoire des empereurs*, who narrated the history of the empire and the church over six centuries – with the most painstaking accuracy and unsurpassed learning – from the written sources, beyond which he did not look. That is the measure of his critical limitations, and his unquestioning acceptance of the authority of the church was only to be expected. It was a gigantic achievement, worthy to rank with Du Cange's, and, like Du Cange's, long the standard authority and certain to remain the basis of all further study in its field. Readers of Gibbon should remember that in long stretches of his book this master of the art of historical composition and spiritual kinsman of Voltaire merely reproduces Tillemont's mosaic panorama in a different style.

At this point the Benedictines entered the lists and matched their great achievements in the Carolingian age. The many handsome folios of the edition of the great church fathers

---

[241] Guyet (1575-1655): Sandys ii 283.

[242] Charles du Fresne du Cange (1626-1688; Sandys ii 289; Pfeiffer, *HCS* ii 133) published his Latin glossary in three volumes in 1678 and his Greek in two in 1688.

[243] Sebastien Lenain de Tillemont (1637-1698): Pfeiffer ii 133.

produced by the Maurists[244] – who not only consulted the best manuscripts but also weeded out spurious matter by sound critical methods – are an enduring work of scholarship, though there is still much to be done and many of the gaps they left remain unfilled. Then came Mabillon,[245] the founder of criticism and at the same time the first man to treat palaeography scientifically. This he achieved during a controversy with the Jesuit Papebroch,[246] in which the antagonism that existed between the two orders may well have played its part; but this admirable pair conducted their dispute in such a noble spirit of disinterested devotion to truth that the affair remains a shining example to posterity, in refreshing contrast to the ugly squabbles of the fifteenth-century humanists and of numerous Dutchmen in the sixteenth and seventeenth centuries. Mabillon's younger contemporary and great friend Bernard de Montfaucon,[247] apart from drawing on the rich stores of the Paris Library, which were enlarged by the collections of the Duc de Coislin and the president of the recently founded Academy, Pierre Séguier,[248] studied manuscripts chiefly in Italy. His *Palaeographia Graeca* created a completely new discipline, and his *Bibliotheca bibliothecarum* provided a conspectus of all the accessible information. Even though these works are seldom consulted nowadays, they have not been superseded. Yet the Many volumes of Montfaucon's *Antiquité expliquée et représentée*

[244] 'The great congregation of the Maurists, named after St Benedict's favourite pupil, St Maurus, during the seventeenth and eighteenth centuries formed a silent army of learned workers, anonymous for the most part, who completed in monumental fashion the last legacy of Erasmus, the task of editing all the Latin and Greek fathers of the Church': Pfeiffer, *AKS* 180 (from his essay 'Humanitas Benedictina').

[245] Jean Mabillon (1632-1707): Sandys ii 293, *SS*² 171; Traube, *Vorlesungen und Abhandlungen* i, 1909, 13f. Pfeiffer, *HCS* ii 131. By challenging the authenticity of the characters, on which the Benedictines' claims depended, the Jesuits forced the Benedictines to embark on detailed palaeographic research. Mabillon's *De re diplomatica* appeared in 1681. He was an original member of the Académie des Inscriptions, founded in 1701.

[246] Daniel Papebroch (1628-1714): see Traube, op.cit. (n.245), 18; *SS*² 171.

[247] Montfaucon (1655-1741; Sandys ii 385; *SS*² 171, Pfeiffer *HCS* ii 131) published his *Palaeographia Graeca* in 1708; see Traube, op.cit., 31f.

[248] Séguier (1588-1672): Sandys ii 287.

*par les monuments* had the equally laudable purpose of introducing readers to the tradition of the monuments, on which nothing had been done worth mentioning north of the Alps apart from Vaillant's[249] work on coins. But further consideration of this branch of learning must wait until we turn once more to Italy.

Among the governments with which the Most Christian King maintained diplomatic relations was the Sublime Porte. As a result, in addition to his envoys, a number of individual travellers (including a few Englishmen, incidentally) found their way to the east. There was also a French Capuchin monastery in Athens next door to the monument of Lysicrates, commonly known as the 'Lantern of Diogenes'. To these links we owe many accounts of the place and, most important of all, the drawings of the Parthenon sculptures – a marvellous stroke of luck, since Morosini's[250] fruitless campaign was about to bring destruction upon them, an event which the Europe of that day could still shrug off without the slightest sense of the irreparable loss it represented. Fortunately, two other men had explored Athens before, an Englishman named Wheler and the admirable Frenchman Jacques Spon.[251] Spon had travelled further afield, observing monuments of every kind and industriously copying manuscripts, so that he can fairly be called the first truly scientific traveller. Moreover he took great trouble to acquaint the world with the outcome of his travels; but the world was not yet ripe for it, and he died in poverty in Geneva. Archaeologists seem to have forgotten him more utterly than he deserves. Apart from anything else, he strove to equip this specialised discipline of 'archaeography' (as he called it) with

[249] J.F.F. Vaillant (1665-1708): Sandys ii 391.

[250] Francesco Morosini, the Venetian general, was besieging Athens when on 26 September 1687 a shell landed in the Parthenon, which the defending Turks were using as a powder-magazine. See Rumpf i 54; Plate 3b shows a plan of Athens drawn by a Capuchin in 1670.

[251] Sir George Wheler (1650-1723) and Jacques Spon (1647-1685): Sandys ii 299; Rumpf i 54. Pfeiffer (*HCS* ii 132, 2) is wrong in accusing Wheler of being a Dutchman, and in accusing Wilamowitz of misspelling his name; in *AKS* 60 he confuses his book with that of Spon. See *DNB* lx. 445 (on Wheler).

a complete set of concepts and to subdivide it into departments corresponding to the various classes of objects with which it dealt. A generation later (1729-31) Michel Fourmont[252] visited Greece at the instance of the French Government, and it is to him alone that we owe the preservation of a large number of inscriptions. Our understanding of his copies and appreciation of his care have increased steadily over the years. That he also indulged in some strange forgeries was conclusively proved by Boeckh, though their purpose remains a mystery; why he boasted in his letters of having destroyed certain monuments, when he did so only on paper, is a psychological riddle.

It says much for the richness of the country's intellectual life that, in a France that was steadily making Catholicism, in one form or another, into its sole religion, Gassendi was able to expound the philosophy of Epicurus without hindrance. This of course would no longer have been tolerated in the latter part of the age of Louis XIV, when Protestantism was violently persecuted and a sceptic like Pierre Bayle[253] had to seek refuge in Holland. The fabulous erudition of Bayle's *Dictionaire historique et critique* renders it not only a mine of biographical information about scholars but also, within the limits of his arbitrary selection of names for inclusion, a useful guide to the current view of the personages of antiquity, and his brilliant writing makes the book a joy to read in spite of all the learned ballast carried. The baptized Jew Jean Astruc,[254] who lived at the court of Louis as physician-in-ordinary, started the analysis of the Torah by distinguishing between the different names of God in Genesis; fruitful criticism of the Bible followed by Richard Simon, Spinoza, Clericus and others.[255] For better or for worse, the point had been

---

[252] Fourmont (1690-1745): Sandys ii 390.

[253] Bayle (1647-1706): *Dictionnaire historique et critique*, 1695.

[254] Astruc (1684-1766) was physician to Louis XV, not Louis XIV; he published his 'Conjectures sur les mémoires originaux dont il paraît que Moise s'est servi pour composer le livre de Genèse' in 1753. So 'followed' is misleading.

[255] Simon (1638-1712; *Histoire Critique du Vieux Testament*, 1678; *Histoire du Texte du Nouveau Testament*, 1689). He was an Oratorian, who found Biblical criticism a powerful weapon against the Bibliolatry of his Protestant

established. The implications were overwhelmingly clear, however long orthodoxy might jib, as the Protestants did until De Wette.[256] But classical scholarship refused to learn from the experience of its sister discipline and preferred to wait until it was itself faced with similar problems.

Anyone who reflects on these developments will salute France as the headquarters of scholarship during these centuries – indeed, one is tempted to say, right from the age of Ausonius and Sulpicius Severus; through the time when Servatus Lupus[257] practised textual criticism according to his lights and later the Sorbonne was the stronghold of mediaeval philosophy, until, in the fullest sense of the term, the French Renaissance had raised humanism, after it had crossed from Italy, to the status of a science. And yet we must not fail to note that scholarship would have died under this very flowering of French classicism – as it almost had once before, at the height of Gothic – if other nations had not picked up the torch and rekindled its dying flame. In France itself the Greek poets, and the true classics generally, ceased entirely to be the objects of scholarly study. The value of the long series of Delphin Classics[258] is purely typographical. Suffice it to say that the moderate productions of Tanaquil Faber,[259] his daughter Anna and her husband André Dacier are the only works in the series worth mentioning; that Hardouin,[260]

---

opponents (Bentley must have known his work; Kenney 40f., Pfeiffer, *HCS* ii 130). Clericus (= Jean Leclerc, 1657-1736; Sandys ii 441; Pfeiffer, *HCS* ii 137, etc.) is more important as a liberal theologian than as a scholar. Spinoza (1632-1677); his *Tractatus Theologico-Politicus* of 1670 contains a history of the text of the Pentateuch that seems to be the earliest history of a text. See S. von Dunin-Borkowski, *Spinoza*, iv, 1936 (cited by Pfeiffer, *HCS* ii 128, n.6).

[256] W.M.L. de Wette (1780-1849), German theologian.

[257] Servatus Lupus: see above, n.77.

[258] The Delphin Classics had as general editor P.D. Huet, Bishop of Avranches (1630-1721; Sandys ii 292; Pattison, *Essays* ii 244f.). Housman calls him 'a critic of uncommon exactness, sobriety, and malevolence' (*Manilius*, i, 2nd edn. 1937, xv-xvi).

[259] T. Faber (1615-72), Anne Dacier (1654-1720) and André Dacier (1651-1722): Sandys ii 291-2; Pfeiffer, *HCS* ii 134-5.

[260] Jean Hardouin (1646-1729): Sandys ii 298; Traube, *Vorlesungen und Abhandlungen* i 31f.

though his edition of Pliny's *Natural History* has some merit, is otherwise merely notorious for his mad theory that practically the whole of Latin literature is a forgery of the late middle ages; and finally, that Menagius[261] compiled some serviceable notes on Diogenes Laertius but was the model for Molière's Vadius. On the other hand, there is one important French scholar who must be mentioned, namely Salmasius;[262] he will be discussed later, because his main work was done outside France.

The native Muse could now flatter herself that she had outgrown her ancient models, and French began to replace Latin in works of learning. Inevitably the question arose whether the Moderns did not now deserve precedence over the Ancients, and though the *Querelle*, begun by Perrault,[263] was carried on passionately by both sides, in practice in France the Moderns emerged victorious. During Voltaire's lifetime the French dropped out completely in all branches of learning; nor have any seminal ideas been forthcoming since. Montesquieu's *Considérations*[264] had only an indirect influence, and the sort of history written by the Abbé Mably,[265] for instance, is scientifically worthless. One writer who came in for criticism during the *Querelle* was Homer; this led to the chance discovery of the ancient evidence casting doubt upon the unity of the *Iliad*, which confronts us so puzzlingly on the threshold of Greek history. The Abbé d'Aubignac,[266] in some highly confused writings which had no effect on contemporary opinion, had put forward some ideas on this subject that were

---

[261] Menagius (= Gilles Ménage, 1613-1692): Sandys ii 290. Wilamowitz refers to *Les Femmes Savantes*; he also inspired the character of the Pedant in La Bruyère.

[262] Salmasius: see below, n.283.

[263] Charles Perrault's *Parallèle des anciens et des modernes* appeared in 1688-92; see Sandys ii 403 and Pfeiffer, *HCS* ii 134.

[264] Montesquieu (1689-1755) published his *Considérations sur la Grandeur et la Décadence des Romains* in 1734.

[265] G. Bonnot, Abbé de Mably, published his *Observations sur les Grecs* in 1794 and his *Observations sur l'histoire de la Grèce* in 1796.

[266] François Hédelin, Abbé d'Aubignac et de Meimac (1604-1676), over-valued by J.L. Myres, *Homer and his Critics* (1958, 47f.); see Adam Parry's introduction to Milman Parry, *The Making of Homeric Verse*, 1971, p.xii, n.1.

destined to bear fruit later; indeed F.A. Wolf[267] may have owed him a greater debt than he acknowledged. The credit for exhuming d'Aubignac belongs to Georg Finsler,[268] for the French had forgotten him, and it is to be hoped that those among them who laud him to the skies without having themselves the remotest conception of the Homeric Question are laughed at in their own country too.

In returning to the Netherlands to examine the successors of Scaliger and Lipsius, we may as well take in Germany. German culture of the time lacked a centre and accordingly exhibits nothing even faintly approaching unity. No single court or city did anything to encourage learning and the arts, even before the disastrous war that virtually put an end to all such activities. Of the universities, Wittenberg sank into insignificance under the tyranny of a bigoted Lutheranism. Nevertheless numerous foreigners of renown taught there briefly, and Erasmus Schmid[268a] deserves honourable mention for his edition of Pindar, in which his achievements as a textual critic are so great that he stands comparison with Turnebus;[269] strange though his exegesis seems to us, his attempt to treat the poems as works of rhetorical art was a challenge which long went unheeded. In Augsburg rich merchants put up money for the purchase of manuscripts; thanks to them the important collection known as the Augustani, could still be formed which is now in Munich. It was put to good use by David Höschel,[270] who produced *editiones*

[267] Wolf: see below, n.422.
[268] G. Finsler (1852-1916) published his *Homer* at Berlin in 1908; Wilamowitz is alluding to 'Un mensonge de la science allemande: Les "Prolégomènes à Homère" de F.A. Wolf', Paris, 1917, by V Bérard (1864-1931).
[268a] Erasmus Schmid (1570-1637) published his *Pindar* in 1616. His method of analysing the poems in terms of the conventions of encomium described by the rhetoricians of the early empire is curiously echoed by the new tendency to explain much in Pindar in terms of encomiastic convention; see *JHS* 93, 1973, 116.
[269] Turnebus: see above n.231.
[270] D. Höschel (1556-1617; Sandys ii 272) had help from Scaliger in his *Photius* and in his *editiones principes* of Phrynichus (1601) and Procopius

*principes* of such important works as the *Bibliotheca* of Photius, Origen against Celsus and a volume of the *Excerpts* of Constantine, and was highly regarded by Scaliger and Casaubon.

In Heidelberg too it was the library that attracted scholars and encouraged them to direct their energies into useful channels. Xylander[271] was its head at one time. Later Janus Gruter[272] found in it a congenial sphere of activity. We are glad to think of this upright and industrious man enjoying it. Life had driven him hither and thither. Pitchforked into England as a child along with his parents, who had had to leave their home in Antwerp for religious reasons, educated at Cambridge and subsequently Scaliger's devoted pupil, Gruter next tried to establish himself in several north-German universities; and after he had settled at Heidelberg, it was his cruel fate to see not only the Palatine library but his own books carried off by the Imperial authorities. He retired to a neighbouring village and died soon afterwards. Gruter published editions of many Latin authors and with his *Lampas* inaugurated the fashion for collecting the writings of earlier scholars; but all that keeps his name alive is the series of inscriptions he compiled under the guidance of Scaliger.

Of the other men of the period before the Thirty Years' War, only Valens Acidalius[273] deserves mention – on account of some first-rate emendations in Plautus which have stood the test of time – and perhaps Martin Crusius[274] of Tübingen for his *Turcograecia*, in which he described contemporary Greece and its people. That Thomas Reinesius,[275] latterly of Leipzig,

---

(1607). On him and on the generosity of Johann Jacob Fugger, see Pfeiffer, *Gymnasium* 71, 1964, 202f. ('Augsburger Humanisten und Philologen') and *HCS* ii 141.

[271] Xylander: see above, n.193.

[272] Gruter (1560-1627): Sandys ii 359; Pfeiffer, *HCS* ii 138. He learned Latin from his English mother, and was educated at Norwich Grammar School and Caius College, Cambridge. See above, n.216.

[273] Valens Acidalius (1567-1595): Sandys ii 273.

[274] Martin Crusius (1526-1607): Sandys ii 270. In 1575 he wrote to Greek scholars in Constantinople to inquire whether Athens still existed.

[275] Reinesius (1587-1667): Sandys ii 364. The manuscript of the *Cena* had been found in 1650 at Trau in Dalmatia, near Split (see Konrad Müller, *Petronius*, 1961, xxviii).

enjoyed a great personal reputation in the seventeenth century through his wide-ranging correspondence, and was rewarded by Louis XIV for his edition of the newly discovered *Cena Trimalchionis*, is of little account, for with all his great plans he never succeeded in producing anything beyond trifles. Caspar von Barth[276] from Küstrin was the right man for the age of roving adventurers. After visiting Italy, Spain and England he spent the latter part of his life as a free-lance scholar in Leipzig and published only a repulsive selection from the monstrous mass of his *Adversaria*. One cannot read him without catching the infection of his muddled thinking and muddled writing – and that is just what he would wish, for he displays the most exotic objects in his shop window in order to create the impression that he has a stock of rare treasures inside. Many of the manuscripts he rummaged through remain untraced, but his frauds are not always due to carelessness. Some are deliberate: for instance, the verses he served up of Vestricius Spurinna.[277] His literary remains, both printed and in manuscript, ought to be thoroughly examined; but it would be difficult to find anyone tough-minded enough for the task.

The best German scholars had already made for Holland, and even those who remained eventually gravitated there. We can therefore pick up the thread of our story in Holland, beginning with Scaliger's successors. Scaliger's last favourite pupil, Daniel Heinsius,[278] who wrote glowing obituaries of him, was too young for such an exalted position. Nor was he equal to it. He made a highly successful career as a teacher and in the service of the States-General, and wrote Latin verses which were much admired, as well as a tragedy; but his achievements as a scholar were no more than average. Hugo Grotius[279] was even more obviously too young. In 1600, at the

[276] Barth (1587-1658): Sandys ii 363.
[277] In 1624 he published an epigram attributed to Vestricius Spurinna, a Roman notable of the second half of the first century A.D.; see Speyer 320.
[278] D. Heinsius (1580-1655): Sandys ii 313.
[279] Grotius (1583-1645; Sandys ii 315; Pfeiffer, *HCS* ii 126) published his *Mare liberum* in 1609 and his *De jure belli et pacis* in 1625. Wilamowitz seems not to understand that Grotius did not set out to become a successor to Scaliger, scholarship not being his main interest. He was in fact a successor to Erasmus; see the references to him in H.R. Trevor-Roper's *Religion, the Reformation and Social Change*, 1967.

age of seventeen, he submitted his *Syntagma Arateum* to the
Master, who was well pleased with it. This book brought
together Aratus and his translators – the only sensible
arrangement – and the youthful editor gave proof of his
incomparable stylistic gift by filling in the gaps between the
fragments of Cicero's version. Later, during a period of
enforced idleness, he translated the poetical extracts in the
*Florilegium* of Stobaeus and the Anthology of Planudes, so
skilfully that for years scholars printed his verses side by side
with the originals. Grotius alone had the makings of a worthy
successor to Scaliger; but life sucked him into its whirlpool,
and he tasted imprisonment and exile. On the other hand,
although Grotius had his detractors, he made his name and
became a man of influence by sheer force of intellect. His end
was sad; he died at Rostock after being shipwrecked on his
return from Sweden, and was besmirched by calumny even in
the grave. The works which keep his fame alive today belong
to other departments of learning, but we should remember
that he also applied his scholarship to the interpretation of the
Bible. The saying '*Aliter pueri Terentium legunt, aliter Grotius*',
which treats him as the type of consummate scholar, made a
deep impression on the mind of Goethe.[280]

Gerhard Vossius[281] would dearly have loved to succeed
Scaliger and was disappointed to be passed over; but he
obtained an important post in Amsterdam instead, which he
filled with distinction. His *De historicis Graecis et Latinis*, one of
the few works of literary history produced in his day,
remained in use down to the middle of the nineteenth century.
His *Aristarchus, sive de arte grammatica* is a systematic treatise, a
sort of encyclopaedia of classical scholarship; we could show
in detail how it looks forward both to Boeckh's well-known
lectures and backward to the Seven Liberal Arts and the
ἐγκύκλιος παιδεία of ancient 'grammar', and also back to
ancient rhetoric. Vossius was exceptional in writing about the
*theologia gentilis*, as he called it, of the ancients, a subject

[280] See E. Grumach, *Goethe und die Antike*, 1949, pp. 79, 207, 330, 333 for
Goethe's allusions to this saying.
[281] G.J. Vossius (1577-1649): Sandys ii 307; *SS*[2] 164; Gruppe 47. (For
Boeckh's lectures, see below, n.458.)

usually avoided. Not that there was any sign that it was
understood, either then or for a long time to come. Anyone
who neither treated mythology as a plaything for poets, and
its deities as symbolical or allegorical figures – which was how
the Latin poets themselves treated them – nor took the line of
the Stoics as described in Cicero's *De natura deorum*, was
anathema to the Fathers and the Neoplatonists. For them the
gods were demons or devils, and paganism represented a lapse
from revealed monotheism – in other words, the gods could
still work miracles, were still real beings, and Van Dale's
denial[282] in his *De oraculis ethnicis* (1683) gave great offence.
Van Dale's rationalistic mind could conceive of no better
explanation for them than priestcraft, which exactly suited the
later rationalists. All in all, the conception of learning we find
in Vossius is immensely superior to the narrow routine of text-
production and *Adversaria*-spawning; but it paved the way for
the *polyhistors* of the next generation.

After a long interregnum another Frenchman, Claudius
Salmasius,[283] was invited to fill Scaliger's chair. His erudition
and width of interests seemed to justify his selection, but he
failed to concentrate his energies on a major work. A most un-
French formlessness in his writings spoils the effect, and his
taste for polemics tends to divert attention from the matter in
hand. A good opportunity came his way in Heidelberg, where,
as a pupil of Gruter, he transcribed the manuscript of the
Anthology of Cephalas, now known as the Palatine. Thanks to
Salmasius it continued to be known as 'the Inedita' down
to the time of Friedrich Jacobs;[284] for though from time
to time Salmasius did communicate an epigram or two, not all
the pressure exerted on him by Scaliger and Casaubon, who
recognised his gifts, could induce him to produce a proper
edition of any part of it except the Pattern Poems,[285] which
caught his fancy by their strangeness. The same sort of
interest led him to write an elaborate commentary on the

[282] A. Van Dale (1638-1708): Gruppe 65.
[283] Salmasius (1588-1653; Sandys ii 185; Pfeiffer, *HCS* ii 122) is known to
English readers for his violent controversy with Milton.
[284] Jacobs: see below, n.435.
[285] Pattern Poems = $T\epsilon\chi\nu o\pi a i\gamma\nu\iota a$ = *Carmina figurata*; the Mouse's Tale
in *Alice in Wonderland* is an example.

poems of Marcellus of Side,[286] which had survived by chance
because they were inscribed on the walls of the Triopion of
Herodes Atticus in Rome. The horribly corrupted *Liber
memoralis* of Ampelius,[287] which he published along with
Florus from a manuscript that has since been lost to view, was
an ideal subject for his kind of scholarship, which is seen at its
happiest in his *Exercitationes Plinianae*. It was the elucidation of
subject-matter rather than textual criticism that attracted
him, and the relation of Pliny to Solinus[288] set him a problem
in literary analysis. Salmasius had studied law in his youth,
which is why he wrote on legal and economic questions. This
involved him in an unequal contest with a practising lawyer,
Desiderius Heraldus,[289] who showed him no mercy.
Significantly Boeckh[290] still finds it necessary to go into these
disputes in great detail in his *Public Economy of Athens*.
Salmasius also had a violent quarrel with Petavius[291] over a
question of dress. Another of his disputes was with Heinsius.
This turned on what was then called Hellenism – i.e.,
basically, the Greek of the Bible. When contrasted with correct
Attic, this was bound to appear a tissue of barbarisms and
solecisms; but since this seemed hard to reconcile with the
dignity pertaining to the word of God, a 'Hellenistic' dialect
was invented. Salmasius was right in denying the existence of
such a dialect; but the arguments on both sides make it plain
that nobody at the time either understood, or could have
understood, how languages develop. In the matter of fame
Salmasius had nothing to complain of, and when Queen
Christina of Sweden wished to attract him to her court she
requested the States-General, through diplomatic channels, to
do her the favour of releasing him for a while. But he was not

[286] Wilamowitz himself published a discussion of these verses (*Kleine
Schriften*, ii 192f.), which were translated by Leopardi (*Tutte le opere*, ed. W.
Binni, 1969, i 428f.).

[287] *c.*200 A.D.; the work is a miscellany of cosmology, geography, history,
etc.

[288] 3rd century A.D.; wrote a *Collectanea rerum memorabilium*, edited by
Mommsen in 1864.

[289] Heraldus (1589-1649): Sandys ii 287.

[290] Boeckh: see below, n.452.

[291] Petavius: see above, n.236.

happy in the north and died shortly after his return.

The Queen, who possessed all the energy of her illustrious father, succeeded in inducing some of the foremost scholars of the day to migrate to her country, and others were selected, doubtless in deference to her tastes, for diplomatic appointments there. Descartes, Grotius and Salmasius were already celebrities when they arrived, but they did not stay long. Two sons of famous fathers, Isaac Vossius and Nicholas Heinsius,[292] formed closer ties with her which survived her removal to Rome, where she held her little Catholic court. Among lesser lights, Meibom[293] at least is worth mentioning, less for his Diogenes Laertius than for the *Scriptores musici*, which has retained its importance to this day. On Sweden itself, as it then was, this colony of scholars could not produce much effect; nevertheless Norrmann,[294] in addition to publishing some Byzantine material from manuscripts that had been carried off to Uppsala as spoils of war, won his spurs as a critic by his edition of the *Rhetoric* of Aristides.

Isaac Vossius acted for Christina in her purchase of manuscripts from which originate the *Codices Reginae* in the Vatican but he also knew how to look after himself; hence the Vossiani at Leyden. Both morally and intellectually unstable, he died a free-thinker and at the same time a canon of Windsor. Of his many ingenious ideas few are still remembered, and scarcely anyone now opens any of his editions. Nicholas Heinsius, whose private means enabled him to preserve his independence, was a man of quite a different stamp. He had already travelled widely, collated many manuscripts and acquired a considerable number by the time he temporarily entered Christina's service. Later he represented his country at the Swedish court and held other public appointments before retiring to devote his leisure to learning. His labours were confined almost entirely to Latin poetry, from Catullus to Prudentius. Apart from his numerous

[292] Isaac Vossius (1618-1689): Sandys ii 322; *SS*² 166. Nicholas Heinsius (1620-81): Sandys ii 323; *SS*² 165; Kenney 57f., whose excellent account atones for a disappointingly brief treatment by Pfeiffer.
[293] Marcus Meibom (1630-1710): Sandys ii 327.
[294] Lars Norrmann (1651-1703): Sandys iii 344.

editions he left a great deal of material on which later scholars relied for their own publications. It is hard to believe that anybody ever had such an intuitive understanding of what these poets, especially Ovid, were trying to say and how they expressed themselves, or to doubt that, so far from rejecting what he put into their mouths as unworthy of them, they would sometimes have admitted that he had even improved on them; for, diligent as he was in consulting manuscripts and though his flair for the true reading served him well, he knew nothing of real textual criticism. He emended, as was customary, *codicum et ingenii ope*, thereby setting an example that was only too widely followed by people who possessed neither his feeling for style nor his *ingenium*. But our abhorrence of inept conjecture must not lessen our admiration for the genius of Heinsius.

Heinsius' counterpart in the domain of Latin prose literature is Johann Friedrich Gronov[295] (Gronovius), who no doubt surpassed him in scientific scholarship. Gronovius came from Hamburg, and his portrait shows a typical north-German face. From his travels in Italy, France and England he brought home collations of manuscripts, among them the Etruscus, thanks to which the text of Seneca's tragedies was restored to its authentic form. Subsequently he had a long and distinguished career as a professor, during his later years at Leyden. Apart from his editions, his *Observationes* marked a considerable advance in the study of Latin prose since Livy, with whom he was at his best; indeed one can fairly say that his work in this field was not superseded before Madvig.[296] The book is in the usual miscellany form; but his methodical treatment and his concentration on the single object of providing an introduction to the language of the period, hold the whole thing together. As recently as fifty years ago German students were still urged to read him for themselves. At the same time he by no means neglected the subject-matter of his authors, and wrote successfully on the Roman coinage.

These men remained the pillars of Dutch scholarship on its textual side for the rest of the century and, as regards Latin,

[295] J.F. Gronovius (1611-1671): Sandys ii 319; *SS²* 165.
[296] Madvig: see below, n.487.

throughout the next century too; there was no real change of direction until Ruhnken.[297] Editions of the classics poured from the press, and scholars working on any of the authors concerned must still consult them; but by and large they are dead. For no important work was done on manuscripts, and the textual criticism was often slapdash, with a few lucky hits among a sad mass of blunders. There were some better men at work than the notorious Burman.[298] Lindenbrog, for instance, another Hamburger and at one time a pupil of Scaliger's, is remembered for his Statius, Oudendorp for his Lucan and Apuleius, Drakenborch for his Livy. There were also some clever ones, like the late-comer Johann Schrader.[299] But the work as a whole represents a decline, even if the reciprocal eulogies and the squabbles more or less balance each other out. The history of scholarship needs to spend as little time here on individuals as with the Italian humanists – who incidentally, are much more interesting as human beings. Greek was very much in the background. The only thing of any value in Jacob Gronovius'[299a] Herodotus is the information on the Florentine manuscripts; his edition of the astrological poem of the so-called Manetho was the *editio princeps*, but there its interest ends. All that was achieved by the German Küster's[300] edition of Suidas was to make this important work generally available. Graevius'[301] Callimachus is not without merit, but its value lies primarily in the collection of fragments contributed by Bentley, and secondarily in the commentary by Ezechiel Spanheim,[302] whose passion for coins

[297] Ruhnken: see below, n.356.
[298] Pieter Burman I (1668-1741; Sandys ii 443) and his nephew Pieter Burman II (1714-1778; Sandys ii 455) are notorious as the authors of numerous editions of Latin authors loaded with useless variants and stale notes copied from earlier scholars.
[299] Friedrich Lindenbrog (1573-1648): Sandys ii 364. Franz van Oudendorp (1696-1751): Sandys ii 454. Arnold Drakenborch (1684-1748): Sandys ii 447. Schrader (1722-1783): Sandys ii 455.
[299a] Jakob Gronovius (1670-1716): Sandys ii 329.
[300] Ludolf Küster (1670-1716): Sandys ii 445; see the references in Monk's *Life of Bentley* (for personal particulars).
[301] J.G. Graevius (1632-1703): Sandys ii 327; the edition of Callimachus had been begun by his son Theodore (d.1692).
[302] Spanheim (1629-1710): Sandys ii 327.

ran away with him even here. Spanheim came from Geneva,
entered the service of royalty at an early age and became
Frederick I of Prussia's first ambassador to England, where he
died. There is no profit in him except as a numismatist; his
Julian is negligible. Graevius, also a German, who was
transplanted to Holland at an early age and became a professor
at Leyden, published editions of several authors, many of them
of the variorum kind, which came into fashion at this time; he
also compiled a *Thesaurus antiquitatum Romanarum* in the manner
of Gruter's *Lampas*, which gave a new lease of life to works of
earlier scholars.

The *Thesaurus* was the precursor of numerous compilations
of the same sort in many volumes. The production of
*Antiquitates*, as they were called in imitation of Varro, had its
uses, inasmuch as their compilers gathered together with
immense labour the literary evidence for innumerable details
of ancient life – some important, others quite trivial – and
helped to reduce them to order. To that extent these scholars'
industry and their forgotten books still count for something;
but since the tradition of the monuments hardly existed for
them, and since they were almost completely ignorant of
source-criticism and very weak in historical criticism, they
could hardly have achieved much more, even if the intellectual
attainments of most of them had been higher than they were.
A typical specimen is Johannes Meursius,[303] who was
responsible for an unprofitable edition of Aristoxenus and
other writers on music from a manuscript for which he was
indebted to Scaliger. Meursius also produced a bad edition of
Chalcidius. Then he flung himself upon Greek – more
particularly Attic – antiquities. His quotations are countless
and the literature is well-thumbed, but there is scarcely an
idea to be found anywhere. The combination on the one hand
of editions of the classics in which the content was almost
completely ignored and on the other of compilations of
'Antiquities' led to a cleavage between verbal scholarship and
the scholarship of 'things' which had disastrous consequences.
The exponents of the former fancied themselves superior
because, they claimed, conjecture required brains, whereas all

[303] Meursius (1579-1639): Sandys ii 311.

the compiler seemed to need was application. The whole conception of these Antiquities, with its emphasis on the accumulation of facts, has obscured the proper understanding of ancient life down to the most recent times, and where it survives, as in most of the so-called 'Private Antiquities', the old chaos still prevails, with the result that many scholars are sadly lacking in any clear conception of ancient life, which can be acquired for the most part only through a study of the monuments. As ability steadily declined, the prestige attaching to knowledge steadily increased, until the accumulation of facts became the highest object of ambition. We can already see this happening in Salmasius, as compared with Scaliger; but, as Heraclitus said long ago, 'much learning does not breed understanding', and it was only Wagner the famulus who said, 'True, I know much, but would know everything.'[304] Daniel Morhof[305] in his *Polyhistor* sums up the ideal of the age – in which German scholarship was at its lowest ebb.

This was also, of course, the age of Leibniz, the first German since Luther to become a figure of European importance. Leibniz too may be termed a *polyhistor*; but at the same time it is true that the prestige of the ancients and more especially of classical scholarship, had sunk very low in the hundred years since Scaliger. Philosophy, mathematics and the natural sciences had far outgrown the Greek science that nurtured them. Modern man had come of age, and in all the arts there was a revulsion from antiquity, as it was then understood: in other words, the spell was broken. Scholarship ought to have adapted itself to the changed circumstances; instead, it preferred to struggle along to the bitter end in the same old rut. The antiquaries' idea of a book was a string of quotations, the scholars' a string of conjectures. The Dead-Sea fruits of high-flown orations and Latin verses, along with learned *Epistles* and the rank growth of venomous polemics, was all that this kind of scholarship was still capable of producing. It was the fag-end of a Heroic Age. Vitality was running low, and only a new supply of sap, in the shape of

---

[304] *Faust* i 601.
[305] Morhof (1639-90): Sandys ii 365.

men with a new outlook and the ability to make others share it, could save the tree from withering completely. Here too, as in philosophy and political theory, the new spirit came out of England.

It is clear to anybody who walks round the magnificent monastic buildings of the Oxford and Cambridge colleges that the changes at the time of the Reformation did not involve a major break with the past as they did in Germany, and the same applies to English humanism. Wycliffe and Roger Bacon were its precursors, even if they produced no immediate effect; and apostles of the new movement like Chrysoloras, Aeneas Sylvius and Poggio were early visitors. They were followed by Erasmus,[306] who found favour with the great and in the universities. Englishmen went to study in Italy and on their return spread the germs of the New Learning when they entered on high office in the Church. In this respect the situation has not changed; witness Cramer and Gaisford[307] in the last century, both of whom were bishops. Sacred and classical philology were still bracketed together, but also still distinguished from each other. One can understand Englishmen's reverence for a figure like Linacre,[308] and it was Greek philosophy that nerved Lady Jane Grey to mount the scaffold so heroically; but English humanism produced nothing, any more than German humanism, that need detain the historian of our science, and this holds good for the age of Elizabeth, and even of Cromwell. Chapman's Homer[309] and

---

[306] He was Lady Margaret Professor of Divinity and lived in Queens' College, Cambridge.

[307] Cramer and Gaisford were not bishops, but deans; see below, nn.339-40.

[308] Thomas Linacre (c.1460-1524; Sandys ii 225; Pfeiffer, *HCS* ii 66) became a Fellow of All Souls in 1484 and studied Greek under Politian in Florence, besides studying medicine in Padua and Vicenza. His translations of the Aristotelian commentaries of Simplicius and Alexander of Aphrodisias and of several treatises of Galen show a good knowledge of Greek for that time. As physician to Henry VIII (from 1509) he was also tutor to the Princess Mary, and besides a Latin grammar wrote a book *De emendata structura Latini sermonis* (1524). He founded the College of Physicians (1518), and is buried in St Paul's.

[309] George Chapman (c.1559-1634; Sandys ii 241) completed his Homer

the Latin verses of Buchanan belong to the history of English literature. Shakespeare was quite untrammelled by any creed, either inwardly or outwardly, which is a much more important point than Seneca's influence on the style, and Plutarch's[310] on the matter, of his tragedies. Milton[311] is the epic poet of Puritanism, but even in subject-matter he is unimaginable apart from Greece and Rome, like the contemporary continental poets, and he stands in the same relation to antiquity as they do. But England was still in the purely receptive stage. Although Casaubon and Isaac Vossius spent the evening of their lives there, they left no disciples capable of carrying on the tradition, unless we count Thomas Gale,[312] who produced the *editio princeps* of Iamblichus' *De mysteriis* from a manuscript obtained from Vossius. Nevertheless quiet study of the Greeks produced precious fruit: if Plato and Plotinus had not been read with inward sympathy at Cambridge, Shaftesbury[313] would never have nourished his mind on that philosophy.

Seventeenth-century England, then, produced nothing beyond a few isolated works which can conveniently be treated, like those from Germany, at the time under the heading of Dutch scholarship. Such were Gataker's[314]

---

in 1611. George Buchanan (1506-1582; Sandys ii 243) was famous in his own day for his Latin epigrams and his Latin version of the Psalms. 'Buchanan, perhaps alone among the Scottish Calvinists, was essentially a humanist, not a preacher': H.R. Trevor-Roper, *English Historical Review*, suppl. 3, 1966, 9). See I. MacFarlane, *Buchanan*, 1981.

[310] On Shakespeare's use of Plutarch, see D.A. Russell, *Plutarch*, 1973, ch.9. On Seneca's influence on Shakespeare, see T.S. Eliot, *Selected Essays*.

[311] Milton (1608-1674; Sandys iii 344) was well enough acquainted with Latin and Greek to make a felicitous emendation at Euripides, *Bacchae* 188 (see Dodds's commentary ad loc.). His Euripidean notes are published in *Museum Criticum*, 1826, 283f.

[312] Gale (*c*.1635-1702; Sandys ii 354), Dean of York. Cambridge Platonists: Sandys ii 353.

[313] Shaftesbury (1671-1713), the Cambridge Platonist.

[314] Thomas Gataker (1574-1654; Sandys ii 341), Fellow of Sidney Sussex, Cambridge. His commentary on Marcus Aurelius (1652) is still useful; see G. Zuntz, *JTS* 47, 1946, 85 (cited by Pfeiffer, *HCS* ii 144, n.2); and Fraenkel (see next note) thinks him Pearson's nearest rival for the honour of being the greatest English classical scholar before Bentley.

elucidation of the Stoic philosophy of Marcus Aurelius, Stanley's[315] Aeschylus, Thomas Gale's *Historiae poeticæ scriptores antiqui*, Potter's[315a] Clement and Lycophron and *Antiquities of Greece* – all highly creditable performances in their day. Henry Dodwell's[316] writings on chronology, both in general and also with special reference to some historians, found a larger public than they deserved, and are long forgotten. We are glad to note, as an earnest of things to come, that as early as 1629 John Selden,[317] whose *De dels Syriis* had won him fame as an orientalist, published the Parian chronological table in his *Marmora Arundelliana*, a description of the collection of Greek marbles which, after many adventures, came into the possession of the earl of Arundel. The subsequent history of the *Marmor Parium* was one of shameful neglect and mutilitation, until finally it found a home in Oxford. Selden was a conscientious worker, but even such a clear and straightforward inscription was more than he could decipher, and nobody was in a hurry to consult the actual tablet – not even Boeckh, if it comes to that, who was the first to explain the meaning of this priceless relic. Joshua Barnes,[318] who edited Homer and Euripides, is remembered today only as a foil to Bentley; but his Homer contained material which was useful in its day. All this work has one feature in common: a trend towards Greek, which not for the first time put new life

---

[315] Thomas Stanley (1625-1678; Sandys ii 351) also wrote a History of Philosophy. Fraenkel (*Ag.* i 40f., 78f.) showed that the best new suggestions in his Aeschylus were due to John Pearson (1613-1686). After being Master of Jesus and then Master of Trinity at Cambridge, Pearson became Bishop of Chester; he wrote a famous *Exposition of the Creed*. We now know that in Fraenkel's words (*Ag.* i 40) 'in range of learning and critical power he is probably inferior to no English scholar save Bentley'.

[315a] John Potter (c.1674-1747; Sandys ii 356), Archbishop of Canterbury.

[316] Dodwell (1641-1711; Sandys ii 357) was Camden Professor of Ancient History at Oxford from 1688 till 1691.

[317] Selden (1584-1654; Sandys ii 342). Jacoby in his edition of 1904 points out that whatever judgment we pass on the quality of Selden's editing, without him the upper part of the inscription would not have been preserved.

[318] Barnes (1654-1712; Sandys ii 357), Regius Professor of Greek at Cambridge and Fellow of Emmanuel. He is said to have persuaded his wife to finance his edition of the *Iliad* by telling her that it was the work of King Solomon.

into scholarship. The cult of the Hellenic, whether he realised it or not, was the mainspring of the philosophy of Shaftesbury, who had a deeper understanding of it, based on temperamental affinity, than others. Shaftesbury developed, and awakened, an entirely new attitude to nature and art, which set up enthusiasm as a counterpoise to the purely rationalistic approach. Though it passed entirely unnoticed among professional scholars both in England and Holland, this was the first dawn that heralded the second coming of true Hellenism.

The year 1691 saw the publication of the *Epistula ad Millium* as an appendix to an edition of the Chronicle of Malalas, of which Oxford possessed the only manuscript. Its author was Richard Bentley,[319] who at twenty-nine was still entirely unknown and living there as tutor to an undergraduate. Nothing like it had been seen before. Not only was it packed with emendations such as no one else could have produced at that time: it contained a collection of the fragments of Ion of Chios, revealed an unprecedented familiarity with the ancient grammarians, including the formidable Hesychius, and, finally, established the completely unknown fact that *synapheia* prevails in Greek anapaestic systems right through to the catalexis. Actually, in this maiden effort[320] we already have the whole of Bentley – the happy knack of the emender, the exact observation which enabled him to arrive at fixed rules, the vision that showed him what the great tasks of scholarship were. Bentley embarked on too many of them but completed none, for no sooner had he made a start on any particular one

[319] Bentley (1662-1742): Sandys ii 401; *SS*² 166; Kenney 71f.; Pfeiffer, *HCS* ii, ch.11. The life by J.H. Monk, Bishop of Gloucester (1831; 2nd edn. 1833; reprinted 1969) is most agreeable reading. R.C. Jebb's *Bentley* (English Men of Letters series, 1882) gives a good account of his scholarship, although its author was as far as possible removed from Bentley in temperament, and tells us less about the wider aspects of his scholarship than Wilamowitz does in these few pages. R.J. White's *Dr Bentley* (1965) is trivial; whoever wants to enjoy the gossip about Bentley's quarrels will find it much more entertaining to read Monk. Pfeiffer has a splendid chapter about Bentley, though I think he exaggerates his importance as a theologian.

[320] The *Epistula ad Millium* was reprinted at Toronto in 1962 with an excellent introduction by G.P. Goold.

than his attention was diverted by another. Each was really beyond the capacity of one man – even the collection of all the fragments of the poets and the complete new edition of the grammarians that the young Bentley projected; the reconstruction of the language of Homer and a critical edition of the New Testament were later added to the list. Much still remains for scholarship to do on all these subjects. How this young man came by such attainments and ambitions is part of the mystery of genius. No teacher showed him the way, and nobody as yet appreciated the greatness of the challenge implicit in his achievements; but in Holland, at least, there were people on whom he made an impression. Graevius asked him to edit the fragments for his Callimachus, and this masterpiece appeared alongside Spanheim's commentary; one cannot imagine a more striking contrast in method.

Meanwhile there had begun the amusing controversy about the Letters of Phalaris, which led to the immortal *Dissertation* of 1697 (2nd edn. 1699). The best way a German can characterise the *Dissertation* is by putting it on a level with the polemical writings of Lessing. That is due to Bentley's masterly style, which he possessed only in his mother tongue but which is so superb that the Latin and even the German translations, which never ought to have been made, can give no idea of it. Considered in itself, it was hardly worth the effort. Leibniz had already detected in his student days that the letters were spurious, and the barrage of learning that Bentley puts up seems to us superfluous. We no longer need to be told that in the Acragas of Phalaris there were no tragedies and no Attic drachmae. In those days people needed to be told, but simple athetesis would have been sufficient. What was in the minds of the authors of the Letters of Phalaris and other similar fabrications which Bentley disposed of, and in what period they were concocted, we are not told, and that is how the matter still stands. At this point, though he was still the object of vicious attacks, Bentley received an appointment worthy of him at Cambridge, as Master of Trinity. His mastership was marred by a long series of unedifying feuds with colleagues and subordinates, and it is obviously kinder to his memory to think of him purely as a scholar. During the rest of his life he produced only three further editions: the

Horace of 1712, the Terence with Phaedrus of 1726 and the Manilius of 1739, three years before his death. The fragments of Menander and Philemon, which he published under an assumed name together with a sharp attack on Clericus, were only an interlude, and of his many contributions to the works of other scholars it is enough to mention those to Davies' *Tusculans*.[321] The Horace[322] is the most widely studied of his works. Its importance most certainly does not lie in the conjectures – the text of Horace requires only a tiny amount of that attention, thank goodness – but in the vigour with which he seizes on the genuine tradition. Similarly his Terence is based on the Bembinus, which Faernus[323] had made known in 1565; but here too we find the gift of metrical observation which enabled him to solve the problem of the nature of early Latin verse. Bentley's papers and working copies contain a mass of observations on many poets, chiefly Latin, which have gradually been made known. He abandoned numerous projects because his efforts to find a reliable manuscript tradition had not succeeded. Those already mentioned required immense labour. Concerning Homer, he got as far as discovering that the digamma was still metrically effective, and as regards the New Testament, not only would he have anticipated Lachmann's recension but he would also have made a useful contribution to exegesis, as his much-applauded sermons of 1713 show.

Bentley's fame was slow to reach Germany; not even Lessing seems to have read him. F.A. Wolf, in his *Analecta*, hailed him as the greatest of all scholars, at the same time broadly hinting that he himself was a sort of Bentley; and the school of Hermann and Lachmann carried on the cult. The fact that in his treatment of the Latin poets Bentley has much in common with Nicholas Heinsius and his circle in Holland should not detract from our veneration for him; but the simple truth is that there is more to scholarship than that. Even to

[321] John Davies (1679-1732; Sandys ii 412), President of Queens' College, Cambridge, edited the Tusculans in 1709.

[322] See D.R. Shackleton Bailey, 'Bentley and Horace', in *Proceedings of the Leeds Philosophical Society*, vol. x, 1963, 105f.

[323] Faernus (= Gabriele Faerno, d.1561): Sandys ii 147.

understand a poem, and a poet, rightly requires other things
than intellect, which was Bentley's only weapon – that is the
lesson to be learnt from his Horatian emendations – and the
man who is obsessed with rules will find it hard to give
individuality its due. The *Dissertation* establishes the historical
facts, but that is only the means to an end. Scholarship of this
kind can purify an author's text, which is certainly a great
achievement and the essential first step; but it cannot bring
his work to life and, in order to do so in the way the author
intended, historical research has to conjure up before us the
whole environment from which it sprang. The discovery of the
digamma was also a great achievement; but the fact that
Robert Wood,[324] in the narrow seas between Chios and
Mount Mimas, suddenly realised the truthfulness of Homeric
descriptions of nature, and on the strength of this wrote in
praise of the Original Genius of Homer, probably had more
influence on the growth of our science of classical antiquity.
The foundation of the Society of Dilettanti[325] and the travels of
Stuart and Revett,[326] who made drawings of the ancient Greek
monuments that were still above ground, began a movement
that approached antiquity from an entirely different angle but
contributed quite as much to the genesis of modern
scholarship.

In his grammatical studies Richard Dawes relied entirely
on observation as practised by Bentley, and Dawes' canons[327]

---

[324] Wood (*c.* 1717-1771; Sandys ii 432) in his *Essay on the Original Genius of
Homer* was the first to argue that Homer was illiterate. See Adam Parry's
introduction to Milman Parry's *The Making of Homeric Verse*, 1971, xiii; cf.
J.L. Myres, *Homer and his Critics*, 1958, 59.

[325] On the Society of Dilettanti (from 1733), see Sandys ii 431.

[326] James Stuart (1713-1788) and Nicholas Revett (1720-1804): Sandys ii
432; Rumpf i 57, etc. They recorded the monuments of Athens; so did
Richard Chandler (1738-1810; Sandys ii 434 and Rumpf i 57).

[327] Dawes (1709-1766; Sandys ii 415), Fellow of Emmanuel. W.W.
Goodwin, *Syntax of the Greek Moods and Tenses*, 2nd edn. 1897, 129, writes:
'We must perhaps leave the venerable Canon Davesianus undisturbed in
the single department of object clauses with ὅπως, although we may admit
an occasional exception even there.' Housman in his review of Bywater's
posthumously printed Oxford inaugural lecture made a polite protest
against the rather excessive praise of Dawes in that work (see Housman,
*Collected Papers*, 1973, iii 1005).

became a mainstay of Greek syntax. Clarke's[328] Homer, which Goethe read, and Taylor's Lysias and Demosthenes were of some importance in their day. Gibbon's[329] relation to Tillemont has already been mentioned. Gibbon was not a 'plodder', as Mommsen put it. His book is not a work of original research; but it is assured of immortality by its brilliant writing and because the author's Voltairean bias can enliven even the driest subject-matter. In the following period critical effort was concentrated on the Athenian drama, essentially because the purest Attic was to be found there; about the only man to approach it as poetry was Thomas Tyrwhitt,[330] whose editions of Aristotle's *Poetics* bears witness to his subtle understanding. Jeremiah Markland,[331] who carried on the old tradition of violent emendation in his edition of the *Silvae* of Statius, did much the same with Euripides. So did Wakefield,[332] whose treatment of the tragedians irritated Porson just as his Lucretius irritated Lachmann.

Samuel Musgrave's[333] editions are on a much higher level, but the first decisive step forward was taken by Richard Porson,[334] who was revered by a circle of adoring disciples. It

[328] Clarke (1675-1729): Sandys ii 413; see E. Grumach, *Goethe und die Antike* i 117 and 122, for Goethe's use of this book. John Taylor (1704-1766; Sandys ii 414), Fellow of St John's and University Librarian at Cambridge.

[329] Gibbon (1737-1794).

[330] Tyrwhitt (1730-1786; Sandys ii 419), Fellow of Merton College, Oxford and Clerk of the House of Commons. The name rhymes with 'spirit'.

[331] Markland (1693-1776; Sandys ii 413), Fellow of Peterhouse, Cambridge. Wilamowitz is unfair to Markland. 'It is probable that Englishmen are right in counting Porson the second of English scholars, but many judges on the Continent would give that rank to Markland. He is the only one except Bentley who has been highly and equally eminent in Greek and Latin; and I believe that Bentley did him the honour, extravagant I admit, to be jealous of him' (Housman, *Collected Papers* iii 1005). By 'English scholars', I take Housman to mean 'eighteenth-century and early nineteenth-century English textual critics'; see C. Collard, *PCPS* 22, 1976, 1f.

[332] Gilbert Wakefield (1756-1801; Sandys ii 430), Fellow of Jesus College, Cambridge. Wakefield is too contemptuously dismissed. Some of his conjectures show real acuteness; see Munro, *Lucretius*, i 19, n.3.

[333] Samuel Musgrave (1732-1780; Sandys ii 418) practised as a physician in Exeter, where Benjamin Heath (1704-1766) was town clerk (Sandys ii 417).

[334] Richard Porson (1759-1808): Sandys ii 424; Pfeiffer, *HCS* ii 159. 'At

was the effect of Porson's work on people that really mattered; he was a university teacher only in name. He took from the tradition only what lay ready to his hand, and his Euripides did not get very far; but by observation he conclusively established the metrical rules of tragic dialogue and did the same for its language. All he completed was his transcription of the Lexicon of Photius; otherwise his life's work consists of admittedly splendid emendations to a rather small number of Greek authors. Of his followers, Peter Elmsley[335] remained faithful to the tragedians but finally went to Italy for the authentic manuscript tradition; his promising career was cut short by an untimely death. The loss of Peter Dobree[336] in the same year, 1825, was an even heavier blow, and the greater part of his work had to be put together for publication from his miscellaneous papers. Dobree was Elmsley's superior both in ingenuity and the width of his interests, which embraced both poetry and Attic prose. As regards Aristophanes, the Ravenna manuscript – first made known to the world by Invernizi in 1794[337] – gave increased confidence to the critics, who found that it confirmed not a few of their conjectures. Apart from these great men the age produced some others who call for little more than passing mention, though here and there their work has merit. Bentley's and Porson's studies in the grammarians were carried further, not only by Dobree in his transcription of the *Lexicon Cantabrigiense*,[338] but by Cramer[339]

---

Cambridge a cult of Porson was founded by Kidd, Dobree, Monk and Blomfield,' writes Sir Denys Page in his brilliant essay 'Richard Porson' (*PBA* 45, 1959, 221f.); he corrects the English over-estimation of Porson. The life of Porson by M.L. Clarke (Cambridge, 1937) is pleasant reading.

[335] Elmsley (1773-1825; Sandys iii 394), of Westminster School and Christ Church, Oxford, later Principal of St Alban's Hall, had very different qualities from those of Porson (see Page, 230); he was less ingenious, but more systematic. He did far more for the texts of the tragedians than the adjective 'promising' suggests.

[336] Peter Paul Dobree (1782-1825; Sandys iii 399), a Channel Islander, Fellow of Trinity College, Cambridge.

[337] Filippo Invernizi (d.1832; Sandys iii 86), a Roman lawyer, rediscovered the manuscript, probably written about 1000 A.D.; for its importance, see K.J. Dover's edition of the *Clouds*, 1968, cviif.

[338] A rhetorical lexicon; O. Houtsma's edition of 1870 is reprinted in *Lexica Graeca Minora*, selected by K. Latte and arranged by H. Erbse, 1965.

[339] J.A. Cramer (1793-1848; Sandys iii 443) was not a bishop, but was

in the industrious transcriptions which fill the eight volumes of his *Anecdota*, and by Gaisford,[340] whose folio editions of Suidas and the *Etymologicum magnum* are useful, though critically inadequate. Thereafter, these studies ceased to be cultivated in England. Gaisford's Herodotus and his *Scriptores metrici* are essentially resumés of other men's work, but they are serviceable and sensibly designed. The praise accorded to Bernhardy's[341] Suidas was quite unjustified, for in judgment Bernhardy was certainly not the superior of Gaisford, on whose collations he relied.

The influence of Bentley immediately made itself felt in Holland, for Tiberius Hemsterhuys[342] had by then already turned his attention to Greek. Hemsterhuys was looked up to by his friends and pupils as the perfect type of a scholar, and Ruhnken made him the subject of a celebrated *Elogium*. His works hardly live up to his reputation, but we must also take account of his contributions to the works of others – as well as his stimulating personality. His great object was to establish a norm of correct Greek as it was understood by the grammarians, from whom the classicists had taken their vocabulary, accidence and syntax since the days of Tryphon. The implication was that the imitators were as valid as models as their Attic originals – a view whose after-effects were long felt; and it is significant that Hemsterhuys edited both Pollux and Lucian – that is to say, the most comprehensive of the lexicons and the cleverest of the imitators. The lexicons now became a favourite subject of study. Blancard[343] produced an

---

Dean of Norwich. He published much valuable material in his *Anecdota Oxoniensia* (1834-7) and his *Anecdota Parisina* (1839-41).

[340] Thomas Gaisford (1779-1855; Sandys iii 395) was Dean of Christ Church from 1831 until his death. His edition of the *Etymologicum Magnum* (1848) is still not superseded. See Lloyd-Jones, *BG*, ch. 6.

[341] Gottfried Bernhardy (1800-1875; Sandys iii 121) completed his edition of 'Suidas'; see above, n.30) in 1853. There is now an excellent modern edition by Ada Adler (Copenhagen, 1929-38).

[342] Hemsterhuys (1685-1766): Sandys ii 447; J.G. Gerretzen, *Schola Hemsterhusana*, Nijmegen, 1940, 77-156. Tryphon: see above, n.22.

[343] I think Wilamowitz has confused S. Blancard (*Lexicon Medicum*, 1832) with J.S. Bernard (1718-1793; Sandys ii 451), whose edition of Thomas Magister's Atticistic lexicon appeared in 1757.

edition of Thomas Magister, Pierson[344] of Moeris, Valckenaer
of Ammonius, Ruhnken of Timaeus. In Paris Ruhnken had
also transcribed the lexicons which were later edited by
Bekker,[345] and they were frequently quoted as they stood in
these transcripts. Alberti[346] started by editing Hesychius,
the best source of information on poetic diction, but his edition
owed a great deal to Hemsterhuys. Hemsterhuys had steered
clear of the poets ever since Bentley proved to him in a
friendly way that he was incapable of dealing with the
quotations from them in Pollux. It is true that he produced
nevertheless an edition of Aristophanes' *Plutus*; but here
there were no pitfalls in the text, the whole play being a model
of pure, straightforward Greek. The addition of scholia was
meritorious in its own day but it is now quite out of date.
All the fuss about etymology and phonetics on which
Hemsterhuys and Valckenaer wasted their energies is
forgotten. Hemsterhuys, in fact, belongs entirely to the past,
whereas the Westphalian Peter Wesseling's[347] Diodorus and
Herodotus (the best elements of which are doubtless
attributable to Valckenaer) can still be consulted with profit,
although as a teacher Wesseling was overshadowed by
Hemsterhuys.

In retrospect, the most important scholar of this school
appears to have been Lodewyk Kaspar Valckenaer.[348]
Valckenaer began his career as an editor of the tragedians

[344] Johann Pierson (1731-1759; Sandys ii 461) published his *Moeris* in
1756. On Valckenaer and Ruhnken, see below. Valckenaer's *Ammonius* of
1739 was superseded only by K. Nickau's edition in 1966; Ruhnken's
*Timaeus* of 1754 is still in use.

[345] On Bekker, see below, n.456. His *Anecdota Graeca* (3 vols) of 1814-21
contain some editions of lexical and grammatical works that are still useful.

[346] Johann Alberti took over the edition of Hesychius from Küster in 1736,
published the first volume in 1746, and left the second to be brought out by
Ruhnken in 1766. Even after the editions of Moritz Schmidt (1857-1868) and
Kurt Latte (vol.i 1953, vol.ii 1966, as far as omicron), the Alberti edition
retains some value.

[347] Wesseling (1692-1754): Sandys ii 453.

[348] Valckenaer (1715-1785): Sandys ii 456. His theories of interpolation in
the *Phoenissae* have been developed in modern times by Eduard Fraenkel
(*Sitzungsberichte der Bayerischen Akademie*, 1965). Like Hemsterhuys,
Valckenaer was a Frisian; on the Frisian university of Franeker, now
Leeuwarden, see G. Zuntz, *PBA* 42, 1956, 242f.

with two plays of Euripides, and perceived the spuriousness of many lines in the *Phoenissae* (athetesis was still quite unusual in those days); he also embarked on the restoration of lost plays. He paved the way for the revival of the neglected subject of Hellenistic poetry by his edition of some poems of Theocritus and, by drawing attention to the fragments of Sophron, gave impetus both to the study of dialects and to research in literary history. His treatise on Aristobulus was published after his death by his son-in-law Luzac, and the effect of its exposure of Jewish forgeries passing under the names of famous poets was long felt. Here, and in the wide range of his critical activities generally, the influence of Bentley's example is clearly seen, as it is in his extension of them to the New Testament.

This is the appropriate place for a mention of the Alsatian Philippe Brunck,[349] for his work on the tragedians and the Alexandrians runs parallel to Valckenaer's. Brunck had been struck by the beauty of their poetry when he was living in Giessen, where he served in the commissariat department during the Seven Years' War. We can see from the elegant production of his editions of the poets that they were intended to give pleasure and not merely to provide instruction in language and criticism; but he also made full use of the Paris library, which the professionals neglected to do. All the tragedians benefited, but especially Sophocles, for the errors introduced by Turnebus from the recension of Triclinius were now finally expunged. The library possessed only inferior manuscripts of Apollonius Rhodius and the scholia; but when finally we get an edition worthy of this poet, Brunck will come into his own.[350] The collection of fragments known as the *Analecta Brunckii* was extremely welcome in its day, the more so as it was the next best thing to an edition of the still unpublished *Greek Anthology*, and the arrangement of the poems by authors has great advantages. Here too Brunck was

[349] Brunck (1729-1803): Sandys ii 395.

[350] Such an edition was eventually published by a distinguished pupil of Wilamowitz, Hermann Fränkel (Oxford, 1961); see his *Einleitung sur kritischen Ausgabe der Argonautika des Apollonius, Abhandlungen der Akademie der Wissenschaften in Göttingen,* 55, 1964, 112-15; and we have now an excellent Budé edition by F. Vian.

guided by his genuine love of poetry, which outweighs the numerous sins of omission and commission for which the pundits despised him.

Brunck and Jean-Philippe D'Orville[351] make a nicely contrasted pair. D'Orville held no teaching appointment either, but after extensive travels lived comfortably on his country estate, where he could afford to employ clever young men like Ruhnken and Reiske as amanuenses, and was accorded full academic status. The stink raised by his feud with the egregious Cornelis de Pauw,[352] in which the taunt of 'Orbilius' was countered with the more apposite one of 'Pavo', has subsided. De Pauw's bad editions are forgotten, whereas D'Orville's Chariton enjoyed a certain esteem for years because, together with rather trivial explanatory notes and other matter, it provides an introduction to the Attic of the imperial period, which then and long afterwards was regarded as quite timeless. It was the *editio princeps*, but D'Orville had made no attempt to transcribe the only manuscripts himself and unloaded a good deal of the work on Reiske.[353]

The case of Xenophon of Ephesus, who had recently appeared in a truly pitiable *editio princeps*,[354] shows us the whole body of Dutch scholars engaged in a joint critical effort, which was summed up in Hofman-Peerlkamp's[355] edition of 1818. The joys of emendation must have blinded these critics to the worthlessness of the object on which their labours were expended. The truth is that the mantle of Hemsterhuys fell directly on Ruhnken[356] – the Pomeranian who became a complete Dutchman and knew how to comport himself with dignity in the distinguished and not over-strenuous role of a *Princeps Criticorum*, the term used of him by F.A. Wolf in the dedication of his *Prolegomena*. Wolf presumably enjoyed the

[351] D'Orville (1696-1751): Sandys ii 454. He was professor at Amsterdam from 1730 to 1742, but then resigned.

[352] Pauw (d.1749); see Fraenkel, *Agamemnon* i 44.

[353] Reiske: see below, n.375.

[354] Ed.pr. of Xenophon of Ephesus by Antonio Cocchi, London, 1726.

[355] Hofman-Peerlkamp: see below, n.501.

[356] Ruhnken (1723-1798): Sandys ii 456. Miss E. Hulshof Pol in her pious *Studia Ruhnckeniana* (Leyden, 1953) tells us that we ought to spell him 'Ruhncken'.

irony,[357] for Ruhnken had not the slightest sympathy with the great intellectual movement among his countrymen of which Wolf regarded himself as the leader. Ruhnken's conception of classical scholarship is most clearly revealed by his editing Muretus. Faultless Latinity meant as much to him as learning; but he must have been a brilliant teacher, judging by several of his lectures that were printed straight from his notebooks. He also made numerous discoveries, without putting them to any use, such as the passages from Longinus embedded in the *Rhetoric* of Apsines;[358] his omission was later made good by Janus Bake.[359] Everything Ruhnken published was faultless as far as it went – for instance, his editions of the *Homeric Hymn to Demeter*, the manuscript of which was stolen by Christian von Matthaei[360] in Moscow and found its way to Leyden; of the Lexicon of Timaeus; and of Rutilius Lupus with a *Historia critica oratorum Graecorum*, which contains useful observations on the Hellenistic age but most certainly does not deserve to be called a history. As the life's work of a Prince of Critics this is somewhat meagre.

The tradition was creditably carried on by Daniel Wyttenbach[361] of Berne – who delivered the customary eulogy on Ruhnken and published a commendable edition of Plutarch's *Moralia* – and after him by Jacob Geel,[362] a man of fine taste but unproductive. It was finally wound up in the most brilliant style by Carolus Gabriel Cobet,[363] after whom no further progress was possible in that direction. Cobet's

[357] Wolf's intention cannot have been ironical; see W. Süss, *Philologische Wochenschrift*, 1936, 1274.

[358] The passages are not from the treatise *On the Sublime*, but the *Ars Rhetorica* attributed to Longinus; they are printed in A.O. Prickard's Oxford text of the former work (1906), though not in D.A. Russell's Oxford text of 1968.

[359] Bake (1787-1864): Sandys iii 278.

[360] Matthaei (1744-1811): Sandys iii 385. See N.J. Richardson, *The Homeric Hymn to Demeter*, 1974, 65f.

[361] Wyttenbach (1746-1820): Sandys ii 461. We still use his lexicon to Plutarch.

[262] Geel (1789-1862): Sandys iii 280.

[363] Cobet (1813-1889): Sandys iii 282; Kenney 117f. *Variae Lectiones*, 1854 (2nd edn. 1873); *Novae Lectiones*, 1858; *Miscellanea Critica*, 1876; *Collectanea Critica*, 1878.

ambition, which he achieved, was to extract from his reading a canon of pure Attic, applicable to thought and style as well as language, and to do the same for the imitation Attic of the imperial period, except that there he also demonstrated its inadequacy as an imitation, point by point. Cobet himself wrote as perfect Greek as Ruhnken wrote classical Latin. He therefore proceeded to demand absolute purity of language and the utmost precision of thought from all his authors, and if they showed resistance he at once suspected foul play. Cobet had done a good deal of work in the libraries of France and Italy, and though he made no systematic study of palaeography he was familiar with the misreadings and miswritings of the Byzantines of the last period. He therefore went back wherever he could to the beautiful manuscripts of the ninth to the eleventh century. But even they did not satisfy him, and they must, therefore, already have been badly corrupted; from which he concluded that though one might confine oneself to the older manuscripts, even their text had been shockingly mishandled by *scioli magistelli, protervi interpolatores*. The purpose of these postulates was to justify his innumerable emendations and rejections.[364] Readers of his *Variae* and *Novae lectiones*, as his great collections of conjectural emendations are entitled, could not fail to be enchanted by their wit, and the lame excuses with which many of the more conservative scholars tried to meet him merely strengthened his hand. His doctrines of the exclusive authority of the oldest manuscripts and of interpolations by foolish scribes and readers found ready acceptance among critics, not only in Holland, with the result that texts acquired a very different appearance.

The content of the works of which Cobet purified the words was a matter of comparative indifference to him; it hardly troubled him at all, and even more rarely to good effect – indeed one might say that as a scholar he would have been completely at a loss if the *magistelli* had not kept him occupied.

[364] Even more fatal to the presuppositions on which much of Cobet's work rested was the discovery of numerous papyri which showed that his belief in 'scioli magistelli' who corrupted the texts during the Byzantine period was unfounded, since the chief corruptions had come into being long before.

The positive gain accruing from his textual criticism was great, and a superabundance of his brilliant emendations has survived, but its main value lies in the necessity it created of dislodging his principles. This was effected by the historical approach to language, which recognises that the Hellenistic age was entitled to speak its own language, so that one can only smile when Callimachus is scolded for not having slavishly imitated Homer. Since Cobet's time the cult of the individual has put an end to the mania for standardisation. It is harder, but also more rewarding, to come to terms with the genius of such great but disparate stylists as Thucydides and Isocrates, Plato and Hyperides; and even the lesser men are entitled to go their own way as long as it *is* their own – indeed, if it comes to that, it is the critic's duty to respect a writer's weaknesses and even his vices. The facile rejection of all later manuscripts so long as one of respectable antiquity is available has usually been proved wrong when the others were subsequently examined, and the remains of ancient books have been the final arbiters against it. Thus the movement that started with Hemsterhuys met its end also in Holland, after it had faithfully fulfilled its mission. Cobet, and with him the majority of his numerous pupils, deliberately rejected the German conception of a science of antiquity.[365] Henricus van Herwerden[366] was an exception, and yet he produced nothing of lasting value that was not in the Cobet tradition; his name will continue to occupy a place of honour in the footnotes to the texts of numerous poets and prose-writers. Of Cobet's own writings the earliest in particular repay constant study, for there is always much to be learnt from the method of such a brilliant man even if we know that it is one-sided, and his method was based on a mastery of language such as only a handful of men have ever possessed or ever will possess.

But for the impetus given to Greek studies in England and Holland, classical scholarship would never have succeeded in

[365] W.G. Rutherford in an obituary in the *Classical Review* (3, 1889, 472) called Cobet 'the greatest classical scholar of this century'. Such an opinion shows the writer's utter failure to understand what had been going on in Germany.

[366] Herwerden (1831-1910) was professor at Utrecht from 1864.

becoming strictly scientific, for nothing can endure that is not built on the rock of linguistic knowledge; but the birth of a real science of antiquity was completely unconnected with the sort of esoteric scholarship we have been considering. The decisive factor was the awakening of a new spirit in Germany, which had an equally powerful effect on poetry and philosophy. The men of this second renaissance discovered the immortal Greek genius, to which they felt themselves akin, and eagerly drank in its life – the enhancing gospel of freedom and beauty. This led inevitably to an involvement with Greek poetry and sculpture which gradually turned into scientific scholarship and finally attained to the historic method. It was only with the help of this last that the 'grammar' of the ancients was finally left behind and the way opened to a real understanding of the past, not merely of antiquity.

Meanwhile there are still some Germans of the age of transition to be mentioned: namely, Johann Albert Fabricius, Johann Matthias Gesner and Johann Jakob Reiske, each of them a self-luminous star and at least equal in magnitude to the much more loudly acclaimed foreign professors. Fabricius[367] came from the electoral duchy of Saxony, where the schools still retained at least something of the tradition of the age of Melanchthon, but he made his career in Hamburg, which had escaped the ravages of the Thirty Years' War. Through its trade Hamburg had stimulating contacts with the outside world. Its grammar-school, the Johanneum, flourished – in fact Hamburg was undoubtedly the most cultured city of Germany. It had already parted with Gronovius to Holland, Holstenius to Rome and Lambecius[368] to Vienna; Lambecius catalogued the splendid library in Vienna, which nevertheless continued to be as little used as ever.

Vienna had a life of its own, which drew its inspiration from Italy. The Jesuit school there produced one scholar of epoch-making importance, who outlived Winckelmann by many years; but though he spent his life dealing with magnificent works of art in all the glory of mint condition, the city was entirely unaffected by him. His name was Joseph Eckhel.[369]

[367] Fabricius (1668-1736): Sandys iii 2.
[368] Peter Lambecius (1628-1680): Sandys ii 365.
[369] Eckhel (1737-1798): Sandys iii 44.

With his *Doctrina nummorum veterum* (1797-8) he put numismatics on an unshakable basis, though he still treated it in isolation from its historical and artistic context, which is one of the reasons why it has remained the most highly specialised of disciplines. Fabricius can only be called a *polyhistor*; yet he has something better to offer than mere encyclopaedic knowledge. The amount of learning he crammed into his *Bibliotheca Graeca* and *Bibliotheca Latina* is positively uncanny; at the same time he is a good counsellor, always mindful of his readers' needs. Everything is concise, clear and well arranged. Fabricius was familiar with the scholars of every age and their works, and so far from confining himself to antiquity, Christian and pagan, he paid due regard to the Byzantines, on whom he brought together a body of material which is none the less valuable for having been left unused. Apart from that, he incorporated in those two works numerous writings which had been published inadequately, if at all, and the index of Greek words to his edition of Sextus Empiricus made it a boon to students almost unparalleled at the time. A man of this calibre also influences by his personality the people round him. His son-in-law, Reimarus,[370] would not have been noted here but for his admirable edition of Cassius Dio; he was, however, also the author of a rationalistic critique of Christianity of which Lessing published 'fragments'. Lessing's[371] membership of this Hamburg circle came to exercise a decisive influence on him in his last period.

Johann Matthias Gesner[372] might almost be called a new *Praeceptor Germaniae*, for he made the Thomasschule at Leipzig a model institution and compiled a Greek Reader for schools (which later gave place to a better one by Friedrich Jacobs). The reader offered a more sensible plan than starting Greek with Xenophon, which sounds so much grander. Gesner also

[370] H.S. Reimarus (1694-1768) brought out the edition at Hamburg in 1750-2; fragments of his 'Apologia oder Schutzschrift für die vernünftigen Verehrer Gottes' were published by Lessing as 'Fragmente des Wolfen-büttelschen Ungenannten' from 1774.
[371] Lessing (1729-1781): Sandys iii 241; see n.414.
[372] J.M. Gesner (1691-1761): Sandys iii 5, Pfeiffer ii 168, 175. Jacobs: see below, n.435.

produced a Latin *Thesaurus*, and the distinction of having inaugurated the first Philological Seminar belongs to him too. No doubt this form of university teaching, which encourages the student to think for himself and invites his cooperation, is now becoming general; but classical scholars have always taken the lead in modifying and developing it. Exercises in which a single teacher does most of the talking should not be allowed to usurp the title of Seminar.[373] Hemsterhuys's invitation to Gesner to collaborate with him in his edition of Lucian constituted a kind of patent of nobility which only the Dutch could bestow at that time. Gesner also published on his own account numerous editions of Latin authors which were useful, but for him no more than by-products. He smoothed the way for Heyne, thereby helping to make Göttingen, founded by Freiherr von Münchhausen, different from the older German universities, and also from Prussian Halle.

On the other hand, Leipzig's ancient prestige was not enhanced under Ernesti,[374] who was at the same time a theologian of the old school. His Cicero and one or two other editions were highly praised; they were undoubtedly useful, on account of their terse, workmanlike notes. Ernesti too possessed encyclopaedic learning and imparted it, and his *Lexica Technologica* have retained their value to the student of rhetoric; but his pedestrian mind was incapable of original, let alone profound, thought, and the domineering way in which he suppressed Reiske,[375] the latchet of whose shoes he was not worthy to unloose, will always

[373] 'The German tradition of the seminar, invented, it would seem, by Heyne and Wolf, greatly developed by Ritschl, carried further by Usener and Bücheler, and perhaps perfected by the generation of Fraenkel's Berlin and Göttingen professors ...'. H. Lloyd-Jones, *Gnomon* 43, 1971, 637 = *BG*, p.216 (in an obituary notice of Eduard Fraenkel, who was taught in Berlin by Wilamowitz and in Göttingen by Friedrich Leo). I should have remembered Wilamowitz' paragraph about Gesner; see Ernesti, *Opuscula Oratoria*, 1767, 478f.

[374] J.A. Ernesti (1707-1781): Sandys iii 11. In fact the technical lexica were by the less celebrated J.C.G. Ernesti (1756-1802; see Sandys iii 13 and Pfeiffer, *HCS* ii 171-2).

[375] J.J. Reiske (1716-1774): Sandys iii 14; Pfeiffer, *HCS* ii 172. On what he did for Demosthenes, see Ulrich Schindel, *Demosthenes im 18. Jahrhundert* (Zetemeta, heft 31), 1963, 14f.

be remembered against him. He was a dignified figure in his wig and gown, however, and Reiske fell under the suspicion of being a free-thinker, because his lack of a Sunday coat prevented his going to church. Perhaps Reiske did not greatly miss either the coat or the sermon, so long as he could spend the time on his Greek or Arabic. Scholars should read his autobiography and his letters – and not only scholars, for we must never forget that Reiske's place is with Winckelmann and Lessing. How they looked down on him in Leyden and Leipzig! How he had to starve and knuckle under, and yet he never lost his resilience! What endless sacrifices he made for learning's sake, regardless of the world's indifference to his merits! Heaven knows, the Graces had not smiled on him in his cradle. All the more creditable that without a single gift of theirs he grew into a lovable man. There can scarcely have been a scholar so many of whose conjectures have been confirmed by a better manuscript tradition, and he far surpassed his contemporaries in the number of authors he studied thoroughly. He procured manuscripts wherever he could, but what helped him far more was his immediate familiarity with any style. He cared nothing for poetry; yet even in Theocritus the most cursory reading produced some brilliant emendations. The extent of his interests lies far beyond textual criticism, as is shown by the explanatory notes in his edition of the *De caerimoniis* of Constantine Porphyrogenitus, an *editio princeps*, and also to his translations, which are worth reading in spite of their clumsiness. His wife deserves her meed of praise too, not as a scholar but as her husband's staunch and devoted partner. In his lifetime only one man rated Reiske at his true worth, but that man was Lessing. What more could he ask?

It is an inspiring thought that so many of our best men worked their way up from the bottom, and that hardship only nerved them for the struggle. Winckelmann[376] also had to

---

[376] J.J. Winckelmann (1717-1768): Sandys iii 21; Rumpf i 58; Pfeiffer, *HCS*, ch.13. Goethe's *Winckelmann und sein Jahrhundert* (1805) is in vol.xiii of the Memorial Edition (Beutler); the great biography by Carl Justi (1832-1912) appeared in 1866 (3rd edn. 1923). An English version of Ludwig Curtius' useful short essay will be found in the volume 'Winckelmann 1768/1968' (Inter Nationes, Bad Godesberg, 1968); see also W. Schadewaldt,

drain to the dregs the bitter cup of want and humiliation
before he found his way to Rome and, though writing in
German, triumphantly made a European reputation for
himself. With Lessing, incidentally, Winckelmann is the first
German who can properly be numbered among our classics in
point of style. He had the good fortune to have Goethe and
Justi for biographers, so that we see him in his habit as he
lived, with all the faults of character, grave as they were,
which enabled him to fulfil his destiny. It was his longing for
ancient Greece, and for the freedom and beauty for which it
stood, that drove him to Italy. He had absorbed enough from
the poets not merely to equip him, in the knowledge of Greek
mythology, with the key to the interpretation of the
monuments, but also to allow him to discover Greek sculpture
through Roman copies and to form a notion of its superb
beauty and grace, which were so remote from the rococo – a
notion merely, for in practice he missed much genuine Greek
work. The admirer of Raphael Mengs[377] remained as blind to
the splendour of the early Renaissance as Goethe on his
Italian travels; so it was too early for him to appreciate archaic
art, and even of Phidias he had no more than a vague
perception. But Winckelmann was the first to look at Paestum
with a just feeling of awe; the massiveness and severity of a
Doric temple would have struck others as outlandish and
barbarous. Archaeology as a branch of the study of art was the
creation of Winckelmann, even if his aesthetic theory has been
discarded, like most of the interpretations that were his special
pride. It was the theory that the admiring world seized on, but
his greatness lies rather in the courage to write a history of art
at all and, moreover, to link it with the history of culture in
general. The errors that scholars such as Heyne were able to
detect in it immediately do not matter at all. In producing a
history of style such as no scholar had ever dreamed of in the
domain of either poetry or prose, Winckelmann set an example
which all succeeding ages should look up to with admiration.

*Hellas und Hesperien*², i, 1970, 37-116; the recent biography by W.
Leppmann, *Winckelmann*, 1971, is disappointing, but Pfeiffer's excellent
chapter makes up for this.
    [377] Raphael Mengs (1728-1779) was an academic painter of great gifts
whom Winckelmann knew at Rome.

It is the source of the sap that has made almost every branch
of our science grow and put forth leaves.

The compilers of Antiquities had looked at the monuments
only insofar as they could serve to illustrate this or that
particular problem. It was in Italy alone that the monuments
impinged everywhere directly, and they were so thick on the
ground that archaeological interest never quite died out,
though it seldom went beyond local investigations and was
concerned solely with Roman objects. Justi has left us a
masterly description of these antiquaries, with their real or
pretended    learning,    who    came    into    contact    with
Winckelmann. They were prime connoisseurs, princes of the
church and the like, with whom we cannot concern ourselves
here because they were content simply to enjoy. But Italy can
also claim to have produced numerous eminent scholars in
this period who, on account of the political and moral
decadence of the age, have a special claim on our esteem –
many more, in fact, than the France of the Encyclopaedists
can show. Most of them were clerics, many of them regulars.
Forcellini,[378] for instance, devoted a long life spent in the
obscurity of the seminary at Padua to the production of the
*Thesaurus Latinus*, dying not indeed before its completion, but
before its publication in 1771, the manner of which grossly
belittled his own part in it. Muratori,[379] the archivist of
Modena, undertook entirely unaided the production of
something for the history of his own country roughly
corresponding to our *Monumenta Germaniae*. Here we are
concerned only with his great collection of inscriptions, a
compilation criticised by his contemporary Scipione Maffei,[380]
who was able to outstrip Mabillon in Latin palaeography
thanks to the discovery of the chapter library of his native city
of Verona. Maffei alone was saved from the narrow outlook of

[378] Egidio Forcellini (1688-1768): Sandys ii 374.
[379] L.A. Muratori (1672-1750): Sandys ii 381. Wilamowitz ought to have
mentioned Muratori's teacher, Benedetto Bacchini (1651-1721); see
Momigliano, *TC*, 121f. and 141f.
[380] Maffei (1675-1755): Sandys ii 381; *SS*² 172. See Momigliano's article
of 1956 (reprinted in *SC*, 255f.) on 'Gli studi classici di Scipione Maffei',
besides the article on 'Mabillon's Italian disciples' (1958, in *TC*, 135f.)
already cited.

his fellows by his extensive travels, though he was also an excellent local antiquary, as well as a man of the world and a poet. Anyone who has visited the charming museum that bears his name will remember the spirit of Greek within it; and indeed the museum contains some inscribed stones which were once brought from the Venetian dominions in Greece along with a few pieces of sculpture. The *Monumenta Peloponnesiaca*, published by Paciaudi,[381] a member of the Theatine Order, describes another collection of the same kind. By this time a profusion of Etruscan antiquities had been dug up in Tuscany, and though they may have lacked artistic appeal they compensated for it by their strangeness, and by the riddle of their unintelligible inscriptions. A Scotsman named Dempster[382] had written a book on Etruria as far back as the beginning of the seventeenth century. It was not published for a hundred years, but from that moment an interest in things Etruscan was regarded as a patriotic duty by the people of Tuscany, among whom Antonio Gori[383] distinguished himself by his zeal and industry. The interest, however, did not yet extend to Etruscan vases; and even Winckelmann who came across them in Naples hardly gave them more than a passing glance. Naples was the home of men like Mazzocchi[384] (publisher of the bronze tablet of Heraclea), Martorelli[385] (author of a bulky tome on an ancient inkstand that was no such thing), and Ignarra[386] (a local antiquary), whose horizon was limited to their native

[381] P.M. Paciaudi (1710-1785): Sandys ii 382). On his *Monumenta Peloponnesiaca*, see Momigliano, *Historia* 2, 1954, 452 (= *Contributo* 197-8), who speaks of Paciaudi's horror at the invasion of the precincts of history, holy to antiquarians like himself, 'by a fanatic gang of philosophers who travelled very light'.

[382] Thomas Dempster (1579-1625): Sandys ii 340. His *Etruria Regalis* was published in 1723-6. For the history of the 'Etruscomania' which caused Greek vases to be taken to be Etruscan for many years, see R.M. Cook, *GPP*², 1973, 289f.

[383] A.F. Gori (1691-1757): Sandys ii 380; Cook, *GPP*², 289.

[384] A.S. Mazzocchi (1684-1771): Sandys ii 384; Cook, *GPP*², 290. The tablets contain an important dialect inscription; see E. Schwyzer, *Dialectorum Graecarum exempla epigraphica potiora*, 1923, 19f.

[385] Giacomo Martorelli (1699-1777).

[386] Niccolo Ignarra (1728-1808): Sandys ii 384.

heath, where, and where alone, they were great figures. How could these men deal with the discoveries resulting from the excavation of Herculaneum, which Charles III energetically promoted, founding an Accademia Ercolana[387] for the purpose in 1736? No foreigners, above all, were to be allowed in – on that they were all agreed. Nevertheless some foreign technicians, fortunately, were employed on the actual diggings. The volumes of the 'Antiquities of Herculaneum' began to appear in 1760, but they were far less effective in spreading the glad tidings than the news-letters of Winckelmann, though these only transmitted the impressions he had received from a cursory inspection. The papyri completely puzzled everybody, and much irreparable damage was done through carelessness and ignorance, until Padre Piaggio invented an ingenious method of unrolling them. [388] The first volume devoted to the papyri appeared only in 1793. It contained Philodemus *On Music*, and we should salute it as a notable academic triumph; but after one or two further volumes no more was heard of the project, and few of the transcripts that reached Oxford saw the light either. The unification of Italy at last brought a man of energy to the helm in the shape of Giuseppe Fiorelli,[389] who published the old reports on the excavations, vigorously promoted the uncovering of Pompeii, and wrote an outline of its architectural history which August Mau[390] and Heinrich Nissen subsequently elaborated. But most of the work still remains to be done, and it is good to think that the sources of new knowledge are in no immediate danger of drying up. The old transcripts of the papyri were now published in a new series of volumes which revived interest in the subject – or rather, to be exact, awakened it for the first time – and in this way an enterprise has gradually been set on foot[391] that promises well but still has a long way to go.

[387] Academia Ercolanense, founded 1755, not 1736; the 'Antichità di Ercolano' began to appear in 1757, not 1760.

[388] See E.G. Turner, *Greek Papyri: an Introduction*, 1968, ch.2.

[389] Fiorelli (1824-1896): Sandys iii 246; cf. Rumpf i 93.

[390] Mau (1840-1909): Bursian 1097, 1136; Rumpf 93, 104. Nissen (1839-1912): Bursian 963, etc.; Rumpf 93.

[391] The purchase of more land at Herculaneum and the invention by Dr

Naples, where the professional scholars were so little capable of profiting by the treasures that had fallen into their laps, did nevertheless produce one man whose philosophical speculations introduced entirely new and stimulating ideas into the study of history: Gian Battista Vico,[392] author of the *Scienza Nuova*. In many respects Vico anticipated the ideas of Herder,[393] and insofar as the Romantic movement entailed a shift of emphasis from the individual to the people, from conscious creation to the impersonal march of evolution, from the highest achievements of culture to its humble beginnings, Vico was its precursor thanks to whom religion and myth come to be understood properly for the first time. The business of explaining figures like Lycurgus and Homer, of determining what is truth and what is error, was also begun by him. The fact that he and others followed these paths independently of one another may well be regarded as an endorsement of his novel contributions to the philosophy of history.

Winckelmann has his place in the history of Italian archaeology in virtue of his *Monumenti antichi inediti* and the Italian translation of his 'History of Ancient Art'. There was also a personal link between him and Ennio Quirino Visconti,[394] the most important member of a Roman family of archaeologists, who leant heavily on Winckelmann in his description of the Vatican collections which had been greatly enlarged by the more recent popes. Visconti's *Iconography*, in which he continued the work begun long before by Fulvius Ursinus, provoked strong criticism. The successor who truly continued Winckelmann's work was Georg

---

Anton Fackelmann of Vienna of a new method of reading carbonised papyri have opened up exciting new possibilities. See the periodical *Cronache Ercolanesi*, directed by Marcello Gigante and first published in 1971.

[392] Giovanni Battista Vico (1668-1744). On Vico's interpretation of Roman history, see Momigliano's paper '*Roman "Bestioni" and Roman "Eroi" in Vico's* Scienza Nuova', *History and Theory* 5, 1966, 3f. (= *TC*, i 153f.). On his importance in the history of philology see M. Gigante, *Bollettino del Centro di Studi Vichiani* 2, 1972, 1f. A good general account in I. Berlin, *Vico and Herder*, 1976.

[393] J.G. Herder (1744-1803): Sandys iii 31. See last note, and cf. n.425.

[394] Visconti (1751-1818): Sandys ii 383; Rumpf 62.

Zoëga,[395] a Dane of Italian extraction who settled in Rome, where he became a complete Roman. He had been a pupil of Heyne's, and as a young man participated in the extravagances of the age; but in Rome, where circumstances compelled him to renounce many ambitions, he became a model of the sovereign art of dealing with every task according to its requirements – briefly or at length, but always appropriately, with nothing superfluous and nothing omitted, and his whole mind focused on the matter in hand. Where the monuments are concerned, an accurate account of the facts is not merely the first step in their interpretation, but half the battle. In this respect Zoëga's work is exemplary, and indeed in his *Bassi Rilievi* he made a series of mostly insignificant works of art the subject of a commentary such as was still unknown in the domain of literature. It is a thousand pities that he published so few of the general ideas he had derived from his work; but this opinion may not be shared by the Egyptologists, who were perhaps even more deeply indebted to him on the Coptic side than students of Arabic were to Reiske. Zoëga must have communicated a great deal by word of mouth. Welcker[396] certainly, and possibly even Wilhelm von Humboldt,[397] were influenced by him, consciously or unconsciously, and the same is doubtless true of the group of highly cultivated men and women in Copenhagen who were associated with the new movement in Germany. Thorwaldsen,[398] for instance, was a close associate.

Zoëga was educated at Göttingen, where Gesner had firmly established classical studies and where Christian Gottlob Heyne[399] now introduced the study of art and the historical approach of Winckelmann. At Göttingen there was a galaxy of notable teachers in every faculty, whose influence on the

---

[395] Johann Georg Zoega (1755-1809): Sandys iii 318; Rumpf 62.
[396] Welcker: see below, n.477.
[397] Humboldt: see below, n.416.
[398] Thorwaldsen: see above, n.6.
[399] Christian Gottlob Heyne (1729-1812): Sandys iii 36; Gruppe 107; F. Klingner, *Studien zur griechischen und römischen Literatur*, 1964, 701. Pattison in his essay on F.A. Wolf (*Essays* i 337f.) portrays Heyne most unfairly; Pfeiffer (ii 171 etc.) is disappointingly brief.

young men who flocked there from all directions with minds
wide open to the new gospel often determined the entire
course of their lives; but it was round Heyne, secretary of the
local academy and editor of its journal, founder of the well-
stocked library and confidant of the Anglo-Hanoverian
government, that the place revolved. Heyne's strength was
that he was at once a born ruler of men and a born teacher.
The hardships of his youth as the son of a poor weaver had left
no mark upon him. So highly was his first book, an edition of
Tibullus, regarded in Holland – though textual criticism was
not his strong point – that Ruhnken, in declining the
invitation to succeed Gesner, recommended Heyne for the
post. Grammar and language were subsidiary, but otherwise
his teaching embraced the whole range of classical learning, as
did his writing. Heyne did not go deep, but he knew by
instinct what ultimately mattered; and anyone who ventured
to write about the genius of such an age as that of the
Ptolemies cannot have lacked the historical sense. His two
great works were his Homer and his Virgil;[400] in his exposition
of these poets he gave his contemporaries what they
demanded, an introduction to the poetry. Heyne had an idea
of the problems posed by Homer, including the genesis of the
*Iliad*, and made a useful contribution to the discussion without
offending against good sense or good taste; he is always worth
consulting. Though he satisfied his times, he was already out
of date before he died, and it was his misfortune to be
ruthlessly thrust aside by ungrateful pupils, a fate which for
years impeded a just appreciation of him. The man who
scattered the seed that bore such various fruit in the persons of
Zoëga, Voss and Wolf, the brothers Humboldt and Schlegel,
deserves to be called a *Praeceptor Germaniae* in a higher sense
than Gesner.

In preparing his edition of Homer, Heyne could have taken
advantage of the Venetian scholia – for Jean-Baptiste d'Ansse
de Villoison[401] published them in 1788, without himself

[400] His *Pindar* (1798) was a useful work at the time, and his *Apollodorus*
(1783; 2nd edn. 1803) contains a valuable collection of mythological
material.
[401] Villoison (1753-1805): Sandys ii 397. See Ch.Joret, *D'Ansse de Villoison*,
1910.

realising what a treasure he had unearthed. Villoison had previously edited the valuable Homeric Lexicon of Apollonius, not to mention the *Eudocia* of Palaeokappa[402] – a case of *carbones pro thesauro*.[403] Before Venice he visited Weimar, of which his *Epistulae Vinarienses* gives an amusing account. The mere fact that a French scholar wrote Latin epigrams on the members of the Duchess Anna Amalia's circle lends the book a sentimental value, and its meagre extracts from manuscripts in the Weimar library look pedantic by comparison. Villoison also travelled in Greece and collected inscriptions, but the Revolution prevented him from benefiting from his journey to the extent he had hoped. As a scholar, Villoison does not rank high. Nor does Jean-Jacques Barthélemy,[404] who in his novel *Voyage du jeune Anacharsis* not only flattered the French by including the leading men of the day in the guise of ancient Greeks, but provided innumerable readers with a vivid picture of Athens at the height of its greatness. It was the first of a series of such historical novels, and we must not underestimate the good these books did, though among the Germans only Georg Taylor[405] (alias Hausrath) possessed the necessary knowledge and literary skill. Kingsley's *Hypatia*, Walter Pater's *Marius the Epicurean*, Viktor Rydberg's *Den Siste Athenaren*, Sienkiewicz's *Quo Vadis?* catered for the widespread interest in the struggle between Christianity and paganism at its last gasp, and the learned scholars who found gross anachronisms on every page had only themselves to blame for neglecting to fill the gap. The versatile Böttiger[406] had already adopted this form with a specifically educational aim in his *Sabina*, and his

[402] Palaeokappa: Speyer 321, n.1.

[403] See Phaedrus 5. 6. 6.

[404] Barthélemy (1716-1795): Sandys ii 392. He also helped to decipher Phoenician inscriptions.

[405] Georg Taylor (pseudonym of Adolf Hausrath, 1857-1909). *Hypatia*, by Charles Kingsley, 1853. *Marius the Epicurean*, by Walter Pater, 1885. *Den Siste Athenaren*, by Viktor Rydberg, 1859. *Quo Vadis?*, by Henryk Sienkiewicz, 1895. Wilamowitz does not mention the greatest historical novel dealing with the ancient world – Flaubert's *Salammbo* (1862). Its historical accuracy has been tested and justified; see L.A. Benedetto, *Le origini di Salammbo*, 1920.

[406] K.A. Böttiger (1760-1835): Sandys iii 74.

example was followed by W.A. Becker,[407] whose *Charicles* and
*Gallus* are based on solid learning. These books are now quite
out of date; but nothing has taken their place, for Ludwig
Friedländer's[408] *Roman Life and Manners*, excellent and
readable as it is, is no real substitute, if only because
nowadays we must have illustrations, as Montfaucon realised
long ago.

We must also consider here a number of men belonging to
the age of transition who stood aside from the main current of
development but nevertheless did commendable work. Johann
Schweighäuser[409] (almost the whole of whose activity falls
within the eighteenth century) lived in Strasburg and had
links with Wilhelm von Humboldt; it is as absurd to assign
such a complete German to France as in the case of Brunck.
Schweighäuser edited a variety of voluminous writers such as
Appian, Polybius, Epictetus and Athenaeus, and finally
Herodotus, with very useful notes; and he took pains to
consult the manuscripts. One must not expect textual
criticism from him; but, excellent scholar as he was, he
possessed something of the spirit of Casaubon, from whom in
many respects he directly derives. No one who has followed in
his tracks will fail to praise him for his sound critical sense.
Gottlieb Wernsdorf[410] of Danzig is mentioned here only
because of his still indispensable *editio princeps* of Himerius,
which he did not live to see in print and which must have cost
him untold labour to produce so far from all facilities. It was
published by his brother Johann Christian, a Professor at
Helmstedt, whose *Poetae Latini minores* had the merit of making
many half-forgotten poems once more readily available.
Johann Gottlob Schneider[411] (who added Saxo to his name)
pursued his own way. It was a thorny path of starvation and
menial employment (his time as Brunck's famulus was
comparative bliss) until he finally obtained a chair at Breslau,
where he was neither happy nor successful as a teacher.

[407] Becker (1796-1846): Sandys iii 67.
[408] Friedländer (1824-1909): Bursian 1194.
[409] Schweighäuser (1742-1830): Sandys ii 396.
[410] Wernsdorf died in 1774, and his *Himerius* was published in 1790 by his brother J.C. Wernsdorf (1732-1793): Bursian 938, n.1.
[411] J.G. Schneider (1750-1822): Sandys iii 11.

Schneider was interested in natural science as well as classical scholarship, and this determined his choice of authors to expound, though his Xenophon also long remained the standard text. Even today we cannot do without his Theophrastus, Oppian, Vitruvius or *Scriptores rei rusticae*, though it was only later that their texts were put on a sound basis. The Greek lexicon into which he put so much hard work gained a vicarious immortality in its numerous progeny: it was enlarged by the amiable Franz Passow,[412] who in his early days at Breslau had a stimulating influence, for example, on Otfried Müller,[413] as an apostle of the new scholarship, but produced nothing of his own that has stood the test of time.

We have at last arrived at the threshold of the nineteenth century, in which the conquest of the ancient world by science was completed. The history of scholarship has once more to pass over the antecedents of the general spiritual and intellectual revival of which the flowering of classical scholarship was one aspect; we cannot after all include Lessing,[414] Goethe[414a] and Herder[415] in our story. Lessing still has something of the humanist and *polyhistor* in him. His contributions to the study of actual works of ancient art are trifling, and his attacks on Klotz and his like only serve to illustrate the depths to which scholarship had sunk in the

[412] Passow (1786-1833): Sandys ii 114. *Liddell and Scott* was originally based upon his Lexicon. The revision of it under the direction of W. Crönert, which ceased to appear after the third fascicle, ending with the outbreak of the First World War, is as far as it goes (as far as ἀνά) the best Greek dictionary in existence.

[413] K.O. Müller: see below, n.478.

[414] See above, n.371. The *Hamburgische Dramaturgie* (1767-9) contains some brilliant criticism of ancient dramas; many readers will find it more interesting than the more celebrated *Laokoon*.

[414a] Goethe (1749-1832). Ernst Grumach's *Goethe und die Antike* offers in a most convenient form a collection of Goethe's remarks about ancient authors. But their influence in him is a complex topic; in English, see Humphry Trevelyan, *Goethe and the Greeks* (1941, reprinted 1981, with an introduction by me (= *BG*, ch.2) ); from the vast German literature of the subject, let me single out Pfeiffer's 'Goethe und der griechische Geist' (*AKS* 235f.).

[415] See above, n.393. See also Bursian 444f.

universities of his day. But what would poetic theory be
without him, especially in its bearing on poetic drama – even
though it was the very one-sidedness of his theory of the visual
arts and arts of discourse, and its very mistakes, that so long
enjoyed canonical authority? Without Herder where would all
research be into the origin of language and the organic
evolution of individual nations and mankind as a whole, all
comparative study of parallel phenomena throughout the
world? In Goethe's Greek studies we see the young man's
enthusiastic devotion to the Greek ideal of beauty. Ancient
art, which Goethe looked at in Italy through the eyes of
Winckelmann, determined his views on art in general, which
were shot through with his scientific ideas. In the *Propyläen* we
find a rigid classicism; yet even there he rounds occasionally
on the Grecomaniacs. His own poetry embodies the Hellenic
ideal as the age conceived and longed to behold it, and the
mature Goethe is the oracle to which we refer all things great
and small for his opinion, including his contemporaries and
their works.

To this trinity, as we realise more clearly every day, we have
to add a fourth in the shape of Wilhelm von Humboldt[416] –
though he was no poet, even in his translations from the
classics, and it was only in his letters that he poured forth his
wisdom freely and simply. It is a purely human wisdom; but
for Humboldt the Greek genius was synonymous with pure
humanity – which means much more than the Humanities.
Throughout his life he turned to it for spiritual refreshment,
and he died with lines of Homer on his lips. We have only to
read his correspondence with Welcker to be amazed at his
depth of knowledge, in which he surpassed even Welcker. A
disastrous change of policy on the part of the Prussian
government robbed him of the opportunity of presiding over
the whole educational system, though not before he had

[416] Wilhelm von Humboldt (1767-1835): Sandys iii 68; Bursian 587f. See
Pfeiffer, 'Wilhelm von Humboldt der Humanist', *AKS* 256f.; cf. *HCS* ii,
Index s.v. He made a vast contribution to the science of linguistics; on his
translation of Aeschylus' *Agamemnon* (1816), see Fraenkel's edition, i 50f.
There is a useful selection from his writings in *Wilhelm von Humboldt: Schriften*
(Goldmanns Taschenbücher, Bd. 1492/3, 1964). See Paul R. Sweet, *Wilhelm
von Humboldt* i (1978) and ii (1980) reviewed by me in *BG*, chs 3 and 4.

created its university; but even in the solitude of Tegel he
remained the leader of the group of men who succeeded,
despite the reaction, in raising Berlin to the position of
intellectual capital of Germany.

The impact of the two Schlegels was more direct.
Friedrich,[417] who was the cleverer, outlined what the next
generation accepted as the ideal organic evolution of Greek
poetry. Schiller[418] followed with his theory of 'naive' *versus*
'sentimental' poetry. However much they needed to be
modified, both books contained truths which the scholars
were incapable of formulating for themselves. It was also at
Friedrich Schlegel's prompting that Schleiermacher[419]
embarked on his translation of Plato. August Wilhelm
Schlegel's[420] dominant influence on the aesthetic appraisal of
Attic drama lasted only too long; his review of Niebuhr's
*History of Rome* was of greater value. But it is not the individual
productions of the period that matter so much as the sense of
history and the sympathy with the primitive, both in religion
and morals, that the Romantic movement, following in
Herder's footsteps, imported into scholarship as a counterpoise to the critical spirit – though certainly that was needed
to unload the dead weight of an indolent acquiescence in
authority.

Finally, Johann Friedrich Voss,[421] the arbiter of classical
translation, must not be cheated of his meed of fame. Even
today there are far too many who think of Homer entirely in
terms of Voss, including some who should know better. Voss
unquestionably had the advantage of his competitors in that
his knowledge of Homer's language was up to the highest
standard of his age, and he achieved a truly consistent style.
He also brought to the editing of Virgil's *Georgics* the expert
knowledge and affection of a countryman born and bred. For
the rest, his later translations and the countless attempts of
the same kind to which his work gave rise contributed little to
the better understanding of the poets concerned, and his

[417] F. Schlegel (1772-1829): Sandys iii 72.
[418] Friedrich Schiller (1759-1805). Sandys iii 71.
[419] Schleiermacher: see below, n.441.
[420] A.W. Schlegel (1767-1845): Sandys iii 71.
[421] Voss (1751-1826): Sandys iii 61.

rationalist attacks on his colleague Creuzer's *Symbolik*, apart
from being distasteful, were deprived of their effect by their
violence.

F.A. Wolf[422] as the friend of Goethe and Humboldt, was
well qualified to describe the comprehensive science of
antiquity that was due to be erected on the foundations laid
by his master Heyne. Wolf founded a classical journal, written
in German, which he dedicated to Goethe. This was a truly
epoch-making event, and Wolf's gross overvaluation of
antiquity can be excused by the spirit of the age. His refusal at
Göttingen on matriculation to allow himself to be entered
except as a 'student of philology' probably sprang from his
dislike of anything connected with theology; it was typical of
the man, if only because he gained his point. In effect, the
impulse he gave to scholarship in a particular direction was
more important than his programme. The Germans still
lacked the indispensable linguistic knowledge and needed to
learn the business of critical scholarship itself, for which Wolf
referred them to Bentley. In his own by no means numerous
editions he achieved very little in this line; but though
Immanuel Bekker, in his first publication, a review of Wolf's
Homer, may have shown himself the better critic, it was
Wolf's teaching that inspired him. When Wolf's *Prolegomena ad
Homerum* was published, it was reasonable to expect that the
promised second part would provide the solution to the
problems raised in the first; but the second part never
appeared, and spiteful attacks on Heyne and Herder were a
poor substitute. The main value of the *Prolegomena* was not that
it raised the Homeric Question, which had been raised long
before, but that it revealed the scholia – in other words, the
history of the text. In Berlin Wolf failed to repeat the success
as a teacher that had made him deservedly famous at Halle;
and when we find him following Markland and condemning
speech after speech of Cicero as spurious he seems almost to
be trying to fool his colleagues. The Berlin circle, in which he
ought to have taken pride of place, did its work without him,

---

[422] Friedrich August Wolf (1759-1824): Sandys iii 51; cf. Pattison's review
of the life by J.F.J. Arnoldt, 1861-2, in *Essays* i 337f.; Pfeiffer, *HCS* ii, ch.14
(perhaps too anxious to defend Wolf against Wilamowitz).

or rather in spite of him; and the leadership in textual criticism of the Bentley type fell to another man, who began under Wolf's influence but later struck out on his own.

Gottfried Hermann[423] remained all his life a typical Leipziger, with the unmistakable rationality of the Saxon. His reverence for his teacher, Friedrich Wolfgang Reiz,[424] has preserved the memory of that able and modest man, who worked with some success on Plautus and Livy. Hermann at first completely surrendered to Kantian logic and maintained the absolute rightness of the standpoint which he adopted as a scholar with its backing. He sharply rejected every alternative, and felt justified in ignoring anything that fell outside the strictly circumscribed field of view with which he had grown up. His *De emendanda ratione Graecae grammaticae*, which was only too influential, is thoroughly dogmatic.[425] Latin, incidentally, was the language in which he habitually expressed himself and the only one in which he had a style of his own. Today the book seems to us no less outlandish than Valckenaer's *Origines Graecae*. His metrical theories were based entirely on abstract logic, which is enough in itself to make them untenable; fortunately his views on mythology attracted no attention. No wonder his conception of poetry and its exposition seemed narrow and superficial to Welcker, who always strove to see things whole, and even more so to the historian Otfried Müller. But happily the Hermann who was so enchanting in private life and in the lecture-room was quite different, and when he declaimed a Greek chorus his hearers were suddenly confronted with its full beauty. Hermann was a *preux chevalier* in every sense of the term, who loved a scrap but always fought fairly. Language and metre were intensely real to him, and the ability to make his pupils feel as he did about them was his special charm; of course, in those who could not rise to his example, verbal scholarship became only too easily as sounding brass or a tinkling cymbal. As a critic, Hermann

---

[423] Hermann (1772-1848): Sandys iii 89f.; Bursian 666, etc. There is a not very adequate life by H. Koechly, 1874; Pfeiffer, *HCS* ii 178-9.

[424] Reiz (1733-90): Sandys iii 18. The colon Reizianum (x-uu-x) is named after him.

[425] *Opuscula* iii 143f.

was the reverse of systematic, and championed the rights of the individual – that is to say, of Anomaly as against Analogy, to which the school of Porson subscribed. This contrast is best shown by Elmsley's *Medea* and Hermann's remarks on it. Hermann often went too far, but it gave him an unrivalled insight into the highly idiomatic diction of Sophocles. His contributions to textual criticism show a combination of boldness and luck in conjectural emendation. Homer, Pindar and the tragedians remained to the end his favourite subjects of study. He was still quite young when, entrusted by Heyne with the metrical part of his Pindar, he presented him with a wealth of critical notes of the finest quality, which indeed only horrified Heyne. Altogether, Hermann's finest and most effective works belong to his early years, and none ranks higher than his edition of the *Orphica*, in which he traces the development of epic style from Homer down to its latest ramifications – an early example of the historical method. Wolf's *Prolegomena* tempted him into trying his hand at the game of dismemberment, and though he had no success with his efforts on the Homeric Hymns or Hesiod part of what he had to say about the *Iliad* is as incontrovertible as it is far-reaching.[426] We have to recognise the limits both of his abilities and of his aims. However right he may have been to recommend the practice of the *ars nesciendi* (as Grotius, incidentally, already had in his adage '*Nescire quaedam magna pars sapientiae est*'), he certainly cultivated it to excess himself; the same is even truer of many of his pupils. Yet his insistence that, in any given case, the critic must know whether his author could have thought or expressed himself in some particular way, still holds good in principle; the trouble is that it can never be known with certainty and, what is more, the very notion can never be more than a pious hope even for the best of us, just as we all go through life saying with Scaliger, '*Utinam essem bonus grammaticus!*'

The young Hermann's teaching at once aroused the interest of many pupils destined to make their mark, and they were

---

[426] On his posthumous edition of Aeschylus (1849) see Fraenkel, *Ag.* i 47f. On his Latin studies, see the same writer's paper on 'The Latin studies of Hermann and Wilamowitz', *JRS* 38, 1948, 28f. (= *KB* ii 563f.).

followed by so many others that we can find room only for a
fraction of them; any selection is no doubt controversial, but
we have no alternative in such a sketch as this. One of the
earliest was Friedrich Thiersch,[427] who made his career in
Munich, where he reformed the schools and introduced the
leaven of the new gospel into the university. The foundation of
the Glyptothek, the collection of vases, and at a later stage the
link between Bavaria and the new Greece of King Otho took
him into a wider world than was provided by scholarship of
the school of Hermann, with the result that he was an
immense influence for good without making any positive
contribution to learning. The most unusual among
Hermann's pupils was undoubtedly Christian August
Lobeck,[428] who founded a school of his own at Königsberg.
Lobeck's eagle eye for points of language, which ranged over
the whole field, gives value to his comparatively early edition
of the *Ajax* and of Phrynichus. In his later, purely
grammatical, works[429] he picked up the threads of the
grammar of the Greeks themselves. The wealth of material
contained in these books and the orderly fashion in which it is
presented makes them still useful today, even when the standpoint from which they were written has long been abandoned
by comparative philology and, indeed, was scarcely tenable
even then. One would never guess that behind the
grammarian there lurked the brilliantly witty and vivacious
person whom we meet in many of Lobeck's delightful
addresses on academic occasions, and his impish humour
constantly peeps out from behind the massive erudition of his
*Aglaophamus*,[430] whose very title has a sting, for in the book
this Thracian votary of Orpheus and teacher of Pythagoras
reveals that behind all Mysteries there is nothing but trickery

---

[427] Thiersch (1784-1860): Sandys iii 110; Bursian 733f. See Pfeiffer,
*Historisches Jahrbuch* 80, 1961, 174f. and also in *Geist und Gestalt*, Munich,
1959, 116f.

[428] Lobeck (1781-1860): Sandys iii 65, astonishingly left out by Pfeiffer,
*HCS*.

[429] Most particularly the *Pathologia Sermonis Graecae* (1843-62, preceded by
*Prolegomena*, 1843).

[430] *Aglaophamus*, 1829; he was not so young at the time of its publication as
Wilamowitz implies.

and superstition. It was a case of youth having its fling.
Among the principal targets of Lobeck's criticism were the
eminent French academician Sainte-Croix[431] (whose work on
the historians of Alexander has some merit) and Hofrat
Creuzer[432] of Heidelberg, whose *Symbolik* was hailed as a
master work that had replaced Natural Religion as the
rationalists conceived it with a Revelation alleged to have been
received in the dark ages and diffused all over the world
through secret cults. Both Creuzer himself and his book were
powerful enough to create an impression and make converts.
The whole work suited the mystical leanings of the later
Romantics and threatened also to befuddle the learned.
Creuzer deserves full credit for his revival of the Neoplatonists,
especially Plotinus, whom Lobeck was also well able to
distinguish from the disciples of Iamblichus and Proclus; and
its influence spread, through Victor Cousin,[433] the editor of
Proclus, to France. In Heidelberg, which for many years was
the headquarters of Romanticism and at whose fountain the
brothers Grimm also drank, Creuzer's position was proof
against the sniping of Voss's *Anti-Symbolik* but could not with-
stand the heavy artillery of *Aglaophamus*. Creuzer outlived his
discomfiture by a generation; Lobeck's book, whose learning
and acumen are equally impressive, still awaits the right kind
of sequel to correct its mistakes, even though Lobeck's brand
of rationalism has long ceased to command support. What
Lobeck lacked was the sense of history, which has to go back
beyond the fantasies of the Neoplatonists to the old Orphism.
Orphism was an attempt to reform religious belief and
worship, and beyond Orphism lies the primitive worship of
the Earth-Mother, of which neither Lobeck nor Creuzer could
have any conception.

August Ferdinand Naeke[434] can claim credit for the right

[431] G.E.J. de Ste. Croix (1746-1806): Sandys ii 397.

[432] Georg Friedrich Creuzer (1771-1858): Sandys iii 65; Gruppe 126f. etc.
Momigliano has drawn attention to the importance of his book *Die historische
Kunst der Griechen* (1803; 2nd edn. 1845); see *Journal of the Warburg and
Courtauld Institutes* 9, 1946, 152f. (= *C* 233f. = *Studies in Historiography*, 75f.
'Friedrich Creuzer and Greek Historiography'.)

[433] Cousin (1792-1867): Sandys iii 251.

[434] Naeke (1788-1838): Sandys iii 109. The *Dirae* and *Lydia* used to be

kind of interpretation in two books published after his early
death: his edition of the so-called Valerius Cato and his
reconstruction of the *Hekalē* of Callimachus. Thus to salvage a
lost masterpiece was no easy task at the best of times, and it
was no doubt the attempt of his friend and colleague Welcker
to do the same for the Prometheus trilogy that prompted him.
Naeke was dealing with a Hellenistic poem at a time when the
exquisite poetry of that age was almost totally neglected;
Theocritus received no more than intermittent attention after
the time of Valckenaer even in England (where his influence is
apparent in Shelley and the Lake Poets), and Callimachus
remained a complete enigma. The Anthology of Cephalas was
finally published at about this time by Friedrich Jacobs,[435]
after the manuscripts had returned to Heidelberg via Paris –
minus several pages, incidentally, which had been deliberately
torn out. This excellent man – who lived his whole life in
Gotha, was popular with all the warring schools and was
looked up to as a sort of patriarch in his last years (he died in
1847) – was just the successor Brunck would have wished. He
produced an edition of Aelian's *Historia animalium* based on the
work of Schneider-Saxo and, in collaboration with Welcker,
editions also of the *Imagines* of Philostratus and of the novel of
Achilles Tatius. In addition he compiled an admirable Greek
Reader and inaugurated a series of editions of the classics with
notes, both for the use of schools. In numerous minor works he
brought the radiant vision of antiquity, as his generation
conceived it, within the reach of a wide public.

The part played by August Meineke[436] in making the
Hellenistic poets accessible was of more permanent value.
Meineke began his study of the fragments of Euphorion while
still a boy at Schulpforta under its excellent, if exceedingly
eccentric, headmaster Ilgen, Hermann's teacher and
Humboldt's friend. Graevius and Ernesti, and more recently

---

attributed to P. Valerius Cato, the critic of the Catullan age. On Naeke's
work on the *Hecale*, see Pfeiffer on Callimachus fr. 230.

[435] Jacobs (1764-1847): Sandys iii 64. Not quite for the whole of his life;
on his Munich interlude (1807-1810), see Pfeiffer, *Geist und Gestalt*, Munich,
1959, 115f.

[436] Meineke (1790-1870): Sandys iii 117; absent from Pfeiffer, *HCS* ii.

Thiersch, Döderlein,[437] Dissen, Nauck[438] and Bonitz, were all old Pforta boys,[439] and it was at Pforta that Jahn was first drawn to the study of archaeology. Meineke afterwards incorporated his Euphorion in his *Analecta Alexandrina*, which rescued more than one forgotten poet from oblivion. In the course of a life of ceaseless toil he three times edited the bucolic poets, and we find his tracks almost everywhere in the literature of the subject; but his great work is the collected edition of the *Comic Fragments* after the manner of Bentley, which was accompanied by a critical history modelled on Ruhnken but incomparably richer in content. It is entirely admirable, and students of the subject should not be content with any inferior edition of the same material.[440] In his old age Meineke published editions of Strabo, Stobaeus and Athenaeus which were hasty productions based on their immediate predecessors, so that only the emendations are his own, though these are legion. By that time, as headmaster of the Joachimsthal Gymnasium and a member of the Academy, he had for years belonged to the harmonious Berlin circle,

---

[437] K.D. Ilgen (1763-1834): see Bursian, 666, n.2. Ludwig Döderlein (1791-1863): Sandys iii 113. Ludolph Dissen (1784-1837): Sandys iii 113. He supplied the commentary on the Nemean and Isthmian Odes to Boeckh's *Pindar*, and later produced his own edition (1830; 2nd edn. 1843).

[438] Nauck: see below, n.552. Bonitz: see below, n.565. Jahn: see below, n.571.

[439] To the list of eminent alumni of Schulpforta, we may add Nietzsche and Wilamowitz himself (see *Erinnerungen*, 2nd edn. 1929, 62f., and W.M. Calder's introduction to Wilamowitz' early work, 'In wieweit befriedigen die Schlüsse der erhaltenen griechischen Trauerspiele?', 1974. The former Porta Caeli of the Cistercians became during the Reformation a Latin school under the protection of the dukes of Saxony; no German school had a comparable record. For a list of the eminent classical scholars educated there, see W. Kranz, *Studien zur antiken Literatur und ihrem Nachwirken*, 1967, 474 (= *Gnomon* 6, 1930, 558). Hermann obtained the appointment as head master of his own teacher, Ilgen (Sandys iii 63), who filled the office with particular distinction. The greeting sent to the school by Hermann on the occasion of its three-hundredth anniversary (*Opuscula* viii 476) is memorable.

[440] Wilamowitz is alluding to the edition in three volumes published in 1880-8 by T. Kock (1820-1891; Sandys iii 155), which he always refused to quote. The unfortunate edition of J.M. Edmonds (1957-61) would certainly have reminded Wilamowitz of the final sentence of the sixth ode of Horace's third book.

while remaining the amiable disciple of Hermann that he had always been. The storms of party strife had abated, but at one time the collision had been violent – as it had to be if the ship of learning was not to run aground.

In 1810, on the foundation of the university, Berlin could muster enough scholars to staff it. F.A. Wolf contributed the lustre of his name, but no more. Schleiermacher[441] was probably the most far-sighted of those who were privileged to advise on the setting up of the new institution, which became a seat of learning in the sense in which Humboldt understood the term – as something quite different from what the universities had been hitherto. Schleiermacher's theology, certainly, was not directed towards historical research, but his philosophy was. His translation of Plato stripped the philosopher of his halo, at the same time clearing away the mists in which, ever since Plato's death, truth about the man himself had been enveloped; and it was Schleiermacher's papers on Diogenes of Apollonia and Heraclitus that awakened interest in the study of the Presocratics. It was Schleiermacher's plan too that Bekker should edit the writings of Aristotle. Heindorf,[442] who brought both modesty and good sense to the study and elucidation of Plato's language, had to start almost from scratch. Among his associates in Berlin were Spalding[443] (who died as early as 1811), esteemed as a Latinist on account of his Quintilian, and, most important of all, Philipp Buttmann,[444] whose rare qualities make him no less impressive as a man than as a scholar. Before Buttmann there existed no doctrine of Greek accidence and word-formation worthy of the name. But for the advent of comparative philology, grammar, for us, would have remained forever exactly as Buttmann left it; his stimulating ideas make Lobeck seem no more than a compiler. Buttmann's *Lexilogus* was as great an advance on ancient 'Etymology' as his grammar was on Herodian, and many passages in his *Mythologus*, in their truly classical style, reveal an understanding of ancient Greek

[441] F. Schleiermacher (1768-1834): Sandys iii 82.
[442] C.F. Heindorf (1774-1816): Sandys iii 82.
[443] G.L. Spalding (1762-1811): Sandys iii 81.
[444] Buttmann (1764-1829): Sandys iii 84; Pfeiffer, *HCS* ii 185-6.

poetry and myth quite equal to that of Welcker and Otfried Müller. Christian Ludwig Ideler,[445] the astronomer 'of the Academy, being an Arabic as well as a Greek scholar, was able to apply his scientific knowledge to antiquity in numerous fascinating inquiries into the names of the stars and constellations and other subjects taken from both scientific and popular astronomy. Finally, in his *Chronologie*, he produced a text-book which is still unsurpassed as a clear statement of the fundamentals of the subject, notwithstanding all that has since been added to our knowledge of the various calendars and cycles. As we read him we realise that it takes an expert to reveal the full extent of the Greek achievement in this field – always assuming, of course, that the expert has the sort of classical background Ideler had. In Ideler's case the spirit of mutual aid among this group of friends no doubt also played its part.

By the accession of Wolf's pupil Immanuel Bekker[446] the group acquired a member who became one of its most valued ornaments, though in his own person he contributed little to it (he was only nominally a teacher) and soon went abroad to carry out the gigantic task of collating the manuscripts looted by the French which were assembled in Paris. After numerous further travels for a similar purpose, he published texts, firmly based on sound manuscript authority, of practically the whole of Attic prose literature down to Aristotle. Bekker never gives the reader anything beyond the barest essentials: of how he arrived at them and whether the task had been laborious or easy – not a word. Consider his achievement in regard to Pollux. We are not told what the various manuscripts from which the text is pieced together contained, and we scarcely need to be. Nobody would deny that Bekker cut down his notes too much and sometimes went astray in his estimation of the witnesses for the text; but the allegation that he never acquired a complete mastery of textual criticism is hardly justified, since in dozens of instances the papyri have led us back to the eclectic type of criticism, in the practice of which he relied on his uncommonly sure sense of style. If only

[445] Ideler (1766-1846): Sandys iii 99; E.J. Bickerman, *Chronology of The Ancient World*, 1966, 96.

[446] Bekker (1785-1871): Sandys iii 85; Pfeiffer, *HCS* ii 181-2.

he had divulged more of what he knew! A story which has come down by word of mouth relates that he and his friends were once reading Demosthenes together when Lachmann proposed a conjectural restoration of a corrupt word. Everyone agreed but Bekker, who remained silent. At last some one said to him, 'But isn't it a splendid emendation?', to which he merely replied, 'In *Demosthenes*?', which was the end of the conjecture for all of them. The only author on whom he ever lectured was Homer; and even there it was only in dealing with points of language that his touch was sure; he ended by following Bentley's example and restoring the digamma in a more wholesale fashion than our text in its existing state can bear, thereby opening the door to still more violent experiments in which certain Dutch and English scholars also indulged. In his old age Bekker published an excessive number of texts which he merely proof-read, confining his corrections in many cases to matters of punctuation, in which he was a great artist: anyone who disagrees merely advertises his own lack of understanding of the language. Bekker seldom expressed any opinion on questions of authenticity; but where he did, as with Lucian, his views are disconcertingly radical.

There was one member of the group who stood out from all his fellows, Barthold Georg Niebuhr,[447] a great father's greater son – even in this respect resembling Scaliger, whose work he admired and himself raised, as it were, to a higher power. Though a Danish subject by birth, Niebuhr chose Prussia as his adopted country and distinguished himself in its public service, from which he afterwards reluctantly retired. He had given no tangible proof of his qualifications as a scholar when Humboldt, always on the look-out for talent, procured his election to the Academy; and it was as an Academician, though not before the Academy, that he delivered the lectures that formed the nucleus of his *History of Rome*, which won him immediate fame. In the eyes of the great

---

[447] Niebuhr (1776-1831): Sandys iii 77; Pfeiffer, *HCS* ii 183. See Momigliano, 'G.C. Lewis, Niebuhr e la critica delle fonti', *Rivista Storica Italiana* 64, 1952, 208f. (= *C* 249f.), especially the section on the reception of Niebuhr in England (*C* 253f.).

public, its principal merit was, and still is, that it killed the
official legend of the period of the kings. Since then people
have been alert for possible precursors and have found them in
Perizonius[447a] and Louis de Beaufort.[448] As though Niebuhr's
contribution was to be assessed in negative terms! He raised
no problem, such as Wolf had in his *Prolegomena*, but set out to
show, first, how the legend had arisen, and secondly, above
all, what had to be put in its place by way of history. We know
now that he did not carry his scepticism far enough and that
his *History* hardly reached the point at which a coherent
narrative of events begins to be possible. The truth is that
what makes Niebuhr great is not the critic, but the statesman
in him – who is aware of what makes the wheels of national life
go round, and is familiar with the exigencies of political and
administrative systems, and therefore takes account of the
things that are usually omitted in the narratives of wars, great
personages and memorable events which fill the history books.
Niebuhr's experience taught him that documents are more
trustworthy than the most enthralling narrative, and that one
must make the most of every scrap of evidence about the life of
the past. Niebuhr saw all history in terms of world history.
The lectures on ancient history which he later gave in Bonn
are probably equal in value to the *History of Rome* as a
contribution to learning, and when the Armenian translation
of the Chronicle of Eusebius came to light he was able to turn
the discovery to immediate account in the most masterly of his
dissertations. A lucky chance drew his attention to Scaliger,
whose example inspired him to try to enlist the support of the
Berlin Academy for the gigantic enterprise of a complete
*Corpus* of ancient inscriptions in all languages, which he
believed might be completed in a comparatively short time. At
that stage of course he was thinking only of material which
was either already published or available in transcriptions,
and only incidentally of exploring Greece. His appointment as

---

[447a] Perizonius (Jacob Voorbroek, 1651-1715; Sandys ii 330) published
his *Animadversiones Historicae* in 1685. See Momigliano, 'Perizonius, Niebuhr
and early Roman tradition', *JRS* 47, 1957, 104f. (= *SC* 69f); cf. W. Den
Boer, *Scaliger en Perizonius*, The Hague, 1964.

[448] Louis de Beaufort published his *Dissertation sur l'Incertitude des cinq
premiers Siècles de l'Histoire Romaine'* in 1738-50.

Prussian Minister in Rome prevented him from personally
taking part in the collection of materials, but while he was
there he did everything possible to further it. The only
immediate result was the start made on the *Corpus inscriptionum
Graecarum*, which Boeckh took over although it interfered with
his own plans. Important though this was in itself, its
significance as the first of the Academy's large-scale under-
takings was even greater. The historian of Rome, who was
passionately devoted to the imperial race, could never feel
happy, as Humboldt had, in the papal city and its caricature
of a state. Art indeed left him cold; but the true explanation of
the contrast lies in the radically different temperaments of
these two great men. Niebuhr himself undertook the task of
carefully cataloguing and describing the remains of the
ancient city, and his letters show how his interest in
contemporary Italian affairs was dictated by the desire to
discover whether anything could be deduced from them
concerning the ancient world. His researches in the libraries
had the same object: and, as is well-known, as soon as he
arrived in Verona he discovered Gaius. Mai's[449] discovery of
Cicero's *De republica* and Fronto had raised hopes of a
substantial addition to existing Latin literature from
palimpsests, and Niebuhr found fragments of Cicero's
speeches in the Vatican and of Merobaudes[450] in St Gallen.
Though he always kept in close touch with scholarship in the
narrower sense of the word, his own inadequate sense of style
is shown by his assignment of Petronius and Quintus Curtius
to the third century, and still more conclusively by the
obstinacy with which he maintained the antiquity of '*Lydia
bella puella*'[451] and other poems of the kind. Niebuhr can be

[449] Angelo Mai (1782-1854): Sandys iii 241; Treves 347f.; *SS*² 175.
Sebastiano Timpanaro, *La filologia di Giacomo Leopardi*, 2nd edn. 1978, has
revealed the ingratitude of this person towards the great poet, who was also the
most considerable Italian Greek scholar since Petrus Victorius (see above,
n.125); cf. G. Pacella and S. Timpanaro, *Gli scritti filologici di Giacomo
Leopardi*, 1969; Treves 471f. Timpanaro in the former book gives a
fascinating description of the Rome of Niebuhr, Mai and Leopardi.
[450] *Pro Fonteio* and *Pro C. Rabirio* (1820). Merobaudes, a Christian poet and
rhetorician, lived in Spain during the fifth century A.D.
[451] 'Lydia bella puella': see A. Riese, *Anthologia Latina*, i 2, xxxix-xli.

forgiven for having sponsored towards the end of his life a
straight reprint of the Byzantine historians, since no publisher
could have borne the cost of a critical edition, and in any case
it would have been impossible to produce one at the time; but
that after his death the Academy should have continued such
an unscholarly enterprise, and that its best men should have
lent a hand to it, is, alas, proof that such treatment was still
considered good enough for the Byzantines.

Boeckh[452] was still in the full vigour of early manhood when
he was appointed to a chair in the new University of Berlin,
where he remained until his death in 1867. Though he came
from Baden, he was no stranger to north Germany, having
studied under Wolf and lived for some time in Berlin, where
he was known to the leading scholars – hence his
appointment. From Heidelberg, where he had held a
professorship, he brought with him neither the Romantic
outlook nor a belief in Creuzer's *Symbolik*; but he had come
under Creuzer's personal influence, and kept in touch with
him even when Creuzer was more or less forgotten. Boeckh
contained a streak which was not exactly philosophical[453] but
might be called Pythagorean. He was attracted by the idea of
astronomy as the foundation of both physical and meta-
physical systems, which accounts for his early work on Plato's
*Timaeus* and on Philolaus; and it was musical theory that led
him to the study of metre, and thence to Pindar. He took a
delight generally in weights, measures and figures. This led to
his revolutionary discoveries in metrology and chronology,
and in his old age he returned to the studies of his youth. But
along with this was the desire for a comprehensive understanding of the life of the ancient world, or rather of ancient
Athens, in all its aspects, and a capacity for burrowing into
every corner of it, insofar as that is possible within the confines
of the study. This capacity is seen at its most amazing in his
handling of the naval records, but the Attic documents

[452] Boeckh (1785-1867): Sandys iii 95; Bursian 687; Pfeiffer, *HCS* ii 181.
Cf. M. Hoffmann, *August Boeckh: Lebensbeschreibung und Auswahl aus seinem
wissenschaftlichem Briefwechsel*, 1901, and Wilamowitz, *Kl. Schr.* vi 49f.
[453] Momigliano (*C* 384) lays the strongest stress on the unphilosophical
nature of Boeckh's thinking.

included in the second volume of *The Public Economy of Athens*[454]
evince it in a more readily accessible form. When that book
first appeared, it was so totally novel, and so far in advance of
anything that had been attempted for any country or period
hitherto, that only a handful of scholars realised its
importance – indeed it seems to have been better appreciated
outside academic circles. It was followed almost immediately
by his Pindar,[455] in which an attempt was made for the first
time to approach the poems as historical documents. Therein
lies its chief value, admirable as his editing of the scholia and
judicious as his treatment of the text may also be. Textual
criticism, in fact, did not greatly attract him; and it must be
admitted that his *Antigone*[456] exhibits no particular gift for
poetry as such, either in the text or in the translation – in fact,
language never meant much to him. His treatment of
inscriptions has the same merits and defects. His elucidations
of their subject-matter, especially where they are in the nature
of records, does exactly what is required and could not be
bettered; but for him the lessons that inscriptions could teach
about the history of the language were very much a secondary
consideration. Above all, Boeckh could never bring himself to
accept as equally valid for inscriptions the principle, already
firmly established in regard to manuscripts, that one must
start from the original. To do this was impossible in the early
stages; and later, when Ross[457] brought him his admirable
transcripts from Greece, Boeckh thought they were all he
needed and refused to admit the claims of epigraphers
working at first hand. Instinctively we think of Boeckh as the
dignified old gentleman in full dress who confronts us in the
famous portrait. There we have the serene sage who
dominated the University and the Academy and initiated
generation after generation of students in the comprehensive
science which he mapped out in his *Enzyklopädie*;[458] but today

[454] *Staatshaushaltung der Athener*, 1817; new edn. by M. Fraenkel, 1886; see D.M.
Lewis, *Acta of the Fifth Epigraphic Congress*, 1967, 35f.

[455] Pindar i 1811; ii 1821; still indispensable.

[456] *Antigone*, 1843; new edn. 1884.     [457]Ross: see below, n.476.

[458] *Enzyklopädie und Methodologie der philologischen Wissenschaften*, 1877; the
book is based on the notes collected for a course of lectures given in 26
semesters between 1809 and 1865; on the historical outlook it displays, see
Momigliano, *C* 177f.

we are no longer content that our work should be based entirely on 'acquiring the knowledge that has been acquired'. Such, for decades, was his exalted position, and he filled it worthily. But the Boeckh who helped the new science to victory was quite a different person. Another good portrait shows us the fighter, determined at any cost to achieve, entirely on his own initiative, the object he has set himself. It was in the first twenty years of his Berlin career that he won his victories and acquired his most important pupils and allies; for, whether he wished to or not, he gathered disciples round him just like Hermann, whom he had reverenced in his youth – but though each had to admit that the other was a force to be reckoned with, it was impossible for them to do one another justice.

Preoccupation with the financial administration of the Athenians led Boeckh to the study of their law, and by setting Athenian legal procedure as the subject for a prize essay, he called into existence the important work in which two competitors, his pupils M.H.E. Meier[459] and G.F. Schömann, collaborated. Whereas Meier obediently followed in the footsteps of his friend and mentor, Schömann covered the whole field of classical studies at Greifswald with great distinction for many years. His *De comitiis Atheniensium* might almost have been written by Sigonius, so remote does it seem from modern ideas, but in its day it was as good as could be expected. Schömann's descriptions of ancient institutions are well written, and provide a careful and judicious summary of the literary tradition. His book on the parts of speech is still the best introduction to ancient ideas on the subject.

Boeckh's choice of the history of rhetoric as the subject in another essay competition proved equally happy, for in giving rise to Leonhard Spengel's[460] admirable Συναγωγὴ τεχνῶν it determined the course of his successful career. No one has come anywhere near Spengel in knowledge of the nature and technique of rhetoric. His editions of the *Rhetoric* of

[459] M.H.E. Meier (1796-1855): Sandys iii 168. G.K. Schömann (1793-1879): Sandys iii 165. *Die Lehre von den Redeteilen nach den Alten*, 1864.
[460] L. Spengel (1803-1880): Sandys iii 180. On his merits and limitations, see R. Kassel, *Textgeschichte der Aristotelischen Rhetorik*, 1971, 106f.

Anaximenes and the *Rhetoric* of Aristotle with explanatory notes remain the best introductions to these topics,[461] and he also produced numerous shorter works of importance. Thanks to his familiarity with the tricks of the Attic orators, Spengel was able to form the first correct estimate of their trustworthiness, but little attention was paid to him. His work on the text of Aristotle and of Philodemus shows how much abler he was than many scholars who have made more noise in the world.

Boeckh's oldest pupil was Eduard Gerhard,[462] who damaged his eyesight collating the scholia for his teacher's Pindar and went to Italy to recuperate. As a result, instead of continuing his excellent work on Apollonius Rhodius and the structure of the later hexameter, Gerhard became Germany's first professed archaeologist. His guiding principle, based on the experience of many years, was: '*Monumentorum artis, qui unum vidit, nullum vidit, qui mille vidit, unum vidit.*' In accordance with this principle he devoted his energies to cataloguing collections and publishing as many monuments as possible. As regards vases, which just then were being dug up in vast quantities, all subsequent work of this kind is based on his; and it would not be too much to say that in his *Rapporto Volcente*[463] he founded the scientific study of the delightful art of vase-painting, which by now has become almost a separate discipline. What attracted Gerhard in these paintings was not their artistic quality but the solid information he gleaned from them; things that were 'merely beautiful' did not interest him. He was usually unlucky with his interpretations, and his mythological speculations were misconceived; yet he succeeded by sheer force of personality not only in securing many treasures for the Berlin Museum, where he finally obtained the appointment he deserved, and bringing on the rising generation of archaeologists, but also in founding our Archaeological Institute, which was ushered into the world after a long period of gestation on the day of the Feast of Pales,

[461] Did Wilamowitz know E.M. Cope's *Introduction to Aristotle's Rhetoric* (1867) or his three-volume commentary (1877)? They are still useful.

[462] Gerhard (1795-1867): Sandys iii 217; Rumpf 69; Cook, op.cit., 295f. etc.).

[463] Rapporto Volcente in *Annali*, 1831.

1829, as the *Instituto di Corrispondenza Archeologica*. It was a noble attempt to bring all the civilised nations of the world together. The French, headed by the Duc de Luynes, [464] gave most valuable help over a long period; so did the Belgian de Witte.[465] The Italians long remained grateful for the existence of an institution which in the face of the dismembered state of their country took the unity of Italy for granted. The Dane Kellermann[466] devoted his short life to the study of epigraphy as a resident in the Institute, and although the English were less forthcoming Millingen[467] was one of the founders and the connection was maintained. The secretaries, however, were all Germans, and without the help of Frederick William IV, who had become the patron of the Institute while still Crown Prince, it would have collapsed financially. In the end it was taken over by the Prussian, and subsequently by the Imperial, government. All through these early years the driving force behind it was the indefatigable and persuasive Gerhard, whose selfless devotion found a way out of every difficulty. The Institute also owed much to Christian Josias Bunsen,[468] a worthy successor to Niebuhr as Prussian Minister, whose description of Rome – another link with Niebuhr – was perhaps the greatest achievement of his career. Excavations gave a great impetus to Roman topography, and Italian archaeologists like Carlo Fea,[469] Antonio Nibby and Luigi Canina knew how to make the most of them. In Germany, the admirable compendium of the literary evidence produced by W.A. Becker[470] without any knowledge of the monuments led to a lively controversy during the forties, since the men who were familiar with the ruins, especially Ludwig Urlichs[471] and Ludwig Preller, felt it incumbent upon them to protest against

[464] Albert, Duc de Luynes (1803-1867): Sandys iii 165.
[465] Jean de Witte (1808-1889): Sandys iii 293.
[466] O. Kellermann (1803-1838): Sandys iii 219.
[467] James Millingen (1774-1845).
[468] Christian Carl Josias, Freiherr von Bunsen (1791-1860).
[469] Fea (1753-1836): Sandys iii 244; Rumpf i 64. Nibby (1792-1839). Canina (1795-1856): Sandys iii 244.
[470] Becker: see above, n.407.
[471] Urlichs (1813-1889): Sandys iii 202. Preller (1809-1861): Sandys iii 239.

such a one-sided approach. All this is long forgotten, and both sides have been given their due; but the deep excavations of the past decade have put an entirely new face on the earliest period of the city's history.

It was only decades later that the Institute in Rome published anything about the east beyond an occasional communication. The Elgin marbles from the Parthenon, the Aeginetan marbles and the Phigaleian frieze[472] had of course found their way to London and Munich respectively and completely transformed current notions of genuine Greek art; but they had been removed from their native country, about which individual travellers, mostly Englishmen, were now the only source of information. The discoveries in Aegina and at Phigaleia were the only ones in which nationals of other countries – the Dane Bröndsted[473] and the Balt Baron Stackelberg – had played a part. Stackelberg's book on Greek graves drew attention to a class of works of art in which the Hellenic spirit finds particularly clear expression, but he is too much given to *Symbolik*. Bröndsted's attractive monograph on Ceos unfortunately had no successors. The Englishmen Gell and Dodwell should also be mentioned, to say nothing of Fellows,[474] the first man to explore Lycia, a country abounding in monuments; but they are all overshadowed by the figure of William Martin Leake[475] who, thanks to his powers of observation and cool judgment – in which he compares favourably with Dodwell – laid the foundations of the geographical and topographical study of the whole of Greece and important parts of Asia Minor. Leake also wrote on the topography of Athens and investigated the demes. Both books were bound to be translated into German, but at first it was only in a few quarters that they were welcomed and used, as they deserved to be, as a starting-point for further

---

[472] The frieze from the temple of Apollo at Bassae (Phigaleia) is in London; see Rumpf 67. On the impression made by the Elgin marbles, see B. Ashmole, *Lectures in Memory of Louise Semple Taft*, 1st series 1967, 179f.

[473] P.O. Bröndsted (1780-1842): Sandys iii 318. O.M. Stackelberg (1787-1834): Sandys ii 218; cf. iii 218.

[474] W.M. Gell (1777-1836). E. Dodwell (1767-1832). Sir Charles Fellows (1799-1860): Sandys iii 443.

[475] Leake (1777-1860): Sandys iii 442.

investigation. All eyes were fixed on the Greek War of Independence, and learned observers as well as volunteers flocked to the scene, while the *Expédition de la Morée* produced a good map of the Peloponnese and a description of the country. Not long afterwards two Germans, Ludwig Ross and Heinrich Ulrichs,[476] received permanent appointments at the new University of Athens. Ulrichs died, leaving behind only a few topographical works, but those first-rate. Ross gave the public a vivid picture of the Greek landscape in his accounts of royal tours and of his travels among the Aegean islands, and where he came across inscriptions either published them himself or sent copies to Boeckh; he had been a pupil of Hermann's, and his lack of historical training gradually became very obvious. All this had the effect of enlarging the horizons of contemporary scholars to include the land of Greece and its people, with the result that they ceased to dream only of seeing Rome. And so it was to Greece that Otfried Müller betook himself, never to return, thereby making the land in which he sleeps into a place of pilgrimage for us scholars; and it was travel in Greece that gave Welcker a new lease of life.

The turning-point in the intellectual life of Friedrich Gottlieb Welcker[477] was his visit to Rome, where he came under the influence of Humboldt and Zoëga. Welcker's equal devotion to ancient art and ancient poetry is in itself enough to make him unique. With Niebuhr, his colleague at Bonn, his relations were never close; nor had he much real sympathy with Boeckh, but their common opposition to Hermann united them. The clash became inevitable when Welcker published his book on Aeschylus' Prometheus trilogy, with its supplementary volume on the satyric drama. It contained a great deal that scholars were justified in condemning, and its sub-title, '*Die Kabirenweihe auf Lemnos*' betrayed a disturbing weakness for *Symbolik*. But the important points in Welcker's study of the Aeschylean trilogy in general and his efforts to penetrate beneath the surface of the Hellenic genius, which

---

[476] Ross (1806-1859): Sandys iii 227. Ulrichs (1807-1843): Sandys iii 227, 371.

[477] Welcker (1784-1868): Sandys iii 216; Bursian 1029; Pfeiffer, *HCS* ii 179.

speaks to us equally clearly in legend, poetry and the visual arts, were at first entirely lost on the school of exact scholarship, though subsequent opinion has come round to him. At this time the remains of the various lyric poets were gradually being collected. Welcker himself undertook Alcman, and all the other collections were indebted to him. Next came his books on the epic cycle and on the Greek tragedians considered in relation to it, which impressed by the copiousness of their matter and the boldness of his imagination; every heap of fragments presented itself to him as a coherent whole. This scholar of fifty-seven, who exhausted his travelling-companions in Greece by his tireless energy, felt the presence of the gods all round him when he finally set foot on their homeland: there they were no mere symbols or abstractions, but living powers.

Otfried Müller,[478] at whose grave Welcker paid the tribute of a passing tear as he climbed the hill of Colonus, had travelled the same path, but with other plans in mind. Müller was Boeckh's favourite pupil and a spoilt child of Fortune. Only just out of his teens when he succeeded to Heyne's chair, he was soon in the good graces of the dignitaries of the Georgia Augusta University. On his visit to England he found himself in a society that habitually looked down on the Germans; but this did not embarrass him, and the impression he created can be gauged from the fact that his *History of Greek Literature* was originally written for the English public. When the perjured king of Hanover expelled the Seven Men of Göttingen,[479] the last thing that Müller – who had expressed his own opinions in the matter quite fearlessly – could have expected was that he would be given every facility he desired for his journey. Nor was production ever any trouble to him either. He found it so easy to switch from one subject to

[478] Karl Otfried Müller (1797-1840): Sandys iii 213; Bursian 1007; Gruppe 157. His *History of the Literature of Ancient Greece* (1840-2) first appeared in English, having been commissioned by the Society for the Diffusion of Useful Knowledge; see Pfeiffer, *HCS* ii 187, n.3.

[479] In 1837 Ernest Augustus, king of Hanover, expelled from the Georgia Augusta University of Göttingen seven professors who had protested against his revocation of the constitution granted in 1833; they included the brothers Grimm.

another, however remote, that in addition to his major historical studies he managed to edit Festus, to compete – to Boeckh's amazement – for the Academy's prize for an essay on the Etruscans and, finally, to write his *History of Greek Literature*, which is not only the most readable in existence but the only one that is a genuine history, for Bernhardy's unwieldy book[480] is neither of these things and Bergk's is only a collection of essays on individual problems. Müller's hastily compiled *Prolegomena to a Scientific Mythology* was also a natural by-product of his historical labours. His doctor's dissertation had shown, even at that early stage, that he was aware that the Greeks were not a homogeneous people but an amalgam of races varying in their natural aptitudes; and his great achievement is to have traced the effects of this on their history, social structure, beliefs and legends. In doing so he put their early history on a sound basis once and for all. True, he never reached the main point – that is to say, the Athenians and the Ionians, whom he consequently underrated – but in his letters from Greece he corrected his estimate of them, and he would probably have been prepared to reconsider his belief that Greek civilisation was completely autochthonous. Müller's early death was a blow to the cause, but he died in harness, and even in that last struggle he helps us understand the heroic age.

Müller was quite at home in textual criticism, as Welcker never was; but he found exclusive devotion to it repellent and temperamentally he was bound sooner or later to clash with Hermann – who in fact provoked the quarrel by not merely attacking Welcker's *Prometheus* but failing to praise Dissen's[481] Pindar. Dissen, who was a colleague of Müller and a friend of Boeckh, Lachmann and Welcker, thirsted for praise and got more of it from his friends than he deserved. But it was Hermann's onslaught on the first instalment of Boeckh's *Corpus* that caused the greatest ill-feeling and unleashed a violent controversy. So, when Müller poached on Hermann's

[480] G. Bernhardy (1800-1862) published a *Grundriss der griechischen Literatur* (1836-45); for T. Bergk see below, n.519. Müller's *Prolegomena zu einer wissenschaftlichen Mythologie* (1820-4; 2nd edn. 1844) was reprinted in 1970.
[481] Dissen: see above, n.437.

most jealously guarded preserves by publishing his edition of the *Eumenides*, no wonder open war broke out, with unqualified persons on both sides fanning the flames. When we look back on the affair calmly, we can see that it was a pointless contest. Hermann was incapable of judging Boeckh's Herculean labours; he either failed to understand, or rejected as uninteresting, Müller's profound observations.[482] On the other hand he was undoubtedly right in most of his strictures – and not merely about the simple construing of a particular passage. The fact is that these two scholars complemented one another. Hermann was like the manager of an ancient estate who fears that a new generation may let it go to ruin. The new science of antiquity has triumphed as it deserved to, but the danger of its cutting adrift from the safe anchorage of linguistic knowledge is always with us. Therein lies the sole reason why we have to keep the memory of that unhappy quarrel alive, and continue to listen to the warnings of Hermann's ghost. The importance of this battle of the schools is that it marked the close of an incomparably fruitful epoch. Müller died. Welcker, who had always been a solitary figure, remained as energetic as ever, but concentrated his powers on the production of his great work on Greek mythology, which appeared in 1862 but made little appeal to that generation. Boeckh continued with undiminished vigour, but left others to finish the *Corpus* as best they could with their antiquated methods, and his last publications were on subjects way off the beaten track. Hermann's criticism became more and more violent. In his editions of Bion and Moschus, which he produced without acquainting himself with the manuscript tradition or examining the question of authorship, he forced out of the poems an arbitrary division into stanzas, creating a bad precedent thereby. In editing the *Bacchides* he harked back to the *Trinummus* of his youth (1810), on the strength of which Ritschl had called him the only critic of Plautus fit to be mentioned in the same breath as Bentley;[483] but by this time

---

[482] Hermann's review of Müller's *Eumenides* (1833) forms Part II of the sixth volume of his *Opuscula* (1835).

[483] On Hermann's work on Plautus, see the article of Fraenkel quoted in n.426.

nobody could obtain a hearing on the subject of Plautus except Ritschl himself. There was no lack of later scholars to carry on the traditions of both schools, and some of the most important ones will be mentioned in due course; but as regards Greek, they did little more than build upon the achievements of their predecessors.

Latin, on the other hand, after a long period of neglect, came to the fore again. But the revival was confined almost entirely to verbal scholarship, on which excessive stress was laid in other fields too. Its leading figures were Karl Lachmann and Nicolai Madvig, and later Ritschl.

Lachmann[484] studied at Göttingen, but really educated himself with a group of friends, which he doubtless dominated. At bottom, he was influenced by the Romantics, with whom at first sight he seems to have little in common. He soon brought out his Propertius, in which he made a clean sweep of all the transpositions and inept attempts to smooth the style that had disfigured the text. Nearby Wolfenbüttel provided the only trustworthy manuscript; from the others he took various readings as he thought fit, and emendation, coupled with an arbitrary new division into books, did the rest. His later Catullus is a riddle to anyone who comes to it unprepared. It is an attempt to reconstruct page by page from the Renaissance copies the only manuscript in which the poems had survived. The justification offered subsequently by Haupt, though highly ingenious, was deceptive, and it needed an arbitrary fiat to get it accepted. But the principle of recension is right. Not only that: it was a great achievement to establish it in the way he did, even if the principle was hardly understood at the time, let alone observed. Lachmann's two contributions to the subject of Greek metre belong to the period between his Propertius and his Catullus; we should gladly ignore these efforts, with their number games, were it not for the harm they did. Lachmann, by common consent, was already the greatest living master of textual criticism in the domain of early German literature, where his immortality is assured, and his Berlin friends

---

[484] Lachmann (1793-1851): Sandys iii 127; Pfeiffer, *HCS* ii 190.

appealed to him to deal with such exceptionally difficult texts as those of Gaius and the *Agrimensores*. He acquitted himself well, but the verdict of Mommsen, who once called him 'the great master of language' was: 'His emendations are splendid – if only he had known something about the subject!' Following in Bentley's footsteps, he tried, as a good Protestant, to provide the Church with a text of the New Testament[485] as transmitted in place of the *textus receptus* – that product of chance and caprice whose every letter is regarded as sacred by the orthodox. He rejected the revered text, and on the basis of the oldest manuscripts and Jerome produced the text that the eastern church has accepted as canonical. He knew that in so doing he was not by any means getting back to the autographs of the New Testament writers, and from deliberate conservatism he left certain corruptions as they stood; for he drew a sharp distinction between recension and emendation (terms which we owe to him) and stated his principle in the preface. Clearly much of the history of the text remains to be written, and it is surprising to find Lachmann disregarding the innumerable ancient quotations. Shortly before his sadly premature death he produced, in his Lucretius,[486] with commentary, the book from which we all have learnt critical method and which every student is required to ponder. Lachmann considered that the tradition of the poem's genesis justified his explaining many of the breaks in continuity by assuming the existence of doublets and detached fragments; in this undoubtedly he went too far. On the other hand, his realisation that Mark's gospel is older than the two other synoptic gospels, which must therefore have been based on it, was a triumph of comparative analysis. His resolution of the *Iliad* into a number of separate lays is modelled on his earlier dismemberment of the *Nibelungenlied*. Both enjoyed a vogue, but neither has stood the test of time,

---

[485] On Lachmann's work on the New Testament, see Metzger, op.cit., in n.648.

[486] The importance of Lachmann's *Lucretius* is not diminished by the brilliant work of Sebastiano Timpanaro, who has shown (*La genesi del metodo di Lachmann*, 1981) that the credit for having invented the method which has been associated with his name belongs in the main to Bernays, Madvig and Haupt.

because they lacked the kind of foundation that can be laid only by historical research. But where would we be without Lachmann? That we must never forget. The impact of his personality and speech on his hearers was so overwhelming that they were sometimes paralysed and sometimes tempted into grotesque attempts to copy him. We have to free ourselves from his leading-strings, but only by first surrendering willingly to him, as he himself prescribed.

Madvig,[487] who was born in Bornholm and rose to the highest offices in the Danish government, was also entirely self-educated. It is in the *Emendationes Livianae* and his edition of Cicero's *De finibus* that his greatness first impresses itself upon us. Madvig was a past-master of classical Roman prose, and his sharp strictures on the slovenly ways into which German academic writing had fallen were well deserved. He was as grimly determined as Lachmann to get back to the genuine manuscript tradition, though in the third decade of Livy he succumbed to the illusion that all authority rests with the oldest manuscript. Madvig was interested in the science of language; but despite his concern with wider and deeper issues, for us he remains primarily the grammarian with a genius for deducing the rules of Latin syntax from classical usage in a strictly logical manner. This approach, broadly speaking, is justifiable with the language of formal prose, though of course not with poetry – but then, Madvig usually steered clear of poetry. His command of Attic prose was not indeed equal to Cobet's, though the harsh terms in which Cobet and others criticised his *Adversaria* for its many mistakes, and even metrical howlers, were quite unfair. His corrections of the text of Greek prose writers such as Plato and Plutarch would be reckoned an important part of any ordinary scholar's work; for him they were merely a by-product. In other work of a quite different kind he reached conclusions that have since become common property – for example, on Asconius, the *tribuni aerarii* and Granius Licinianus.[488] The book of his old age on the constitution and

[487] Madvig (1804-1886): Sandys iii 319. Cf. H. Nettleship, *Lectures and Essays* ii, 1895, 1f.; Kenney 110.
[488] Granius Licinianus is a minor Roman historian of the Antonine age.

administration of the Roman state is based on methods and materials that were no longer adequate even in 1880, but this we gladly overlook. Madvig is an imposing figure in his combination of Olympian calm and clear judgment, which inspires complete confidence. His sole concern was for the truth, and he led the way to it directly, so that his influence went far beyond his immediate audience and fellow-countrymen. He was far too many-sided ever to have thought of forming a school.

Friedrich Ritschl[489] was an entirely different sort of man in temperament, talents and character. Ritschl studied at Halle under Reisig,[490] whose early death makes it impossible to judge whether in his more mature works he would have succeeded in his aims, though he was an admirable teacher. Ritschl's first love was Greek. His dialectical skill was already apparent in his discussion of Orus and Orion,[491] which explains why his erroneous findings were long accepted. Considering their date (1838), his inquiries into the Pisistratean recension of the Homeric poems and into the library and librarians of Alexandria were outstanding, and they contain casual observations on the development of the Greek epic that are very apposite.[492] At this point certain marks in a late manuscript of Plautus turned his thoughts in a new direction. Plautus was now to be the most fruitful part of his activities, his only other important work being on the literary career of Varro. Ritschl abandoned his Greek studies completely, just at the point where they could have helped him with Plautus. He was the first person to make use of the Ambrosian palimpsest found by Mai, and in a letter to Hermann from Milan, written in the first fine rapture of discovery and creative effort, he outlined the programme of his

---

[489] Ritschl (1806-1876): Sandys iii 139; life by O. Ribbeck, in two volumes, 1879-81; see Wolfgang Schmid, op.cit. below in n.528.

[490] Christian Carl Reisig (1792-1829): Sandys 108.

[491] Ritschl took the grammarian Orus, who was his discovery, for a contemporary of Herodian in the second century A.D.; R. Reitzenstein (*Geschichte der griechischen Etymologika*, 1897, 287f.) showed that like Orion he belonged to the fifth century A.D.

[492] They also contain some unfortunate mistakes; see Pfeiffer i 6, n.5, and 100, n.2.

life's work. Bentley and Hermann were his models in
scrupulous attention to language and metre. In that respect
everything was still to do. Ritschl realised that he had to
reconstruct Old Latin and that he had to do it in quite a
different sense from Scaliger. He was alive to the importance
of inscriptions and for a while worked at them with
Mommsen; the archaic inscriptions available were all too few,
and he steered clear of the Italic dialects. Today, though so
much has developed differently, the reader is still spellbound
by his *Parerga Plautina* and his introduction to the *Trinummus*;
and even where his critics have refuted him, their work could
not have been done without him. No wonder people were
transported by the wealth of observations so brilliantly
presented. Nine plays appeared in quick succession; and then
there was an end. Ritschl lived another twenty-two years,
during which time the scientific study of Plautus which he had
inaugurated marched on to even further triumphs, mainly
through C.F.W. Müller,[493] whose knowledge of Latin has
been credited by one good judge as almost unequalled. After
his deplorable quarrel with his colleague Otto Jahn,[494]
as a result of which he left Bonn for Leipzig, Ritschl dwindled
into a mere teacher, repeating his old lectures year in year out.
A supporter who prophesied the end of the classical school of
Bonn proved wrong, for it reached its height only under
Ritschl's pupils Bücheler and Usener;[495] but as a teacher
Ritschl has had few equals, and he deliberately set out to form
a school. This could hardly have failed to provoke reaction.
That he succeeded is attested not only by the number of his
disciples (the *Symbola in honorem Frederici Ritschelii* [495a] was the

[493] C.F.W. Müller (b.1830; Bursian 829), a pupil of Lobeck and Lehrs.

[494] A good account of the quarrel is given by A. Körte, *Die Antike* ii, 1935,
211f.

[495] Franz Bücheler (1837-1908): Sandys iii 481; F. Leo's memorial speech
is reprinted, together with other tributes by his friends, in *Wesen und Rang der
Philologie*, Stuttgart, 1969. He edited Petronius and Juvenal, and did
important work on the Italian dialects and on Latin inscriptions. Hermann
Usener (1834-1905): Sandys iii 184; see Eduard Schwartz, *Gesammelte
Schriften* i, 1938, 301f. and 316f. He made an important contribution to the
study of ancient philosophy and ancient religion; his *Epicurea* (first
published 1887) remains the standard collection of Epicurean fragments.

[495a] *Symbola Philologorum Bonnensium in honorem F.R.*, 1864-7; the

first miscellany of its type, whose justification may be doubted), but by the fact that they followed obediently in his tracks, from which only the best were ever able to depart. There is something magnificent, reminiscent of Scaliger, about his method of providing for the requirements of his subject by allotting specific fields of research to other scholars, and setting themes for them. Thus the remains of Ennius were collected by Vahlen,[496] of the Latin dramatists by Ribbeck,[497] and of the Twelve Tables by Rudolf Schöll;[498] the grammatical fragments of Varro were to be published by A. Wilmanns[499] and of Suetonius by Reifferscheid.[500] Significantly enough, none of this activity was in the cause of Greek studies. The Viennese Academy's decision to undertake a critical edition of the Latin Fathers is also attributable to Ritschl's influence.

To the school of Ritschl textual criticism was everything, a

---

*Commentationes Mommsenianae* followed in 1877. Scholars should not forget that Wilamowitz called in question the justification for *Festschriften*, which complicate the task of bibliographers, go out of print quickly and soon cease to be available; see Sterling Dow, *Harvard Library Bulletin* 8, 1954, 283f., reprinted in Dorothy Rounds, *Articles on Antiquity in Festschriften: An Index*, 1962, 551f.

[496] Johannes Vahlen (1830-1911) published his *Ennius* in 1854; the second edition, immensely more cautious and not always the better for that, appeared in 1903. He also made a great contribution to the understanding of Aristotle's *Poetics* and wrote numerous articles and notes about both Greek and Latin literature. Housman's justified protest against the excessive conservatism in textual criticism of Bücheler and Vahlen, whom he called 'men of wide learning and no mean acuteness, but without simplicity of judgment' (*Manilius* i, 2nd edn. 1937, xliii) should not prevent English people from recognising the achievements of these scholars. On Vahlen, see Wilamowitz, *Kl. Schr.* vi 53f.

[497] Otto Ribbeck (1827-1898): Sandys iii 188. His *Scaenicae Romanorum poesis fragmenta* (first published in 1852-5, 3rd edn. 1897-8, last reprinted 1962) has still not been superseded (on A. Klotz, *Tragicorum fragmenta*, 1953, see O. Skutsch, *Gnomon* 26, 1954, 465f.).

[498] Rudolf Schöll (1844-1893): Sandys iii 198; not to be confused with his father Adolf or his brother Friedrich.

[499] August Wilmanns brought out his edition of Varro's grammatical fragments in 1864; Bursian 938-9.

[500] August Reifferscheid (b.1835; Bursian 848) published his edition of Suetonius' grammatical fragments in 1860. As late as 1881 he was working on a second edition, but this never appeared.

bias shared with Lachmann and Madvig, not to mention
Cobet, and always characteristic of Hermann. As a result
scholarship came to be more and more closely identified with
conjectural emendation. The dismemberment of the classics,
usually on grounds entirely divorced from their subject-
matter, and the rejection of whole works as spurious
proceeded drastically. Unlimited reliance was placed on the
'philological method', the *via ac ratio*, which many people
regarded as a magic wand: with its aid alone, the doors of
every treasure-house would spring open at a touch. Unhappily
the gold was often pinchbeck; and the worst was that these
errors were not of the kind that benefit learning by being
eliminated. That one in a thousand of the conjectures put
forward in the periodicals, and even texts, of that period was
correct would be a generous estimate. Athetesis ran riot in the
Greek tragedians, and in Cicero. The Dutchman Hofman-
Peerlkamp,[501] who had remodelled Horace to fit his own ideas
of logic, now found enthusiastic imitators. Lachmann's belief
in the hidden efficacy of number and Hermann's exaggerated
emphasis on strophic correspondence were applied to the
dialogue of tragedy, the plays of Seneca and heaven knows
what else. One had only to find the division, it seemed, to solve
at one stroke all the critical problems in Hesiod and
Theocritus, and even in the elegies of Tyrtaeus and
Propertius. Unfortunately there seems to be no way of
eradicating the numerical superstition, which always crops up
again in a new form. Harsh as it may sound, the only possible
verdict on these complacent believers in the Method is that
they were totally devoid of both historical sense and a sense of
the possible. The last idea they had was to enter into another
man's mind; they could hardly spare the time to acquaint
themselves with their author's diction before they began
correcting it. Their only excuse is that the old belief in
classical literature's absolute perfection was still unshaken, so
that when they found much in it that they could no longer
admire, they concluded that there was something wrong,
which called for treatment – if necessary, by cauterisation and

---

[501] Petrus Hofman-Peerlkamp (1786-1865): Sandys iii 276. On his way
with Horace, see E. Fraenkel, *JRS* 36, 1946, 189.

the knife. This can be observed most clearly with Horace and Sophocles.

It is enough to describe the tendency in general terms; as Euripides puts it, one should let the dead be dead. It only remains to mention briefly some other scholars of the period who did work of lasting merit, and there are quite a few. But first we must look at England and France. Both countries were slow at first to import verbal scholarship, though it still has its votaries in England today. The only true English counterpart of Cobet was Charles Badham[502] who, despite his services to Platonic scholarship, was never properly established in England and ended his days as the leading representative of classical scholarship in Australia. At the same time humanism lived on in the humanities which were the staple of university education – in a system in which the outward forms of churchmanship were constant, scholars were made bishops and a future cabinet minister might owe his first step on the political ladder to his Greek verses. In this way sound learning and a life-long devotion to the classics were fostered in England, where nobody repudiated Virgil because he was not Homer; and although we can point to no leading figure between the deaths of Elmsley and Dobree and the eighteen-seventies, there was no doubt a great deal more to be learnt in England about the interpretation and general understanding of the classics – though only the classics – than was commonly supposed in Germany. Some eccentric performances there certainly were; but even they can teach us something, and much that is worthless in itself may nevertheless be useful to a wider public. Travellers and excavators did much to further the progress of archaeology, as at Halicarnassus and Cnidus. Sir Charles Newton,[503] the discoverer of Cnidus, wrote as

---

[502] Badham (1813-1884): Sandys iii 407. 'Badham, the one English scholar of the mid-century whose reputation crossed the Channel, received from abroad the praises of Duebner and Nauck and Cobet, but at home was excluded from academical preferment, set to teach boys at Birmingham, and finally transported to the Antipodes': Housman, *Manilius* i, 2nd edn. 1937, xlii.

[503] Newton (1816-1894): Sandys iii 443. In 1855, after H.G. Liddell had declined it, Newton was offered the Regius Chair of Greek; this was, of course, long before English universities had chairs of archaeology. Newton

enthralling an account of his travels as Ross of his. But Englishmen still tended not to study the history of art.

In France, where interest in classical antiquity was discouraged under the educational regime of the First Empire and the Restoration, the genius of Champollion[504] created Egyptology, and even the younger generation of Germans betook themselves to Sylvestre de Sacy[505] to be initiated in Semitic studies. Diez,[506] on the other hand, was the father of Romance philology, and Immanuel Bekker[507] published editions of the Provençal and Old French epics. Greek also came to France from Germany. When the estimable publisher A. Firmin Didot,[508] who himself wrote on Aldus Manutius and Musurus, started his series of Greek classics with Latin translations in the old manner, the retention of which is characteristic, he drew his editors mainly from Germany – the Clarendon Press, incidentally, often did the same – and by far the best volumes in it are those produced by the indefatigable Friedrich Dübner and Carl Müller.[509] Finally, it was Henri Weil[510] of Frankfurt who brought about the welcome revival of Greek studies in Paris. German labours in the historical sphere are scarcely conceivable without the help of Müller's *Fragmenta Historicorum* and his unfinished *Geographi minores*, and the new edition of Stephanus' *Thesaurus* by Carl Benedict Hase[511] and the brothers Dindorf[512] is equally indispensable. The celebrity

---

declined, and the choice fell on Jowett, who chose to retain a post for which he was not well fitted after his election as Master of Balliol in 1870 and until his death in 1893. See Lloyd-Jones, *BG*, ch. 1.

[504] J.F. Champollion (1790-1832), the great Egyptologist who by means of the Rosetta Stone began the decipherment of Egyptian hieroglyphics.

[505] De Sacy (1758-1838), the great Arabist.

[506] Friedrich Christian Diez (1794-1876).

[507] Bekker: see above, n.446.

[508] A.F. Didot (1790-1876): Sandys iii 273.

[509] Dübner (1802-1867): Sandys iii 272. We still depend on his edition of 1842 for the greater part of the ancient scholia on Aristophanes. Carl Müller (Sandys iii 272-3; Bursian 898) edited the *Geographi Minores* (1855-61); he is not to be confused with C.F.W. Müller (see above, n.493).

[510] Weil (1818-1909): Sandys iii 258; on his work on Aeschylus, see Fraenkel, *Ag.* i 56.

[511] K.B. Hase (1780-1864): Sandys iii 272.

[512] On the Dindorfs, see below, n.534.

of the archaeologists Quatremer de Quincy and Raoul Rochette[513] was short-lived; but Jean-Antoine Letronne,[514] who was overshadowed by them all his life, made a lasting contribution to every subject he set his hand to and, in particular, gave a stimulus to archaeology in the best manner by the collected *Inscriptions de l'Egypte*, which he inaugurated, and by numerous articles which testify to his integrity and good sense as a critic. On the appearance of a manuscript – the only manuscript – of the most important of the lesser geographers, he produced an excellent edition. The useful all-rounder Jean-François Boissonade[515] covered a wider field, and his *Anecdota* possess permanent value as a contribution to Byzantine studies. Emile Littré's[516] *Hippocrates*, which belongs to a mere passing phase in this great scholar's triumphant career, is a first-rate piece of work and awakened an interest in the study of ancient medicine which was taken up only much later in Germany. The world also had to wait long for anything comparable to Henri Martin's *Etudes sur le Timée de Platon*.[517] On the other hand, Le Bas's[518] collection of inscriptions was nothing more than raw material.

Theodor Bergk's[519] inexhaustible fertility in conjectural emendation and his tireless efforts to improve his own productions would in themselves be enough to make him the most considerable figure among Hermann's later pupils. Both these characteristics are exemplified by his great work, the *Poetae lyrici Graeci*, to which his collection, the first, of the

[513] A.C. Quatremer [*sic*] de Quincy (1755-1849): Sandys iii 263. Rochette (1783-1854): Sandys iii 264.

[514] Letronne (1787-1848): Sandys iii 264: he published his edition of the *Periplus* of Scylax in 1826.

[515] Boissonade (1774-1857; Sandys iii 249); he published the *editio princeps* of Babrius (in 1844) and the five volumes of *Anecdota Graeca*.

[516] Littré (1801-1881): Sandys iii 252.

[517] T.H. Martin (1813-1884): Sandys iii 256; his *Études sur le Timée de Platon* appeared in 1841.

[518] Philippe Le Bas (1794-1860): Sandys iii 264.

[519] Bergk (1812-1881): Sandys iii 146. The first edition of *Poetae Lyrici Graeci* appeared in 1843, the fourth in 1878-82; for the melic, elegiac and iambic poets the reprint of 1914-15 with Rubenbauer's indexes is still not entirely superseded. Bergk's history of Greek literature appeared in four volumes between 1872 and 1887 (index 1894).

fragments of Anacreon was a prelude. There is little critical recension to be found either here or elsewhere in his work, and much that is arbitrary; but his interests ranged over a wide field, extending from early Latin to the Monumentum Ancyranum and, in his last years, after he had retired from his professorship at Halle and was living at Bonn, to the topography of Roman Germany. Other subjects treated by him – almost always with success and always with originality – include the oldest Greek metre, mythology and astronomy, Empedocles and the papyrus of Chrysippus, the Hellenistic poets and the Philostrati. Each topic in turn completely absorbed his attention, so that his *History of Greek Literature* inevitably disintegrated into a series of self-contained essays.

Lachmann himself could not have carried out a more rigorous recension than Hermann Sauppe[520] produced for his and Baiter's joint edition of the Attic orators, to which he added an admirable volume of scholia and fragments. For Lysias, where Bekker had been deceived by an interpolated manuscript, Sauppe had already demonstrated in his celebrated *Epistula critica* that the Palatine manuscript was the one source that mattered. His texts of Demosthenes and Isocrates, on the other hand, are a classic example of exaggerated respect for the principle of sticking to the best manuscript. His interests also included politics and law as reflected in the orators and led him to the study of inscriptions, the Athenian constitution and topography, while he continued to give proof of his linguistic knowledge in the textual criticism of a large number of authors, so that his selected works deserve to be more widely read. His sketch of Velleius, a work of his youth, his analysis of the sources of Plutarch's *Pericles*, and his disentanglement of the sophist Antiphon from the orator of the same name, to take only a few examples, are first-rate performances.

In themselves, the achievements of Hermann Köchly[521] scarcely warrant special mention, for his criticism is usually

[520] Sauppe (1809-1893): Sandys iii 163; see Wilamowitz' obituary notice of him (*Kl. Schr.* vi 3f.). The mystery of the two Antiphons continues to perplex scholars even now.

[521] Koechly (1815-1876): Sandys iii 132; we still use his *Manetho* of 1868, despite the useful Loeb edition by W.G. Waddell (1940).

wild, though he has his occasional moments of inspiration. His attempts to deal with the *Iliad* in the manner of Lachmann are futile, and the inadequacy of the edition of the Greek writers on tactics which he produced in collaboration with Rüstow as military expert is not due solely to his lack of knowledge of the manuscripts. Köchly was something of a pioneer in the study of the later Greek epic however; for Manetho, for instance, we are still dependent on him. Otto Schneider's[522] *Nicandrea* is a different matter; it is equally judicious in its treatment of the text and in its handling of the literary problems involved. But in his Callimachus Schneider followed Meineke's example and was far too free in altering the text, a proceeding that was not conducive to the reconstruction of the poems, of which he collected the fragments with the greatest care. Tycho Mommsen[523] published an edition of Pindar in which every scrap of material bearing on the text was made available, even where it served no practical purpose – something that had never yet been done for any author, though we must wonder whether such prodigious industry was really worthwhile.

Moritz Haupt,[524] Hermann's son-in-law and pupil and Lachmann's friend and successor, was Lachmann's staunch and dedicated disciple in both German and classical scholarship and judged his mission to be the spreading of his master's gospel. Haupt's first publications were devoted to the development of Lachmann's ideas on the recension of Catullus, on which he based his own work on the poet, and in his elegantly produced editions of the *Triumviri amoris*[525] and of Horace he still held closely to Lachmann. These were followed by his Virgil, but we must note that in the *Appendix Virgiliana*,

---

[522] Otto Schneider (1815-1880): Sandys iii 157; on his *Callimachea* (1870-73), see Pfeiffer, *Callimachus* ii, 1953, xlvii, etc.

[523] Tycho Mommsen (1819-1900): Sandys iii 152. His *Pindar* appeared in 1864 and his *Beiträge zur Lehre der griechischen Präpositionen*, a work of great learning, in 1886-95.

[524] Haupt (1808-1874): Sandys iii 134; see H. Nettleship, *Lectures and Essays* i, 1885, 1f.; Kenney 110f. Wilamowitz at the start of his career was given the task of preparing his *Opuscula* (1875-76) for publication (see *Erinnerungen*, 2nd edn., 176).

[525] *Triumviri amoris*: see above, n.212.

instead of basing himself on the sound manuscript tradition, he emended the vulgate *e codicibus et ex ingenio*. His treatise on Calpurnius Siculus and Nemesianus will always be regarded as the model of a triumphantly successful piece of research; his treatise on the *Epicedion Drusi* was once regarded in the same light, but now we think of it as a particularly instructive example of much learning producing the wrong answer. In his later years the obligation to produce a short dissertation as a prelude to the *Indices lectionum* prevented him from carrying out larger plans, but in the *Indices* themselves he covered the whole field of classical literature, with special emphasis on Latin, and although in time conjectural emendation came to predominate, the reader is always conscious of his feeling for language and style. Everything Haupt wrote bears the impress of his forceful personality and passionate devotion to the cause of truth and right conduct as he saw them.

It was under Haupt's supervision that Lucian Müller[526] wrote his valuable *De re metrica poetarum Latinorum*. This augured well, but Müller's great gifts were fatally marred by faults of character, and it requires great effort to plough through the mass of his repulsively polemical writings for the sake of the occasional good things to be found in them.

Boeckh's successor, Adolf Kirchhoff,[527] must also be included in this period, since his best work belongs to it in point of time and character. As a pupil of Lachmann, Kirchhoff distinguished strictly in his recension of Euripides between the different families of manuscripts; once again this strictness was dearly bought, since he carried it so far as to ignore completely the apparently less trustworthy manuscripts. At first he let himself go in conjectural emendation, but later he swung too far in the other direction. In his Plotinus he showed himself a brilliant emendator, but he carved up the *Enneads* savagely. In his examination of the *Odyssey* he followed and improved on Lachmann's methods; it is odd that later, in his edition of Hesiod's *Works and Days*, he

[526] Lucian Müller (1836-1898): Sandys iii 189; his *De Re Metrica*, 2nd edn. 1894, is still useful.

[527] Kirchhoff (1826-1908): Sandys iii 478; see Wilamowitz' memorial speech (*Kl. Schr.* vi 40f.).

should have returned to the hypothesis of separate lays. Converted to epigraphy by Boeckh, he remained in charge of the *Corpus Inscriptionum Graecarum* for decades, edited the opening volume of the new Attic series and wrote important explanatory appendices to it. Even greater value attaches to Kirchhoff's history of the Greek alphabet, on which all subsequent work is based. If we add to these his Umbrian and Oscan studies and his studies of the runic alphabet of the Goths, we are left with a body of work of which every part contributed to the advancement of learning and some parts gave it fresh impulse, and which is so extensive that one may fairly doubt whether anybody ever accomplished more in so many fields in so short a time; that we must always remember to his credit.

Jacob Bernays[528] occupies a unique position. Hermann Usener, who knew Bernays intimately, has given us such a masterly sketch of him in his preface to the collected minor works[529] that a reference to it is all we need give here: it contains all there is to be said, if we read between the lines. Bernays' elegant and subtle style makes everything he wrote a joy to read; more's the pity that he gradually degenerated into a server-up of trifles. His treatises on Aristotle's theory of drama are still controversial; but as an example of method his greatest achievement perhaps was to have disentangled the fragments of Theophrastus on Piety embedded in Porphyry. It looks obvious now, but at the time it pointed to a method of source-analysis that leads to the recovery of lost works. Some

[528] Bernays (1824-1881): Sandys 176; see Momigliano, 'Jacob Bernays', *Proc. of Royal Netherlands Academy*, 1969; also Wolfgang Schmid, 'Bonner Gelehrte', *150 Jahre Rheinische Friedrich-Wilhelms-Universität zu Bonn, 1818-1968*, 1968, 137f.; Hans Bach, *Jacob Bernays: ein Beitrag zur Emanzipations-geschichte der Juden und zur Geschichte des deutschen Geistes im 19. Jahrhundert*, 1974.
[529] *Gesammelte Abhandlungen*, 2 vols, 1885. See Wilamowitz' *Erinnerungen* 2nd edn., 87, for an interesting account of his relations with Bernays in Bonn. Bernays's connections with England had historical importance. He made friends with Mark Pattison, who shared his interest in Scaliger (see above, n.206). Through Pattison he met Ingram Bywater (1840-1914), whose first book, a collection of the fragments of Heraclitus, shows his influence; so does Bywater's later important work on the *Poetics* and *Ethics* of Aristotle.

years later Ingram Bywater,[530] a scholar whose perspicacity matched his learning, succeeded similarly in discovering fragments of the Aristotelian *Protrepticus* in Iamblichus, which led to further discoveries in the same compilation.[531]

The Lobeck tradition was carried on by Karl Lehrs,[532] whose first publications gave promise of a great career. His *De Aristarchi studiis Homericis* will always retain its relevance. Many of Lehrs's popular essays can also be recommended, for this uncompromising classicist possessed a sense of beauty, even if his energies were devoted mostly to dry subjects. Only in his *Herodiani scripta tria* does Herodian himself come to life as a person; Lentz's reconstruction, an unskilful piece of work built on shaky foundations, was inspired by Lehrs and followed him slavishly.[533] Lehrs's *Quaestiones epicae* also contains good things, but in his treatment of Hesiod's *Works and Days* are to be seen the first signs of that destructive spirit which was responsible for his incredible mishandling of Horace and the *Heroides* of Ovid.

Wilhelm and Ludwig Dindorf[534] lived in Leipzig as free-lance scholars. Wilhelm in particular made editing his trade; Ludwig excelled him in attention to the finer points of language, but was less well known. Wilhelm was able and dexterous, knew his Greek thoroughly and took care to keep abreast of current fashion, as his repeated editions of the tragedians show. This won him a higher reputation than he deserved. If good materials were at hand he used them, but if not he managed without, so that his editions vary greatly in value. None is definitive, and his work for the Clarendon Press (Clement and the Homeric Scholia) did harm to the

---

[530] Bywater was Regius Professor of Greek at Oxford from 1893 to 1908; the memoir by W.W. Jackson (1917) contains much interesting matter.

[531] On the present state of opinion regarding the *Protreptikos*, see I. Düring, *Aristotle's Protrepticus*, 1961.

[532] Lehrs (1802-1878): Sandys iii 107; his brother, F.S. Lehrs, was a friend of Wagner, and tried to teach him Greek.

[533] Lehrs' edition of Herodian appeared in 1848, that of August Lentz twenty years later.

[534] Wilhelm Dindorf (1802-1883): Sandys iii 144. Wilamowitz in his *Aeschylus* of 1914 called him 'dexterrimus ille editionum caupo'. That is a little hard; for a balanced judgment, see Fraenkel, *Ag.* i 53. Ludwig Dindorf (1805-1871): Sandys iii 144.

reputation of German scholarship. Finally he sank so low as to steal from the admirable Sophoclean Lexicon of Ellendt.[535]

At a time when many Greek authors appeared in editions that were unsatisfactory for their hasty and careless preparation and obtuse or captious criticism (Poppo's[536] bulky Thucydides and Stallbaum's[537] Plato are typical of the obtuse, all Rudolf Hercher's[538] editions of the captious variety), nevertheless soundly based and careful editions of many Latin prose-writers were also published, containing really valuable notes even when they were intended primarily for schools. It is enough to mention the best of these editors: Karl Halm[539] (Cicero, Quintilian, the *Rhetores Latini*), Roth[540] (Suetonius), Friedrich Haase[541] (Seneca and Tacitus), Heinrich Keil[542] (Pliny's *Letters*, the *Grammatici Latini*), Martin Hertz[543] (Aulus Gellius, Priscian, Livy) and Nipperdey,[544] whose Caesar was admired for the consistency with which he adhered to a single family of manuscripts, though this in fact was a weakness. Nipperdey's commentary on the *Annals* of Tacitus, on the other hand, had the merit, unusual at that time, of not concentrating on Tacitus' language at the expense of the history. Mommsen's *Solinus*[545] showed how a compiler has to be treated to make him serviceable, but few, unfortunately, followed Mommsen's example. The poets fared less well. Even Ovid,[546] Manilius and Lucan had to wait long

---

[535] F. Ellendt, *Lexicon Sophocleum*, 1834, 2nd edn., revised by H. Genthe 1872, last reprinted 1958.

[536] E.F. Poppo (1794-1866): Sandys iii 159. A third edition of his *Thucydides*, revised by J.M. Stahl, appeared in 1882-8.

[537] G. Stallbaum (1793-1861): Sandys iii 161.

[538] R. Hercher (1821-1878): Sandys iii 185.

[539] Halm (1809-1882): Sandys iii 195; see Pfeiffer, *Geist und Gestalt*, 1959, 119f.

[540] K.L. Roth (1811-1860; Bursian 959-60) published his *Suetonius* in 1858. The notice in Sandys iii 517 is confused; see Bursian 1149.

[541] Haase (1808-1867): Sandys iii 137.

[542] Keil (1822-1894): Sandys iii 202.

[543] Hertz (1818-1895): Sandys iii 199.

[544] Nipperdey (1821-1875): Sandys iii 117.

[545] See n.288 above.

[546] The manuscript tradition of Ovid's amatory works was not established before E.J. Kenney's Oxford edition of 1961; since then, F. Munari has discovered an important new manuscript (*Il Codice Hamilton 471 di Ovidio*,

for their manuscript tradition to be established. Exegesis lagged behind still further, though Rudolf Merkel's[547] *Fasti* made a useful contribution, even if Merkel failed to do justice to Ovid as an artist. The same weakness is even more apparent in his Apollonius Rhodius, where his elaborate *Prolegomena* deal with one aspect only of the poet's language.

Karl Friedrich Hermann,[548] on the other hand, who taught with great success at Marburg and Göttingen, devoted his life to work of an entirely different character from that of the textual critics we have been discussing. Hermann was a deeply learned man, and his volumes of antiquities, into which he packed a vast amount of material skilfully organised, must have met a need, judging by the number of times they were reprinted. But such handbooks are soon forgotten. More important were his revision of the text of Plato, and certainly his *Life of Plato*, which was the first attempt to understand the development of Plato's thought, in contrast to the approach of Schleiermacher, or even Ast. Schneidewin[549] was a colleague at Göttingen; the two men died at about the same time and may be said to have upheld the Göttingen tradition in their aversion to the exclusive pursuit of textual criticism. Not that the Göttingen school by any means abjured it totally – witness Ahrens and Adolf Emperius,[550] who was an excellent critic, as his edition of Dio Chrysostom shows; it was only Emperius' early death that prevented his commentary from coming to anything. Schneidewin also engaged in textual criticism, in his editions of the Greek lyric poets – which Bergk took over forcibly – and of the newly discovered *Elenchus* of Hippolytus, in which he collaborated with the theologian Duncker. Schneidewin's main object, however, was interpretation,

---

Rome, 1965). The first real apparatus criticus to Lucan appeared in the edition of C. Hosius (1st edn. 1892; 3rd edn. 1913). The first edition of Manilius that supplied adequate information about all the four main manuscripts was that of M. Bechert (1900; see Housman, *Manilius* i, 2nd edn. 1937, xxii, for the use Bechert made of his advantage).

[547] Merkel (1811-1885): Sandys iii 193.
[548] K.F. Hermann (1804-1855): Sandys iii 162.
[549] F.W. Schneidewin (1810-1856): Sandys iii 120.
[550] A. Emperius (1806-1841): Sandys iii 120; he also made a good contribution to the textual criticism of Aeschylus. Ahrens: see n.557 below.

which was certainly a merit, though he was not very profound. His edition of Sophocles cannot be described as important, though many generations of schoolboys first read the poet in it.[551]

By a freak of fortune, Schneidewin was succeeded as editor by a scholar of exactly opposite type, August Nauck,[552] who was interested only in the critical side, claiming that Sophocles could never have written anything that was not absolutely perfect; what constituted perfection was of course a matter for the editor's taste. Nauck was already a man of exceptionally wide reading when he produced his edition of the fragments of Aristophanes of Byzantium, which is still authoritative. Subsequently, while he and Kirchhoff were assistant masters at the Joachimsthal Gymnasium, he turned his attention to Euripides, of whom he ranks as one of the best emendators. His *Fragmenta tragicorum Graecorum* is the last word in completeness, reliability and convenient arrangement.[553] When he accepted a chair in St Petersburg, his development as a scholar ceased, as his valuable editions of Porphyry and Iamblichus, his treatment of the text of Homer – in which he followed Bekker – and his numerous critical articles all bear out. It is thanks to Nauck's teaching that Russia has produced a succession of respectable Greek scholars since his day.

Latin Grammar was still treated very much on traditional lines. Hand[554] even used an old book by the sixteenth-century scholar Tursellinus as the basis of his work on the particles. (Compare Hermann's use of the Jesuit Vigerus'[555] book on Greek idioms.) Latin was still studied too much in isolation,

---

[551] Wilamowitz is a little hard on Schneidewin; for more favourable judgments, see Denys Page, *Poetae Melici Graeci*, 1962, vi, and Fraenkel, *Ag.* i 54.

[552] Nauck (1822-1892): Sandys iii 192.

[553] 2nd edn. 1889; even now, after the publication of so much material, it is only partially superseded for Aeschylus and not at all for Euripides. His revision of Schneidewin's *Sophocles* contains highly intelligent work; he was much too ready to emend, but his conjectures, even when they must be rejected, often stimulate critical thinking.

[554] F.G. Hand (1786-1851; Sandys iii 117) published in four volumes (1829-45) his work based upon the old book of H. Tursellinus (b.1545; Sandys ii 369).

[555] Fr. Vigerus (1591-1647): Sandys ii 287.

# 148    *History of Classical Scholarship*

while the other Italian languages remained untouched. The
seal was broken by Mommsen with his *Dialects of Southern Italy*,
which was a splendid book, however much he may have
repudiated it in his old age. Umbrian was discovered shortly
afterwards by Aufrecht[556] and Kirchhoff. Kirchhoff also
carried forward Mommsen's pioneer work on Oscan.
Heinrich Ludolf Ahrens[557] had begun to use the new methods
on the Greek dialects as early as 1839, when there were still
very few available inscriptions. Though handicapped early on
by eye trouble, Ahrens did good work on the bucolic poets,
made numerous contributions to etymology, and finally took
up Cypriote; he was a scholar of much independence who
never received due recognition. Karl Wilhelm Krüger[558]
surpassed his predecessors in exact knowledge of Attic syntax,
and his Greek Grammar, which superseded Buttmann's in the
schools, marks a definite advance, though his logical
distinctions are confusing. His editions of Herodotus, Arrian
and Thucydides with grammatical notes are equally good,
and the Thucydides, a concise and straightforward work,
leaves both Poppo and Johannes Classen[559] far behind.
Thucydides was the wrong subject for Classen, an amiable
and venerable pedagogue, a classicist in the best sense of the
word, whose observations on Homeric usage are some of the
finest studies of their kind. As regards accidence, of course,
everything is obsolete that ignores the science of language founded
by Bopp.[560] To have won acceptance for the science is the chief
title to fame of Georg Curtius;[561] his own books, once a house-
hold word, are out of date, but only because of the rapid
strides that have since been made in his department. It was

[556] T. Aufrecht (1822-1907); see Sandys iii 478; on Kirchhoff, see above, n.527.

[557] H.L. Ahrens (1809-1881): Sandys iii 120; Pfeiffer, *HCS* ii 187-8); 'a
very great grammarian and a masterly editor': Fraenkel, *Ag.* i 55.

[558] Krüger (1798-1874): Sandys iii 119. *Griechische Sprachlehre für Schulen*
(5th edn. 1875-77) is still extremely useful, especially since his *Thucydides*
(2nd edn. 1858-60) constantly refers to it.

[559] Classen (1806-1891): Sandys iii 159; *Thukydides*, 3rd to 5th edn.,
revised by J. Steup, 1900-22.

[560] Franz Bopp (1791-1867): Sandys iii 205. Some would say its founder
was Wilhelm von Humboldt (see n.416, and Pfeiffer, *HCS* ii 185).

[561] G. Curtius (1820-1885): Sandys iii 207.

inevitable that grammar should cease to be the preserve of classical scholars, because it is no longer possible to deal with phonology and morphology in the context of a single language.

In ancient philosophy the main emphasis during the period was on Aristotle; this was a triumph for Bekker's edition. Adolf Trendelenburg[562] embraced the whole Aristotelian system, with special emphasis on the logic. Theodor Waitz[563] expounded the *Organon*, Schwegler[564] and Bonitz[565] the *Metaphysics*, Aubert and Wimmer the zoology. The *Rhetoric*, *Politics* and *Poetics* were the province of pure scholars. The main aid to interpretation was Bonitz's *Index*, which by its very limitations showed perfectly how such things should be done. Bonitz also evinced his superiority to Schleiermacher as an expositor of Plato in his attractive studies of several of the dialogues. Ast's[566] *Platonic Lexicon* is unsatisfactory, though unfortunately still indispensable. Ast had a sound knowledge of Plato, and his emendations also were sound, but he inaugurated the fashion for athetisation.

Of the Presocratics, the philosophical poets were edited by the Dutchman Simon Karsten,[567] and Bernays left his mark on the study of Heraclitus, especially (as we have seen) by his use of the newly discovered fragments in the *Elenchus* of Hippolytus. Meanwhile Krische[568] pointed the way to a proper assessment of the Pythagoreans with his dissertation on their political aims. Hellenistic philosophy, on the other hand, was still neglected. All this achievement pales into insignificance beside Eduard Zeller's[569] great *History of Greek Philosophy*. It was Zeller who showed where the theological

[562] Trendelenburg (1802-1872): Sandys iii 174.

[563] Waitz (1821-1864): Sandys iii 174.

[564] Schwegler (1819-1857): Sandys iii 174. His Roman history (1853-8) was important.

[565] Hermann Bonitz (1814-1888): Sandys iii 174. *Index Aristotelicus*, 1870.

[566] G.A.F. Ast (1778-1841): Sandys iii 112. We now have a *Word Index to Plato*, Brandwood, 1976.

[567] Karsten (1802-1864): Sandys iii 289.

[568] A.B. Krische published his *De societatis a Pythagora in urbe Crotoniatarum conditae scopo politico* in 1830. See Bursian 920.

[569] Zeller (1814-1908): Sandys iii 477.

150    *History of Classical Scholarship*

school of Tübingen had the advantage over the philologists by following the course of an intellectual movement through the persons of its leading figures: in other words, in addition to sorting out the different dogmatic systems to which it gave rise, studying its historical context. That was in the true Aristotelian spirit. Zeller's book had the same orientation. His influence was incalculable and is still felt, even where scholarship has moved away from him. May heaven preserve us from any attempt to bring him up to date by revision, like a schoolbook! Such a masterpiece should be left as the author wrote it; for we are interested in what he has to say even on matters which he would judge differently if he were alive today.[570]

Archaeology was still a poor relation among university departments. It was almost completely unrepresented at headquarters, and Bonn was the only place that possessed a museum of plaster casts devoted to teaching. It had been inaugurated by Welcker. The curator was now Otto Jahn,[571] who was also in charge of the classical teaching and quite capable of running both. At one time Jahn devoted himself almost entirely to Latin epigraphy, and he later published a number of Latin texts from the manuscripts with some help from Lachmann. But this was not his true bent. He had an overmastering urge to expound, and he did so in his edition of Persius, of which it may be said, as Scaliger said of Casaubon's, that the sauce was better than the fish. He also produced editions of Cicero's *Orator* and *Brutus*, in which he showed he understood better than his predecessors that the author's purpose had been to defend his own views in face of the rising tide of narrow Atticism. To accompany his lectures Jahn

[570] The revision by Wilhelm Nestle appeared in 1921-3; the last reprint was in 1963.

[571] Jahn (1813-1869; Sandys iii 220) made a greater impression on Wilamowitz than any other professor who taught him in Bonn; see *Erinnerungen*, 2nd edn., 86f. and Eduard Schwartz, *Gesammelte Schriften* i, 1938, 317-19. Nietzsche's special patron at Bonn had been Ritschl, who was responsible for his becoming a full professor at Basle at twenty-four, and the quarrel between Jahn and Ritschl (see above, n.504) descended to their eminent pupils; Jahn had annoyed Nietzsche by criticising Wagner, and nothing in the *Birth of Tragedy* angered Wilamowitz more than an unkind allusion to Jahn. Jahn also found time to write the classic biography of Mozart. See Lloyd-Jones, *BG*, ch. 14; cf. M.S. Silk and J.P. Stern, *Nietzsche on Tragedy*, 1981.

issued a number of well-chosen and well-produced texts which, in their revised form, are still deservedly popular. When he wrote on the monuments, particularly on sarcophagi and vase-paintings, and on minor objects of all sorts, he expounded them in the manner of Zoëga. The result was applied classical scholarship rather than expert art criticism. Art criticism may rank higher in the intellectual scale, but cannot ignore what the artist or craftsman was trying to create or represent. Unfortunately these writings, which have never been collected, are little read, but Jahn's studies on the dovecote at the Villa Pamphili, for example, the Ficoroni casket, the rape of Europa and the Evil Eye are worth reading. Of Jahn's literary remains his book on the Greek *Bilderchroniken*, which were really a development of book illustration, was completed by his nephew Michaelis,[572] and his great plan for a collection of sarcophagi was taken up by the Institute. Nor must we overlook the ground he broke in his lectures. The consensus among later scholars on the nature of Hellenistic poetry and art and the change-over to classicism, the general ideas underlying Carl Dilthey's[573] admirable dissertation on Callimachus' *Acontius and Cydippe* and Helbig's[574] book on the Pompeian wall-paintings, and the parts of Couat's *Poésie Alexandrine*[575] taken from German books on the subject – all ultimately derive from Jahn. The picture is no longer adequate, but still represents the accepted view.

The credit for bringing the artistic side of archaeology up to standard belongs to Heinrich Brunn,[576] who studied under Welcker and Ritschl and, in his *History of the Greek Artists*, produced something approaching a *historia critica* in the grand style. In Rome, where he was secretary of the Institute, Brunn found his true vocation in the task of analysing the style of

---

[572] A. Michaelis (1835-1910).

[573] Carl Dilthey (b.1839), brother of the philosopher Wilhelm Dilthey; on his *De Callimachi Cydippa*, 1863, see Pfeiffer, *Callimachus* ii, 1953, xlvi.

[574] W. Helbig (1839-1915) published his *Pompeianische Wandmalerei* in 1868-73.

[575] A. Couat (d.1899) published *La Poésie Alexandrine* in 1882; the English translation by James Loeb appeared in 1931 (see Pfeiffer, *AKS* 151, who points out that Couat, like a much more important scholar, Erwin Rohde, thought that Hellenistic poetry contained a 'romantic' element).

[576] Brunn (1822-1894): Sandys iii 221; Rumpf 80.

sculptures and allotting them their places in the development.
The truth is that archaeology is faced with masses of works by
unnamed artists and masses of artists of whom there are
records but no known works. It must try to discover their
connections, though there are always likely to be some of each
that are not easily disposed of. We may imagine the rejoicing
and expectations that were aroused by the identification of the
*Doryphorus* of Polyclitus, the *Tyrannicides* of Critius, the *Eirene
and Plutus* of Cephisodotus, the *Apoxyomenos* of Lysippus and
the votive statues erected at Athens by Attalus I of Pergamum
– discoveries in which Carl Friedrichs[577] played an important
part before his untimely death. In his later days in Rome and
afterwards at Munich, Brunn trained the next generation of
archaeologists, who were able to deal with genuine Greek
work quite differently from their master. Brunn himself to the
end of his life remained so unfamiliar with archaic art that he
actually mistook authentic Attic vases for Etruscan copies.
Incredible as this may seem now, it should serve to remind us,
as we contemplate the wealth of our modern collections, how
much truth the founding fathers of archaeology managed to
glean from the scanty materials at their disposal.

Insofar as mythology consists of heroic saga, Welcker and
Otfried Müller had done pioneer work, but too little attention
was paid to the religious side of mythology, as a result of the
rise of a new theory of symbolism. It is to be hoped that
Nägelsbach's[578] otherwise useful *Homeric Theology* will prove to
have been the last attempt to find, or seek, analogies with
Christianity. The hunt for Indo-Germanic gods and the over-
estimation of the Indians were mainly, though not entirely,
responsible for the growth of a new kind of symbolism, which
saw the sun and the moon, the winds and the clouds in everything and, preoccupied with myth, forgot all about cults;[579]
with it went a crazy etymology, which turned Hermes into
Sarameyas and the Centaurs into the Gandharva. It was on

[577] Friederichs (1831-1871): Sandys iii 115; Rumpf 80.
[578] Nägelsbach (1806-1859): Sandys iii 106.
[579] Max Müller (1820-1900), at one time Professor of Comparative
Philology at Oxford, strongly believed in all this. So, unfortunately, did
W.H. Roscher (1845-1923); his invaluable *Lexikon der klassischen Mythologie* is to
some extent infected by it. On Müller, see Lloyd-Jones, *BG*, ch. 13.

this nature-symbolism that Ludwig Preller based his books on Greek and Roman mythology. Yet they were not only widely used but retained their usefulness, and were even worth recasting after his death.[580] This excellent scholar did service also to Roman topography and, through the source-book in which he collaborated with Heinrich Ritter, to the *historia philosophiae Graecae.*

Since neither Boeckh nor Otfried Müller's interests lay in that direction, political history was still where Niebuhr had left it, when suddenly from England came, first, Fynes Clinton's[581] *Fasti Hellenici* and *Fasti Romani*, which were long indispensable, and subsequently Grote's[582] epoch-making *History of Greece*, which treated Athenian democracy in terms of modern liberalism. The book is based on a conscientious study of the literary sources, and the writing is highly effective, in the manner of political pamphleteering. That indeed is what is is; but here at last was political history handled by a man who understood politics. This was a great advantage, for it cleared the air and forced even those most reluctant to face facts into recognising what the real forces are that govern the affairs of nations. This explains why Ernst Curtius'[583] *History of Greece*, in spite of the success its style secured it, contributed nothing to the advancement of learning; for it was steeped in the same old classicism that inspired Kaulbach's[584] painting *Die Blüte Griechenlands*, and the author, whom no one could fail to respect as a man, never outgrew his faith in that ideal conception, but proclaimed it to his dying day. Apart from securing the excavation of Olympia, Curtius' chief merit lies in his exploration of the country, which he brings most charmingly before the reader, especially in his book on the Peloponnese but also in essays such as that on road-making;

[580] L. Preller: see above, n. 471.

[581] Henry Fynes Clinton (1781-1852): Sandys iii 439. He received much assistance from Gaisford, and an extremely learned correspondence between the two men is preserved in the library of Christ Church, Oxford.

[582] Grote (1784-1871): Sandys iii 438; Momigliano, 'Grote and the study of Greek history', Inaugural Lecture at University College, London, 1952. (= *C* 213f. = *SH* 56f.); M.L. Clarke, *George Grote*, 1962.

[583] E. Curtius (1814-1896): Sandys iii 228.

[584] F.A. von Kaulbach (1850-1920), Munich academic painter.

his *History* is redolent of the scent of the Greek countryside. Heinrich Kiepert[585] too, as a result of his wanderings, became the cartographer of the ancient world. Many workers in other fields, especially collectors of inscriptions, have cause to thank him, for without his maps we should all be helpless.

The first mature historian of Greece in Germany was Johann Gustav Droysen,[586] who had enough of the poet in him for the task – his Aristophanes is as masterly as his Alexander. Nor did he shrink from detail, but worked on papyri even at that early date and demonstrated the spuriousness of the documents cited in Demosthenes' speech *On the Crown*. Anyone writing on the Hellenistic age treads where Droysen first trod. Droysen showed great boldness in building up his history of a period of which no continuous narrative has come down to us, though it represents the zenith of Greek power. So far no one has been able to reverse his assessment of the great conqueror, and documents by the hundred have confirmed his bold combinations more often than could humanly have been expected. Had Droysen carried his *History* further, Mommsen would never have painted so misleading a picture of the Hellenistic world by looking at it exclusively from the Roman point of view.

Arnold Schäfer's[587] book on Demosthenes is a work of unimpeachable learning but, one might add, essentially a scholar's book. Schäfer was shackled by his belief in a hero who can do no wrong, as Tillemont was by his Catholicism. At the same time the book remains as much a standard work

[585] Kiepert (1818-1899): Sandys iii 227. Unfortunately his unsurpassed atlases (*Atlas Antiquus*, 1859; *Atlas von Hellas*, 1872) have long been out of print. See n.168 above.

[586] Droysen (1808-1884): Sandys iii 230; Pfeiffer, *HCS* ii 188-9); see Momigliano, 'Per il Centenario dell' "Alessandro Magno" di J.G. Droysen', *Leonardo* 4, 1933, 510f. (= *C* 263f.): 'J.G. Droysen between Greeks and Jews', *History and Theory* 9, 1970, 139f. (= *QC* 109f.); also 'Genesi storica e funzione del concetto di ellenismo', *Giornale Critico della Filosofia Italiana* 16, 1935, 10f. (= *C* 165f.). Droysen invented the concept of a 'Hellenistic age'; we have to put it in this way in English, because for us the word 'Hellenism' means something quite different. The famous translation of Aeschylus first appeared in 1832, that of Aristophanes in 1835; both have been many times reprinted.

[587] Schäfer (1819-1883): Sandys iii 169.

as Tillemont's – something that critics who try to demolish him by political arguments always have to learn afresh.

Wilhelm Drumann's[588] history of Rome during the transition from the republican to the monarchical constitution collected and sifted a mass of material. It was shapeless certainly, but put together with enormous industry and care. Moreover, though the biographical treatment no doubt suited the character of the period and the records that have come down to us, it meant also that the author's conception of events was governed entirely by his opinion of the actors, and there he was a fanatical partisan. It is too often forgotten how much Drumann influenced Mommsen, and today scarcely anyone would deny that in consequence Mommsen's portrait of Cicero – and not only of Cicero – is a gross distortion, not to say a travesty, of the truth.[589] Drumann's history is as much a work of advocacy as Grote's – or as a speech of Cicero – but the orator alone is completely excused by the nature of his profession.

Finally we may mention Max Duncker's *History of the Ancient World*.[590] Not that it was of much importance in itself – but its linking of the East, about which so much was known by now, with the Greeks was a sound idea, and for this reason the book made a great impression. It could hardly produce a lasting effect, however, because the author remained an amateur in all the many fields in which he aspired to a historian's expert knowledge. Apart from anything else, a man must be able to read oriental records in the original before he can hope to succeed in such an attempt.

But enough of names. Their enumeration has been no less irksome to the author than to his readers, and yet there will no doubt be complaints that some name or other has been omitted. Of the work of the last fifty years it is possible to

---

[588] Drumann (1786-1861): Sandys iii 233; *Geschichte Roms in seinem Übergang von der republikanischen zur monarchischen Verfassung* (1831-44).

[589] The portrait of Cicero we find in Sir Ronald Syme's *Roman Revolution* (1939) is not so very different, despite all the differences between him and Mommsen.

[590] Duncker (1811-1886): Sandys iii 230.

provide only a general survey, without mentioning
individuals. Such a course is permissible because, among
other things, the old division into opposing schools is past, and
scholars now form a single world-wide commonwealth;
America too is beginning to set up museums and furnish its
quota of energetic workers in many fields.[590a] Scientific
scholarship has been steadily adapting itself to the age of
large-scale enterprise. Meanwhile one man who devoted his
superlative abilities to the service of this commonwealth and
set the machinery of co-operation in motion deserves separate
mention: Theodor Mommsen.[591] Mommsen read law at the
university, and the study of historical jurisprudence opened
his eyes to the need for a *Corpus inscriptionum Latinarum*, though
Jahn, in his concern to preserve Kellermann's literary
remains, early nourished the ambition of producing it himself.

Mommsen's first work was a spirited disquisition on the
Roman tribes, in which he criticised Niebuhr's *History* from a
lawyer's point of view, foreshadowing his *Roman Public Law*.
Then he headed south. His immediate task was to learn
epigraphy, which required a pilgrimage to San Marino. There
he sat at the feet of Bartolommeo Borghesi;[592] for once Luigi
Marini[593] had indicated the correct method, especially in his
*Atti dei Fratelli Arvali* and his *Papiri Diplomatici*, Borghesi had
shown his unrivalled familiarity with the whole body of
available inscriptions. This he did in his book on the *Fasti
consulares*, or lists of magistrates with their official careers, for
which epigraphy is the prime source. Mommsen learnt the
practical side of an epigrapher's work in his wanderings up
and down the kingdom of Naples. These brought him many
hardships, but at the same time made him familiar with the

[590a] Even when it was written, this was an understatement; still, it helps
one to appreciate the vast American achievement of the last fifty years.

[591] Mommsen (1817-1903): Sandys iii 197. The literature about
Mommsen is enormous. The biography by L. Wickert (from 1959) gives a
large amount of interesting information, but cannot see the wood for the
trees. See Alfred Heuss, *Theodor Mommsen und das 19. Jahrhundert*, 1956 and
Eduard Schwartz, *Gesammelte Schriften* i, 1938, 218f.; Wilamowitz, *Kl.
Schr.* vi, 11f.

[592] Borghesi (1781-1860): Sandys iii 244; Treves, 829f.

[593] Marini (1742-1815): Sandys ii 382.

country and its inhabitants, besides affording him a glimpse of pre-Roman times – of the Messapians and Oscans. In Rome he plunged into the battle over topography which was at its height, and personally conducted the struggle with the Berlin Academy over the *Corpus*; the trouble was that Boeckh could never be made to see what publication of a document entailed. It was only when Mommsen returned after several agitated years spent in quite different sorts of activity – when in the teeth of the Academy's opposition he published his *Inscriptions of the Kingdom of Naples*, and when his contributions to the transactions of the Leipzig Academy on epigraphy (still worth reading as an introduction to the subject) aroused general admiration – that opposition was silenced. His *History of Rome*, on the other hand, was written while he was Professor of Law at Zürich and later at Breslau; so far from being the product of spontaneous impulse, it was almost a stop-gap to fill a period of enforced leisure. For laymen it will always remain his masterpiece and be read like Gibbon – as indeed it should be, though with appropriate reservations. Its popularity was due only partly to its intrinsic merits. Partly, as with Grote, it was due to the introduction of contemporary political ideas – though also, of course, partly to its learning and style, and to the author's personality as revealed in his loves and hates.

Having reached the limit he had set himself on artistic grounds with the dictatorship of Julius Caesar, Mommsen broke off and turned to those studies which are the necessary preparation for writing the history of Rome as it should be written: chronology, the coinage, sources, and constitutional history. These are treated in his *Römische Forschungen*, and the new light thrown on them all gives the book a much wider interest than the title suggests. Then came *Roman Public Law*, in which Mommsen the jurist too wrote his own kind of history. Here, in making the fullest use of the inscriptions that were being assembled in the gigantic *Corpus*, he was collecting the materials for his history of the Empire. That he wrote only the fifth volume will always be of regret to laymen, but Mommsen knew better: he returned in time to the love of his youth to write, in his eighties, his *Roman Criminal Law*.

Philologists, historians and jurists are all indebted to Mommsen's minor works. His teaching has not been superseded in any department, for the correction of an occasional wrong conclusion hardly detracts from the effectiveness of the whole. More than to anyone else, we are grateful to Mommsen that our conception of Roman history from Romulus to Caesar is totally different from the account he himself gave of it.

The *Corpus* would not have been practicable without foreign help. French scholars assisted at the outset and again at the end. While Wilhelm Henzen[594] remained at its head the Institute in Rome was a familiar haunt of Italian scholars; and Giovanni de Rossi,[595] a true friend, took charge of the Christian inscriptions. As for Mommsen, the Italians regarded him almost as one of themselves. The *Corpus* could flourish only as long as all concerned acknowledged a single master. Mommsen put forward many more schemes than were ever carried out; for example, the *Prosopographia imperii Romani*. In connection with the *Monumenta Germaniae* he initiated, directed and to a large extent himself edited the series of *Auctores antiquissimi*, without which the *Thesaurus linguae Latinae*, another enterprise that owed its inception to his prompting, could never have been undertaken; nor could the Roman Institute have survived or the German *limes* been explored without his intervention. He was also the driving-force behind the *Association des Académies*, at one of whose meetings, to the astonishment of the French, he argued vainly for a *Corpus nummorum*. That was too much to ask for, and in the form in which it was started, at his instance, in Berlin, it would scarcely have been feasible even if somebody had stepped in to organise it internationally; for the French go their own way, and England has always maintained its pre-eminence in numismatics. Specialists of Imhoof-Blumer's[596] exceptional quality are in a class by themselves and not born in every century. In the world of science co-operative enterprise is no substitute for individual initiative – nobody knew that better than Mommsen – but often the individual will be able to carry out his plans only as a participant. He

---

[594] Henzen (1816-1887): Sandys iii 219.
[595] G.B. de Rossi (1822-1894): Sandys iii 247.
[596] Friedrich Imhoof-Blumer (1838-1920).

will need the help of a learned corporation, which has the advantage that it does not die and can therefore ensure continuity in the indispensable collection of material. That is much; but it is the man who puts it all into shape who matters in the long run. Large-scale enterprise necessarily entails the co-operation of all civilised nations. Anyone who does not see that does not know the meaning of scholarship – and anyone who sees it but nevertheless tries to make difficulties is guilty of the sin against the Holy Ghost. But he is not mocked and in him we trust.

The *Instituto di Correspondenza Archeologica* was the first attempt at an international association of its kind, and when it became the German Institute and established itself also in Athens, the French reorganised their *Ecole* on the same pattern and the English, Americans, Austrians and Italians soon followed suit. The Greeks deserve the warmest thanks for allowing everyone a free hand and later their active participation. Over long years there was much more co-operation than competition in Athens, and that can never be totally forgotten. The uncovering of Olympia by the Germans[597] marked the end of the era of indiscriminate pillage and the introduction of sound methods of excavation, which were subsequently perfected on many sites. Every nation dug away at some piece of classic ground to the best of its ability, and eventually the discoveries of papyri in Egypt by the natives led to an organised search for these precious objects.[598] Finds of every description multiplied amazingly, and the stones and remains of books and documents have put an entirely new face on Greek literature. The monumental tradition goes back much further than the arrival of the Indo-Germanic immigrants in the two peninsulas, and the barriers which formerly isolated the historical memory of Europe from Asia and Egypt have been swept away; even if we still treat European history as beginning with Homer, we have cast our minds back as far as Menes,[599] or even further. Crete has been

[597] Olympia excavations, 1875-80; see Rumpf 95.

[598] See Turner, op.cit., in n.634.

[599] Menes was the legendary Pharaoh of the First Dynasty who was supposed to have united Upper and Lower Egypt by conquering the Delta.

revealed as the centre of an advanced civilisation which radiated in all directions during the second millennium B.C.;[600] and, nearer our own times, we can no longer separate what is Roman from what is Byzantine or Teutonic, or what is Greek from what is Syrian or Arab. The barriers have been lowered too between archaeology, classical and Christian, and scholarship. The monumental and literary traditions are inextricably intertwined. The science of antiquity is no longer classical, nor even claims to be. It is what it should be, an organic whole. Even so it falls within the ambit of an all-inclusive historical-cum-literary science, which it borders and by which it is also influenced. Archaeology, at the same time, is a part of the general study of art, Teutonic law throws light on Greek, and we look for analogies everywhere. We can even get Attic tragedy into sharper focus by contrasting it with modern.

The expansion of large-scale enterprise and the new discoveries have exercised an increasingly decisive influence on scientific scholarship. Excavation of ancient sites and the scrutiny of every scrap of evidence brought up from the earth have been so prevalent that the shortest way to describe the progress achieved is to glance briefly at the territories of the former Roman Empire. This development would have seemed fantastic not merely to Hermann and Lachmann but even to Boeckh; Otfried Müller would have understood and welcomed it. We now recognise Egypt and Mesopotamia[601] as the cradles of civilisation. Egypt provides the yardstick by which to date the Cretan-Mycenaean finds. Both free-standing sculpture and the column originated there; so, ultimately, did our alphabet. From Babylon came astronomy, and in its wake astrology, the latter containing an admixture of Egyptian elements.[602] It is only in our own day that this

---

For a modern treatment of the problems concerning him, see W.B. Emery, *Archaic Egypt* (Pelican Books, 1961; reprinted, 1972).

[600] Sir Arthur Evans (1851-1941) was excavating in Crete between 1899 and 1907; his work at Knossos was followed by that of the Italians at Phaistos.

[601] See G. Roux, *Ancient Iraq* (Penguin Books, 1966).

[602] See F. Cumont, *Astrology and Religion among the Greeks and Romans*, 1912

important pseudo-science and pseudo-religion has been investigated and properly understood, thanks to the magnificent work of a few pioneers. Our knowledge of the Hittites[603] and other gradually Hellenised peoples of Asia Minor has reached a point at which we can look forward to the day when, with the discovery of the key to the language, a flood of light will be shed on ancient Cretan civilisation, and at the same time on the age of the Greek heroes and sea-rovers, even though that age speaks to us primarily and essentially through its art. Only now that the gulf between the Heroic age and the age of Homer, with its geometrical style, is unmistakable has it become possible to understand the historical background of the epic sagas.[604] By no means all the chief places in the Hellenised coastal strip of Asia Minor and on the islands have been uncovered, but enough has been revealed to enable us, not indeed to visualise the old Ionia, but to gain a more vivid impression of the land as it was in Hellenistic and Roman times,[605] while from inscriptions there and in the mother country, where the destruction has almost invariably been greater, we have been able to build up the history of the Hellenistic age stone by stone.[606]

Architecture had entirely new building-types to work on, such as the town hall, the library, the fortified city and the lighthouse. We still do not know the purpose of the *tholos* at Epidaurus,[607] and there is conflicting opinion about the various theatres. There seems to be no immediate prospect of reconciling the evidence of the plays, as interpreted by the commentators, with the theories of the architects. What is new is that we can trace the whole lay-out of a town, whether it resulted from haphazard growth, as at Athens and Rome, or

(paperback edition, 1960); O. Neugebauer, *The Exact Sciences in Antiquity* (paperback edition, 1957).

[603] See O.R. Gurney, *The Hittites* (Penguin Books, 2nd edn. 1954).

[604] See G.S. Kirk, *The Songs of Homer*, 1962 (abbreviated version called *Homer and the Epic* in paperback, 1965); C.M. Bowra, *Homer*, 1972.

[605] See J.M. Cook, *The Greeks in Ionia and the East*, 1962.

[606] M.I. Rostovtzev, *Social and Economic History of the Hellenistic World*.

[607] This is still true; see the balanced account of the various theories given by Alison Burford, *The Greek Temple Builders at Epidaurus*, 1969.

from deliberate planning, as at Priene and Pompeii.[608] Now that Pompeii is no longer unique, its true significance is at last being recognised. The rubbish-heaps of the Acropolis dating from the Persian Wars have yielded precious remains of archaic art and through them certain firm dates.[609] At first people looked only at the paintings on the vases, because they were the richest source of information about the heroic sagas and everyday life. This aspect is perhaps unduly neglected today; but it is entirely right that pottery, of which we possess examples from every period, should now be seen as the most abundant and authentic source for the history of craftsmanship.[610] At the same time, certain inferences regarding the major arts can be drawn from the paintings, and now that we also have the painted gravestones of Demetrias and various other objects, mostly Etruscan, the production of at least an outline of the history of ancient painting no longer seems beyond the bounds of possibility.[611] Some of the gaps can be filled from the rich burials of South Russia, where the development of a culture can now be traced from the Ionian civilisation down to Byzantine times.[612] It also fanned out far into the north, though it is not for nothing that the Goths were also long established there; this Graeco-Scythian civilisation is still wrongly treated as a subject on its own.

The soil of southern Italy and Sicily[613] has yielded little that adds to our knowledge of the Greek past, but it has provided a great deal of information about the earlier inhabitants. In the Terramare of North Italy and in Samnium and Apulia, not to

[608] See R.E. Wycherley, *How the Greeks Built Cities*, 2nd edn. 1962; paperback.1967.

[609] See H. Payne and G.M. Young, *Archaic Marble Sculpture from the Acropolis*, 2nd edn. 1950; R.J. Hopper, *The Acropolis*, 1971.

[610] See R.M. Cook, *GPP*, 2nd edn. 1972. For an account of the work of Beazley, which has transformed the subject, see B. Ashmole, *Proceedings of the British Academy* 56, 1970, 443f.

[611] C.M. Robertson, *Greek Painting*, 1959.

[612] See John Boardman, *The Greeks Overseas* (Pelican Books, 2nd edn. 1973), ch.6. Fundamental studies on Greek archaeology in the Black Sea area are those of Sir Ellis Minns, *Scythians and Greeks*, 1913 and M.I. Rostovtzev, *Iranians and Greeks in South Russia*, 1922.

[613] See Boardman, op.cit., ch.5; also L. Bernabo Brea, *Sicily Before the Greeks*, 2nd edn. 1968.

mention Etruria, excavation, reduced to a fine art by the
Italians, has also brought so much to light that the need for a
solution to the ethnological problems involved has become
pressing. The time is ripe for a comprehensive account of the
culture of the Apulians, Oscans and Etruscans. The essential
aim in each case is to penetrate beneath the superficial
Hellenism to the native bedrock, and although Livy's
traditional version of events down to the war with Pyrrhus is
proving less and less dependable, especially since we now
possess two actual inscriptions dating from the period of the
kings,[614] Italian history is revealed to us by the monuments.

Roman, and to some extent even Punic, Africa was
wonderfully well preserved all through the period during
which the country was a desert. Whole cities are still standing.
Mosaics mark the sites of the country-houses, and the pattern
of agricultural holdings round Carthage can still be traced in
the boundary-lines of the allotments.[615] Inscriptions have
multiplied a hundredfold in the last fifty years, enabling us to
reconstruct the world of Apuleius and Augustine – and what
an uninspiring world it was! Spain, with its Iberians and
Celts, is only just beginning to be revealed, but the influence of
Massilia, and even of earlier Greek settlements, is already
unmistakable.[616] The Elche[617] head rose out of the earth like
Pandora: what will come next? The camp in which Scipio and
Polybius sat before Numantia is known again,[618] and its
discovery has moved the Spaniards themselves to join the
general search. Roman civilisation of the Rhine valley far
beyond inner Gaul, the splendid buildings of Trier,[619] the forts
and palisades of the *limes*,[620] the cult of the Mother and the

[614] See A. Alföldi, *Early Rome and the Latins*, 1967 (rev. R.M. Ogilvie, *Cl. Rev.* 1966, 94), and A. Momigliano, *JRS* 57, 1967, 211f. = *Quarto Contributo* 487f.); Momigliano, 'Interim report on the origins of Rome', *JRS* 53, 1963, 95f. (= *TC* 545f.).

[615] G. Charles-Picard, *La Civilisation de l'Afrique romaine*, 1959.

[616] C.H.V. Sutherland, *The Romans in Spain, 217 B.C.-117 A.D.*, 1939.

[617] A fifth-century bust of a woman in Madrid; see *Monuments Piot*, iv, 1897, plate xiii, or *Enciclopedia dell'Arte Antica* iv, 1961, p.73; it has been thought to show Greek influence.

[618] Adolf Schulten, *Numantia*, 1905-1912.

[619] E.M. Wightman, *Roman Trier and the Trevori*, 1970.

[620] C.M. Wells, *The German Policy of Augustus*, 1972.

deities of the cross-roads, the network of highways – all these
are being discovered and examined, and together they present
a vivid picture to the imagination. This investigation – which
has taught men to recognise the sites of wooden buildings by
the colour of the soil – is being extended beyond Roman to
free Germany, and the day will come when the exact location
of Varus' defeat will finally be identified. Just as the
innumerable independent nations were welded together to
form one Empire, so there grew up an Imperial art, essentially
uniform in spite of its provincial overtones; but controversy
still rages over the question whether oriental influences
predominated in its later developments or whether Rome
remained the artistic capital. Whatever the truth, Byzantium,
the New Rome, was essentially the heir of orientalised
Hellenism and as such time and time again impressed the
superiority of its ancient culture upon western Europe, until it
finally handed over the literature, and with it the intellectual
heritage, of ancient Greece to the keeping of the west. We now
have a separate Byzantine scholarship, which will make a
fruitful contribution to the study of antiquity only when it
begins to study the Byzantines for their own sake.

What an immense variety of tasks we are confronted with
by this successful exploration of the monuments! Archaeology
and history have coalesced so completely that the study of art,
to say nothing of the careers of individual artists, has come to
occupy an even less important place in archaeology than the
classics occupy in the history of literature. The assembling in
vast *corpora* of the mass of archaeological material – which, for
inscriptions, has been attempted but not accomplished – is an
unattainable ideal. This makes the achievement of the one
scholar who had a truly synoptic view of the whole and who
tried to reduce it to order by main force (the only way) all the
more deserving of admiration. We shall therefore name him,
though his tragically brief career belongs to a period later than
our limit – Adolf Furtwängler.[621]

Though new accessions in the way of literary monuments
have been less numerous, their effect has been comparable.
What did we know of Roman municipal law before the

[621] Furtwängler (1853-1907): see Rumpf 119f., etc.

discovery of the bronze tablets of Salpensa,[622] Malaca and Urso? All that piecing together of constitutional references in the grammarians with which we had to be content before was made superfluous by the discovery of Aristotle's *Constitution of Athens*.[623] Our assessment of what we possessed of Pindar[624] and the Lesbian poets has changed completely since, in addition to newly discovered work of theirs, we were given Alcman,[625] Corinna, Bacchylides and Timotheus.[626] And how much more clearly do we see Plautus' Roman quality now that we are able to compare him with Menander![627]

It is the same with Christian literature. Here the newcomers are the *Didache*, the *Gospel and Apocalypse of Peter*, the *Psalms of Solomon*, Aristides' *Apology*, much of Hippolytus and various other Gnostic writings; also the tombstone of Abercius.[628]

[622] Lex Salpensana: charter of the modern Facialcazar near Utrera. Lex Malacitana: charter of the Spanish town that is now Malaga, issued by Domitian. Lex Ursonensis: charter of the town that is now Osuna, based on an act issued by Mark Antony on behalf of Julius Caesar. See E.G. Hardy, *Three Spanish Charters and other Documents*, 1912.

[623] Published from a papyrus in the British Museum in 1890. The main contribution to its exploitation was made by Wilamowitz, *Aristoteles und Athen*, 1893.

[624] A fair number of fragments of Pindar, Sappho and Alcaeus from papyri were published during Wilamowitz' lifetime; a good many more have appeared since.

[625] The famous Mariette papyrus containing part of a maiden-song by Alcman was published in 1863 (see Denys Page, *Alcman: The Partheneion*, 1951). Since Wilamowitz' death other important fragments have been discovered.

[626] Wilamowitz himself published important fragments of Corinna and Timotheus. Most of what we have of Bacchylides comes from a papyrus in the British Museum published in 1897, though other new fragments have been published since.

[627] Wilamowitz did important work on the great Cairo papyrus of Menander, published in 1907; since his death extensive new fragments have been discovered (see the OCT by F.H. Sandbach, 1972, and the commentary by A.W. Gomme and F.H. Sandbach, 1973). Since the death of Wilamowitz papyri have increased our knowledge of early Greek lyric (Archilochus, Stesichorus), Greek tragedy and Hellenistic poetry (especially Callimachus), and many other Greek authors.

[628] The *Didache* is a brief early Christian manual of ethics and behaviour, probably of the second century A.D. The only manuscript, written in 1056, was discovered in 1875; see Chadwick *EC* 46. Fragments of the apocryphal gospel and apocalypse attributed to St. Peter, both probably written during

Classical scholars gave much-needed help in collecting the pre-Nicene writings, and also clarified the history of the post-Nicene church by ending its intolerable divorce from the history of the Empire.[629] Nor is that all. Others besides the foolish dabblers who have turned Jesus into an Aryan, or amused themselves by disputing his existence, have been busy with the subject of Christian origins, and much zeal and erudition have gone into the reconstruction, from later phenomena, of a mystery religion, half Greek, half oriental, which is supposed to have exercised a decisive influence on the development of Christian dogma. Though the case is far from conclusive, the fact remains that the investigation of the religions of the Imperial period – Mithraism[630] and the cults of Jupiter Dolichenus[631] and the Sun-God – has demonstrated the existence in Christianity of an admixture of elements derived from these religions, perhaps even of an analogy between Christianity and them. The inscriptions relating to the Roman army are especially important as showing its orientalisation, but they throw light also on what one may call the official religion of the Empire; and, even more than the papyri, the inscriptions of the Imperial period have enabled us to understand the genesis of the colonate – in other words, the relapse into serfdom, which so long remained a riddle.[632]

---

the second century A.D., were found at Akhmim in Egypt in 1886-7; in 1910 an Ethopic version of the gospel was discovered. A Greek version of eighteen psalms attributed to Solomon, but actually written during the first century B.C., was found in 1891. Part of an Armenian version of the second-century *Apology* of the Christian author Aristides was published in 1878; a Syriac version followed in 1891. The sole manuscript of the *Refutation of All Heresies*, by Hippolytus (170-236) was found in 1851; it contains important fragments of Heraclitus. Abercius, Abbot of Hierapolis in Phrygia, composed his own epitaph, containing an autobiography, in about 182 A.D. (see Chadwick, *EC* 278); it was published by W.M. Ramsay in 1883.

[629] Wilamowitz must have had in mind the great classical scholar and great authority on the early Church, Eduard Schwartz (1851-1940; see Pfeiffer, *Geist und Gestalt*, 1959, 133).

[630] See F. Cumont (1868-1947), *The Mysteries of Mithra*, 2nd edn. 1903 (paperback, 1956).

[631] The local Baal of Doliche in Commagene, identified with Jupiter, became the centre of an important cult.

[632] The fullest modern treatment is by A.H.M. Jones, *The Later Roman*

The inscription from Gortyna[633] setting out Cretan family law would in itself have been sufficient to tempt the jurists to the study of Greek law, a subject they had not touched before outside the country of Cujacius and Heraldus. It was only the first of such discoveries. Then came the papyri, which not only created the profession of papyrologist – reading the cursive is a special skill – but also finally disposed of the theory – which Mommsen could still propound as a candidate for his doctor's degree – that students of law do not need Greek. Today they know that Greek is indispensable for both the Twelve Tables and the Digest, and Greek Law has become a separate discipline.[634] Our knowledge of Greek administration is derived from the Egypt of the Ptolemies, which has its peculiarities; but even in the Ptolemaic fiscal system there is much, in its principles at least, that may be regarded as conforming to the general Greek pattern. And it is not only from the time of Augustus on that the Romans followed Hellenistic precedents: in Sicily they did so as soon as it became a Roman province.

From the linguistic point of view Latin inscriptions are unrewarding except as evidence of grammatical and phonetic decay. Nevertheless they have taught us a proper view of vulgar Latin, on which the Romance languages are based. Meanwhile the myth of an African Latin has been exploded, though only recently. A field has been opened up which Latin and Roman philologists, meeting half way, can both cultivate, and a new generation has restored the idiom of living speech to its rightful place, even in those authors whose texts have only too often been made to conform with the rules of the literary language.[635] This has encouraged fineness of ear among textual critics, and it is bound to emphasise the

---

*Empire, 284-602*, 1964; the shortened version is *The Decline of the Ancient World*, 1966.

[633] The famous inscription with the fifth-century law code of Gortyn in central Crete was first published (in part) in 1863; other parts followed later. See R.F. Willetts, *Gortyna (Kadmos*, Suppl. 1), 1967.

[634] On the importance of papyri for the study of Greek law, see E.G. Turner, *GP*, Index, s.v. Law, Greek; cf. H.I. Bell, *Egypt*, 1948.

[635] Wilamowitz is thinking of the work of the Swedish school of Latin scholars centring on Einar Löfstedt (1880-1955).

distinctions between periods, so that different people will no longer be able to assign, for instance, the *Peregrinatio Aetheriae*[636] (another discovery of our day) to different centuries.

A Greek official document, such as the text of a law or an excerpt from the record of a conference,[637] is always a highly studied piece of writing, and the same can be said of royal edicts[638] and the private correspondence of educated people, so that these records on stone or paper compensate us to some extent for the loss of Hellenistic prose. Attention has been paid mostly to phonology and accidence, and only to a small extent to word-formation and syntax; but the distinction between Hellenistic and Attic (including artificial Attic) prose has become so clear that it can no longer be overlooked, and anybody with a flair for language should be confident enough to date a piece of literary Greek to the nearest hundred years – at any rate before A.D. 300, difficult though it may be, in dealing with the later, entirely artificial, prose to catch the exact sense in which by that time even educated people used the old words. We must acknowledge that although substantial progress has been made towards a history of the language such as Lobeck, Bekker and Cobet never dreamed of, we still have far to go.[639] Any archaeologist would say the same of the history of style in the visual arts.

The discovery of set *clausulae* in the *kola* of a period and the transition from a quantitative to an accentual system of scansion has taught us important lessons about prose style in both languages, and has provided us with a criterion which is often decisive where the text or genuineness of a passage is in

[636] The *Peregrinatio Aetheriae* is the record of a pilgrimage to the Holy Land written in vulgar Latin by the abbess of a convent in Spain during the late fourth century A.D.; it was discovered in Arezzo and first printed in 1887. Löfstedt's commentary (1911) marks a new stage in the understanding of vulgar Latin and of the light which it can throw on Latin of an earlier period. The text is edited by W. Heraeus (4th edn., Heidelberg, 1939).

[637] See now R.A. Coles, *Reports of Proceedings in Papyri*, Brussels, 1966.

[638] See C.B. Welles, *The Royal Correspondence in the Hellenistic Period*, 1934.

[639] See A. Debrunner, *Geschichte der griechischen Sprache* ii (Sammlung Göschen 114), 1954; A. Meillet, *Aperçu de l'histoire de la langue grecque*, 6th edn. 1943, 241f.

doubt.[640] The avoidance of hiatus had been noticed earlier –
another useful observation, though it has been put to
improper uses. On the other hand, attempts to tie the great
masters of Attic prose to hard and fast rules are doomed to
failure. The microscopic examination of language, whose
practitioners here often delighted in compiling statistical tables of
average percentage frequencies, has sometimes achieved
results. But equally often it has proved deceptive, because the
mind cannot be mechanised. We must not despise little things
– but neither must we forget that they are little.

Richard Westphal was undoubtedly a clever man. But his
attempts to base metrics firmly on musical principles, while
arousing lively interest, failed in the long run to satisfy textual
critics. Though the controversy continues, agreement has
happily been reached about the practical application of the
theory.[641]

Finally, a word on the effect of these new discoveries on
textual criticism.[642] We now possess evidence about epic
language from the sixth century onwards which shows that it
remained the same throughout the ages. We also have remains
of ancient books dating from every period since the end of the
fourth century, so that we know in what form the tragedians
reached the library at Alexandria. We marvel at the technique
of book-production which attained perfection there. We follow
its subsequent course from generation to generation, and we
observe the increasingly chaotic state of orthography which
led to the reforms of Herodian, the decline of the papyrus
industry, and the replacement of the roll by the codex. In the
manuscripts intended for scholars we note the addition of
variant readings and the slow growth of accentuation and

---

[640] See P. Maas, *Greek Metre* (Eng. edn. 1962; corrected impression 1966),
Index, s.v. Formal prose; E. Norden, *Die Antike Kunstprosa*, 5th edn. 1958. E.
Fraenkel, *KB* i 27f.; *SB Munich*, 1965, Heft 2; *Leseproben aus Reden Ciceros und
Catos*, 1968.

[641] R. Westphal (1826-1892): Sandys iii 157; see Sandys for bibliography.
Sandys' view that Westphal and Rossbach's *Theory of the Musical Arts of the
Greeks* (3rd edn. 1885-7) is 'a masterpiece which marks an epoch in the
study of the subject' is not now widely held.

[642] On the present state of textual criticism, see M.L. West, *Textual
Criticism and Editorial Technique*, 1973; cf. *SS²* 186.

other aids to correct reading, while scholia consisting of
extracts from separate commentaries begin to fill the margins.
Fragments of surviving writings are more important to the
critic than the new discoveries, because they enable him to
judge the Byzantine tradition. We see the difference it made to
a book whether it enjoyed the protection of the 'grammarians'
or was reproduced without that safeguard. Thus, in the case of
Demosthenes, we find we are no better off in regard to his
speeches, but have benefited in regard to one spurious
letter.[643] Xenophon's *Economicus*,[644] on the other hand, is
another matter; there the variety of legitimate openings for
conjecture scattered through the book is obvious. It seems
scarcely credible that incompetence should still dare to claim
that the safest course is to keep to the tradition, as though it
were not the critic's business first to test the reliability of the
tradition and then to act accordingly. Anyone who is
incapable of working his way back from the surviving
manuscripts to the author's autograph, which was innocent of
both word-division and punctuation, had better leave textual
criticism alone. The would-be critic must be familiar with the
corruptions that attended the transition from the ancient
book-hand to the minuscule of the age of Photius, when words
began to be separated and punctuation was introduced, and
with the disfigurements due to the crabbed Byzantine cursive
of the final period. Armed with this knowledge he will know
what to make of the transmitted text. A great deal of what
passed for emendation is concerned with alterations which do
not touch the real transmitted text at all, and the mere
removal of an error due to misreading of the ancient handwriting leaves the actual tradition untouched. But textual
history, which has taken its place alongside *recensio* and
*emendatio*, means more than that. When we have got back to
the archetype via its surviving descendants, we are usually left
with a single copy dating from late antiquity. Recension is
then at an end; but emendation does not follow immediately,

[643] On P. Lit. Lond. 130, containing the third epistle of Demosthenes, see
G. Pasquali, *Storia del Testo*, 2nd edn. 1952, 294.

[644] On P. Oxy. 227 (= P. Lit. Lond. 151), containing Xenophon,
*Oeconomicus*, see A.W. Persson, *Zur Textgeschichte Xenophons*, 1915, 48-9.

except where the time that elapsed between the author's lifetime and the archetype is a complete blank.

Even then account has to be taken of general changes in script, orthography and the like, and at that stage it often emerges that the archetype contained variant readings, as we can see with our own eyes in ancient manuscripts of Herodas[645] and Cicero's *De republica*, where it has sometimes led to the perverse rejection of either the first or the second hand. Actually, we have a free choice in such cases; but what if several ancient copies of the work had survived and their texts differ? It then becomes necessary to distinguish between the corruption of a single text and discrepancies between different redactions, which are by no means confined to the classics; but we ought only to speak of 'redactions' when the divergencies are on a more serious scale than the minor variations found in the same book. If the evidence indicates that there really were separate redactions, the one before us may equally well be either a complete revision, in which case we can properly speak of interpolation, or the result of the vicissitudes experienced by the text before some scholar fixed it. In this context we shall do well to recall how the works of Goethe and Kleist have fared even in the era of the printed book. Textual criticism of this kind is impossible without recourse to the ancient grammarians, particularly with the classics. There the standard Alexandrian edition is a second archetype which we have to reconstruct, and if there was more than one edition, we are faced once more with the problem of where variants end and interpolation begins. Here again there will have been an interval between the author's lifetime and the standard edition, during which the text was unprotected.

Our possession of manuscripts of Homer, Plato and Euripides dating from that interval can teach us almost all we need to know about critical method. The only Latin author who sets us a problem of that kind is Plautus, and in his case we could never have found our way without the textual history

---

[645] On the various hands in the British Museum papyrus of Herodas, see I.C. Cunningham, *Herodas: Mimiambi*, 1971, p.17; on those in Cicero, *De republica*, see K. Ziegler's preface to his Teubner edition of 1960.

of Greek literature to guide us.[646] On the other hand, the
single example of Virgil's *Aeneid*[647] is enough to show what
strange adventures an ancient book could undergo which
appeared in an age of the most advanced technique of book
production and was immediately taken over by the
professional scholars. Callimachus and his contemporaries
must have fared much the same. The New Testament,[648]
especially the Gospels, after remaining entirely unprotected
for centuries, had its text more or less fixed, though in a
somewhat violent fashion, but fortunately the traces of other
redactions were not completely obliterated. The additional
evidence provided by translations and the earlier quotations
puts the history of its text on a par with Homer's, to which it is
the nearest parallel in spite of all the differences between
them. The way it corrects the errors into which Lachmann's
method led him is particularly instructive.

What then has really emerged from all this? In the first
place, that the Byzantines did their work well; but what they
were able to achieve depended on the ancient copy which
came their way. That, not the Laurentianus, is the archetype
from which all manuscripts of Aeschylus and Sophocles are
descended. (Incidentally, it is purely by chance that the same
manuscript contains them both.) The suspicion that any good
reading in a later manuscript must be the product of
conjecture has in many cases not been confirmed. For
instance, the Arabic version of Aristotle's *Poetics* has indeed
shown that the book was already as incomplete as it now is at
a very early stage (and probably from the beginning), but the
supremacy of the Parisinus has been undermined.[649] True, we
have lived to see a conjectural reading rejected in spite of

[646] See F. Leo, *Plautinische Forschungen*, 2nd edn. 1912, reprinted 1966,
ch.1.

[647] See R.A.B. Mynors' preface to his Oxford text of Virgil, 1969, and the
review by E.J. Kenney in *CR* 21, 1971, 197f. Wilamowitz' statement about
Callimachus is born out by the earliest manuscript of his we possess, the
new third-century or early second-century papyrus in Lille.

[648] See B.M. Metzger, *The Text of the New Testament: Its Transmission,
Corruption and Restoration*, 1964.

[649] See the preface to R. Kassel's Oxford text of the *Poetics*, 1965. The
supremacy of the Parisinus has been undermined not only by the discovery
of the Arab version, but by that of the importance of the fourteenth-century

confirmation, which only shows how far an inflexible method, backed in this case by hostility to the critics, could lead men astray. Secondly, we now know that in Imperial times the classics were handed on by a sound literary tradition in the form they had assumed in a standard text, a fact which did not exclude the possibility of variant readings; but of course there were careless copies going about too. There is seldom anything to be learnt from manuscripts of Homer dating from these centuries unless they contain rare variant readings, whereas up to the time of Augustus there were still places where the text fixed by the Alexandrian scholars had not yet penetrated.[650] Where there are several markedly divergent redactions, as with Herodotus[651] and Thucydides, and also some of the public speeches of Demosthenes,[652] it means that no 'grammarian' had produced a standard edition. This accords with what we know of the practice in schools. We try to use the compilers from Didymus onwards as a means of getting back to the great Alexandrian scholars. As to what lies still further back, there is no direct manuscript tradition on which we can base our researches.

It is often said that recent discoveries have reduced the whole idea of conjectural emendation to an absurdity, which is certainly not the case. On the contrary, they have confirmed many conjectures and often revealed defects which had been overlooked – in other words, which ought to have been removed by conjectural emendation. Indeed the main thing we have gained from them is precisely that the historical tradition has given us a clearer understanding of where and how it is legitimate, nay incumbent upon us, to resort to

---

codex Riccardianus 46, both due to D.S. Margoliouth (1858-1940; see G. Murray, *PBA* 26, 1941); see *Analecta Orientalia ad Poeticam Aristoteleam*, 1887; *The Poetics of Aristotle*, 1911.

[650] Cf. S. West, *The Ptolemaic Papyri of Homer*, 1967.

[651] Herodotus papyri: see A.H.R.E. Paap, *De Herodoti reliquiis in papyris et membranis Aegyptiis servatis*, 1948. On Thucydides papyri: see J.E. Powell, 'The papyri and the text of Thucydides', *Actes du Vme. Congrès International de Papyrologie*, Brussels, 1938, 344. Aristarchus did write a *commentary* on Herodotus, and perhaps on Thucydides also; see Pfeiffer, i 224-5.

[652] On Demosthenes papyri: see H. Erbse in *Geschichte der Textüberlieferung der antiken und mittelalterlichen Literatur*, 1961, 264.

conjecture. Even without the discovery of ancient books the reaction against the excesses of a criticism run mad was bound to come, and though excesses in the opposite direction were inevitable they are none the less to be deplored. At the same time the recognition, in Germany too, of the obligation to explain the classics – and not only for the benefit of schoolboys – and the production of a number of exemplary editions has helped to bring the critics to their senses. Subject-matter and style now receive proper attention, and editors concentrate less upon single words. Moreover, scholars are learning to respect individuality, instead of insisting on conformity to a fixed ideal, and as the demand for absolute perfection implicit in the canonical authority of antiquity has given way to the historical approach, an understanding has arisen of much that one may deplore but must forgive. Anybody who is inclined to think that textual criticism has little left to accomplish must admit, if he looks about him, that the attempt to understand the idiosyncrasies and the historical significance of even the most widely read authors has only just begun. And though the external form of their works may be tolerably well established, few have set out to fathom their inner form. A complete understanding of the details is always essential, but only for the sake of grasping the whole, and once the whole is grasped, it in turn throws a flood of light on the details.

There has also been a healthy revulsion from the practice of rejecting whole works as spurious. The genuineness of the speeches of Gorgias, Antisthenes,[653] Alcidamas[654] and Herodes Atticus is scarcely contested nowadays, and certain public speeches of Demosthenes which have been a stumbling-block have ceased to be so once their political character has been understood. All Cicero's speeches and his correspondence with Brutus[655] are genuine. So are the letters

[653] The genuineness of the *Ajax* and *Odysseus* attributed to Antisthenes is defended by the latest editor of his fragments, F. Decleva Caizzi (*Antisthenis Fragmenta*, 1966, 89f.)

[654] The *Odysseus* attributed to Alcidamas is not generally thought genuine; still less the Περὶ πολιτείας attributed to Herodes Atticus (see U. Albini, *Erode Attico Περὶ πολιτείας* , 1968.

[655] Markland (see above, n.331) in 1745 cast doubt on the authenticity of the letters to Brutus and of the speeches *post reditum* (Sandys ii 413); F.A. Wolf echoed his suspicions (Sandys iii 58). Madvig set at rest these worries.

of Sallust.[656] Even the *Culex* and the *Ciris*[657] have their champions, whose arguments cannot be lightly dismissed; but the treatment of some other poems in the *Appendix Virgiliana* shows that the pendulum is swinging too far in the other direction. The same applies to numerous testimonia which we are once more being asked to take on trust, even when they vouch for 'Plutarch', *De fluviis*; and the opinion has even been expressed that we cannot afford to reject any tradition whatever – which is equivalent to saying that it is legitimate to pay in bad money when you are short of good.

There is a strange contrast between this trend and the sweeping rejection, by many historians, of things that men like Eratosthenes, on the strength of evidence we no longer possess, accepted as established fact, especially in regard to chronological data. One example has been the discarding of the lists of Olympic victors, which nobody now does;[658] and the same may be said of the refusal to admit that the historian can learn anything of value from the study of the heroic sagas.[659] That is a laborious business, of course, and requires tact. It is far less trouble to wipe the slate clean, because you can then draw upon it whatever you like – except that these modern designs have a way of soon getting wiped off again.

Considerations of content and style alike have constrained us to allot the individual work and the individual author their place in a historical sequence, and this has led to a fruitful study of the various species and styles of discourse, such as the dialogue,[660] the diatribe, the *consolatio* and so on. Thereby the

[656] Eduard Meyer thought so (*Cäsars Monarchie und der Prinzipat des Pompeius*, 2nd edn. 1919, 563); but now opinion has swung the other way (R. Syme, *Sallust*, 1964, 318f).

[657] Not many people now accept the *Ciris* or the *Culex* as by Virgil. On the *Culex*, see Eduard Fraenkel, *JRS* 42, 1952, 1f. = *KB* ii 181f.; on the *Ciris*, R. Helm, *Hermes* 72, 1937, 78f. and R.O.A.M. Lyne, *Ciris*, 1978.

[658] The Olympic victor lists present a complicated problem, but there seem to be no good grounds for doubting their authenticity; see F. Jacoby, *Atthis*, 1949, 58f. (with notes); T. Lenschau, *Philologus* 91, 1936, 391.

[659] Again a vexed question; see for instance the discussion of the Trojan War between M.I. Finley, J.L. Caskey, G.S. Kirk and D.L. Page in *JHS* 84, 1964, 1f. Finley seems to me right in holding that the modern tendency is to exaggerate the value of saga as a source of history; but hardly any modern scholar would deny it all historical value.

[660] *Dialogus:* R. Hirzel, *Der Dialog*, 2 vols, 1895 is still valuable.

first steps have been taken towards arranging the whole body
of ancient literature in groups and elucidating it by the
comparative method. The great virtue of this approach is that
it removes the pernicious dichotomy between Greek and
Latin; for this cosmopolitan literature is bilingual from the
time of Augustus onwards. The investigation of subject-matter
has led to the search for sources, and to their critical
evaluation, not merely in compilations like those of the
grammarians, which can be of use only if one puts the
scattered elements together and traces them back to their
original authors, but in the whole of the later historical and
philosophical literature. From this large portions of the
content of many lost works have been recovered, and no doubt
a great deal more of the kind remains to be done. There is, of
course, no sovereign method here either, no skeleton key
which will unlock all doors, and many people have gone
astray, as they have in textual criticism, through their belief in
a single, universally valid pattern of perfection and their
consequent failure to appreciate the individual quality of
writers so important but so different in their methods as
Cicero and Plutarch. In this respect too, however, we seem to
have turned the corner.

The philosophers have been busy studying the Presocratics
and the Sophists, stimulated by the appearance of a reliable
edition of the collected fragments;[661] but their special merit is
that for the first time they have made the Hellenistic schools,
the Stoa (down to Epictetus) and the Garden,[662] intelligible
from the historical, and thereby also from the philosophical,

---

Investigation of the diatribe was intensive after Wilamowitz published
*Antigonus von Carystos* in 1881; on its value, see the good summary by
Günther Schmidt, *Der kleine Pauly* ii 1577-8. *Consolatio*: the old monograph of
C. Buresch of 1887 has now been improved on by R. Kassel, *Untersuchungen
zur griechischen und römischen Konsolationsliteratur* (Zetemata, heft 18), 1958.

[661] The first edition of H. Diels' *Fragmente der Vorsokratiker* appeared in
1903; 8th edn., revised by W. Kranz, 3 vols, 1956.

[662] H. Usener's *Epicurea* appeared in 1887, H. von Arnim's *Stoicorum
Veterum Fragmenta* (4 vols) between 1903 and 1924. See now M. Pohlenz,
*Die Stoa*, 1949-55; good account of Epicurus and bibliography in Wolfgang
Schmid's article in *Reallexikon für Antike und Christentum* 5, 1961f. See A.A.
Long, *Hellenistic Philosophy*, 1973.

point of view. If, as seems likely, the name of Posidonius is frequently taken in vain these days, since his responsibility for everything attributed to him cannot possibly be maintained, that is no more than an inevitable passing phase.[663] The truth is that the general outlook and speculative opinions associated with his name belong to the sphere of religion and have in fact had a great influence on Christian thought. It is highly significant that this development, and indeed the whole movement of mind which culminated in the triumph of the oriental religions – in other words, the spiritual life of the Imperial period, which even Mommsen entirely omitted in his description of that world – is the subject of close study at the present day. The growth of the new discipline of Comparative Religion under the leadership of a number of brilliant men has been even more vigorous. It sets out to explore the primitive forms of belief and worship out of which the official religions of the Greeks and Romans grew, and investigates all the many manifestations of faith and superstition that are enshrined in moral codes, religious observances and popular customs, in language and legend – in a word, folklore, to use the name we have adopted, along with the substance, from England.[664]

Just as research of this kind entails a descent to the masses from the rarefied atmosphere of polite society in an effort to understand unliterary, irrational, unsophisticated humanity, so other scholars have turned aside from classical art and literature to investigate the exact science and technology of the ancients, which were so long neglected. Their mathematics and astronomy have made a particularly good showing, thanks mainly to Danish scholars[665] but also to a self-taught

[663] Brief account of Posidonius by A.D. Nock, *JRS* 49, 1959, 1f. (= *Essays on Religion and the Ancient World*, ii 1972, 853f.) using the article by K. Reinhardt in *RE* xxii 1953, 560f. Vol.i of *The Fragments of Posidonius*, ed. L. Edelstein and D.A. Kidd, appeared in 1972.

[664] Wilamowitz must have been thinking of scholars like F. Cumont, J. Bidez and M.P. Nilsson (see above, p.xxv).

[665] Wilamowitz has in mind the work of the Danes A.B. Drachmann (1860-1935), H.G. Zeuthen (1839-1920), and J.L. Heiberg (1854-1928), and the Frenchman Paul Tannery (1843-1904); there was also the Englishman Sir Thomas Heath (1861-1940). Archimedes, $Περὶ τῶν μηχανικῶν θεωρημάτων πρὸς \ Ερατοσθένην ἔφοδος$, 1907. Work on the Berlin Corpus and on the Hamburg lexicon of medicine continues.

Frenchman of genius; the discovery of a new work by
Archimedes has helped too.[666] Their medicine has not been
overlooked either; but in that field the essential spade-work, in
the form of a critical edition of the doctors, on which a start
has only just been made, remains to be done. The botanical
works of Theophrastus are in the same case, but new light has
already been thrown on them by a book that combines
technical knowledge with classical scholarship.[667] Such
collaboration between entirely different disciplines and skills
is exactly what is needed to fill the numerous gaps of this kind
and has already achieved notable successes in the
technological sphere; for example, in the reconstruction of
ancient artillery.[668]

This long, and yet all too cursory, survey will have shown that
over the past fifty years science has been busily engaged in
recovering the life of antiquity in all its aspects by means of the
historical method. How, if at all, it can extend its conquests,
who would venture to say? But if we look back over the
distance scholarship has travelled in the course of the
centuries, we shall not despair of its vitality, even if the outlook
is less hopeful than it was in the days when the co-operation of
the whole civilised world was still a reality.

What classical scholarship is, and what it should be, are
clear from its history. Has this long parade of its worthies
taught us what a scholar should be? All those mentioned have
been selected because they served the cause of learning, but
they differed greatly in intellectual power and character, in
interests and abilities. So the most modest definition will
probably be the best. A scholar may do any number of things,
and may do them in any number of ways; but there is one
thing he must *be* if he is to achieve anything that will endure,
and that is *vir bonus, discendi peritus*.[669]

---

[666] A methodological treatise which proves that Archimedes anticipated
the integral calculus was published from a Jerusalem palimpsest in 1907;
see Fraser, *PA* i 1972, 405f.; text in Heath, *Method of Archimedes*, 1912,
reprinted in *Archimedes*, 1955.

[667] Wilamowitz seems to be thinking of O. Kirchner, *Die botanischen
Schriften des Theophrastos von Eresos*, 1874. See now G. Senn, *Die Pflanzenkunde
des Theophrastos von Eresos*, 1956.

[668] See E.W. Marsden, *Greek and Roman Artillery*, 1969.

[669] Cato defined the orator as 'vir bonus, dicendi peritus'.

# Bibliography and abbreviations

*ASNP*   *Annali della Scuola Normale Superiore di Pisa*

Browning, *BS*   R. Browning, 'Byzantine Scholarship', *Past and Present* 8, 1964, 3f.

Bursian   C. Bursian, *Geschichte der classischen Philologie in Deutschland von den Anfangen bis zur Gegenwart*, 1883

*BZ*   *Byzantinische Zeitschrift*

Chadwick, *EC*   H. Chadwick, *The Early Church*, 1967 (Pelican History of the Church, i)

*CIEC* i   *Classical Influences on European Culture, AD 500-1500*, ed. R.R. Bolgar, 1971

*CIEC* ii   *Classical Influences on European Culture, AD 1500-1700*, ed. R.R. Bolgar, 1976

*Cl. Rev.*   *Classical Review*

Cook, *GPP*   R.M. Cook, *Greek Painted Pottery*, 2nd edn., 1972

Fraser, *PA*   P.M. Fraser, *Ptolemaic Alexandria*, 3 vols, 1972

Fraenkel, *Ag.*   Eduard Fraenkel, *Aeschylus, The Agamemnon*, 3 vols, 1950 (new impression, with corrections, 1962)

Fraenkel, *KB*   Eduard Fraenkel, *Kleine Beiträge zur klassischen Philologie*, 2 vols; 1964

Geanakoplos, *GSV*   D.J. Geanakoplos, *Greek Scholars in Venice: Studies in the Dissemination of the Learning of Byzantium to Western Europe*, 1962

Geanakoplos, *BELW*   D.J. Geanakoplos, *Byantine East and Latin West*, 1966

*GRBS*   *Greek, Roman and Byantine Studies*

Gruppe   O. Gruppe, *Geschichte der klassischen Mythologie und Religionsgeschichte*, 1921 (Supplement to Roscher's *Ausführliches Lexicon der Griechischen und römischen Mythologie*)

*JHS*   *Journal of Hellenic Studies*

*JRS*   *Journal of Roman Studies*

*JTS*   *Journal of Theological Studies*

Kenney, *CT*   E.J. Kenney, *The Classical Text: Aspects of Editing in the Age of the Printed Book*, 1974 (Sather Classical Lectures, vol. 44)

Lloyd-Jones, *BG*   H. Lloyd-Jones, *Blood for the Ghosts*, 1981

Momigliano, *C*   A. Momigliano, *Contributo alla storia degli studi classicai*, 1955

Momigliano, *SC*   A. Momigliano, *Secondo contributo alla storia degli studi classici*, 1960

Momigliano, *TC*   A. Momigliano, *Terzo contributo alla storia degli studi classici e del mondo antico*. 2 vols, 1966

Momigliano, *QC*   A. Momigliano, *Quarto contributo alla storia degli studi classici e del mondo antico*, 1969

Momigliano, *Quinto C*   A. Momigliano, *Quinto contributo alla storia degli studi classici e del mondo antico*, 1975

Momigliano, *SH*   A. Momigliano, *Studies in Historiography*, 1966

Pattison, *Essays*   Mark Pattison, *Essays*, 2 vols, ed. H. Nettleship, 1889

Pfeiffer, *AKS*   Rudolf Pfeiffer, *Ausgewählte Kleine Schriften*, ed. W. Bühler, 1960

Pfeiffer, *HCS*   Rudolf Pfeiffer, *History of Classical Scholarship* i, 1968, ii, 1976

*PBA*   *Proceedings of the British Academy*

*PCA*   *Proceedings of the Classical Association*

*PCPS*   *Proceedings of the Cambridge Philological Society*

*RE*   *Pauly-Wissowa, Realenzyklopädie der Altertumswissenschaft*

*RIFC*   *Rivista Italiana di Filologia Classica*

*RSC*   *Rivista Storica Italiana*

Rumpf   Andreas Rumpf, *Archäologie* i (Einleitung: historischer Uberblick) 1953 (Sammlung Göschen, Bd. 538)

Sandys   J.E. Sandys, *A History of Classical Scholarship* (vol.i, From the Sixth Century B.C. to the End of the Middle Ages, 1903; vol.ii, From the Revival of Learning to the End of the Eighteenth Century in Italy, France, England and the Netherlands, 1908; vol.iii, The Eighteenth Century in Germany and the Nineteenth Century in Europe and the United States of America, 1908): reprinted 1964

*SB Munich*   *Sitzungsberichte der Bayerischen Akademie*

*SS*   L.B. Reynolds and N.G. Wilson, *Scribes and Scholars*, 2nd edn., 1974

Speyer   W. Speyer, *Die literarische Fälschung im heidnischen und christlichen Altertum*, 1971

Treves, *SAO*   Piero Treves, *Lo studio dell' antichità classica nell' Ottocento*, 1962

Turner, *GP*   E.G. Turner, *Greek Papyri: An Introduction*, 1968

Weiss, *HE*   R. Weiss, *Humanism in England during the Fifteenth Century*, 1941

Weiss, *RDCA*   R. Weiss, *The Renaissance Discovery of Classical Antiquity*, 1969

Wilson, *ABP*   N.G. Wilson, *Anthology of Byzantine Prose*, 1971.

# Index

Foesius, Anutius, 45
Forcellini, E., 97
Fourmont, M., 62
Fraenkel, E., xxv
Fra Giocondo, 33
Fränkel, H., 87 n.350
Friedländer, L., 104
Friedrichs, C., 152
Frobens, 43
Fulvius, Andreas, 32
Furtwängler, A., 164
Fynes Clinton, H., 153

Gaisford, T., 76, 85
Gale, T., 77-8
Gassendi, P., 62
Gataker, T., 77
Gaza, T., 25
Geel, J., 89
Gelenius, S., 43
Gell, W.M., 125
George of Trapezus, 25
Gerhard, E., 123-4
Gernet, L., xx
Gesner, C., 45
Gesner, J.M., ix, 92-4, 101-2
Gibbon, E., 59, 83, 157
Gildersleeve, B.L., xxvi
Glareanus, H., 43-4
Goethe, J.W. von, ix, x, 42, 68, 83, 105-6, 108
Gori, A., 98
Gothofredus, J., 47
Graevius, J.G., 73-4, 80, 113
Gratius, O., 40
Gregory Nazianzen, 5
Gregory of Corinth, 8
Gregory of Tours, 14
Gronovius, J.F., 72
Gronovius, J., 73, 92
Grosseteste, R., 19
Grote, G., xxii, 153, 155, 157
Grotius, H., 58, 67-8, 71, 110
Gruter, J., 33, 52, 66, 69, 74
Grynaeus, S., 43
Guarino, 3
Guyet, F., 59

Haase, F., 145
Halm, K., 145
Hand, F.G., 147
Hardouin, J., 63
Hase, C.B., 54, 138
Haupt, M., 130, 131 n.486, 141-2
Headlam, W., xxiii, xxiv
Heerwagens, 43
Heindorf, C.F., 115
Heinsius, D., 67, 70
Heinsius, N., 71-2, 81
Helbig, W., 151
Hemsterhuys, T., 85-6, 88, 91, 94
Henzen, W., 33, 158
Hercher, R., 145
Herder, J.G., ix, 100, 105-8
Hermann, G., x, xiv, xxi, xxii, 81, 109-11, 113, 115, 122, 126, 128-9, 133-4, 136, 139, 141, 147, 160
Hermann, K.F., 146
Herodian, 5, 7, 13
Hertz, M., 145
Herwerden, H. van, 91
Heyne, C.G., ix, 94, 96, 101-2, 108, 110, 127
*Hisperica Famina*, 14
Hofman-Peerlkamp, P., 88, 136
Hölscher, U., xxxi
Holstenius, L., 39, 92
Höschel, D., 65
Hotomanus, F., 47
Housman, A.E., xviii, xxi-xxiv
Huet, P.D., 63 n.258
Humboldt, W. von, x, 101, 104, 106, 108, 113, 115, 117, 119, 126
Hutten, U. von, 40, 41

Ideler, C.L., 116
Ignarra, N., 98
Ilgen, K.D., 113-14
Imhoof-Blumer, F., 158
Inghirami, C., 37
Invernizi, F., 84 n.337

Jackson, H., xxii
Jacobs, F., 69, 93, 113
Jacoby, F., xxv
Jaeger, W., xxvii, xxviii